I0434867

Muscatatuck
National Wildlife Refuge

Comprehensive Conservation Plan Approval

Submitted by:

Marc Webber   9/4/09
Marc Webber   Date
Refuge Manager

Concur:

Matthew D. Sprenger   9/9/2009
Matthew D. Sprenger   Date
Refuge Supervisor, Area 2

Thomas C. Worthington   9/9/2009
Thomas C. Worthington   Date
Acting Regional Chief, National Wildlife Refuge System

Approve:

Charles M. Wooley
Acting Regional Director   _Charles Wooley_   9/10/09
Thomas O. Melius   Date
Regional Director

Muscatatuck
National Wildlife Refuge

Comprehensive Conservation Plan

Table of Contents

List of Figures and Tables

Chapter 1: Introduction and Background

Introduction

The Muscatatuck National Wildlife Refuge (NWR), established in 1966, manages 7,802 acres in Jackson, Jennings, and Monroe Counties of Indiana (Figure 1). The Refuge also administers nine conservation easements totaling 130.5 acres in five Indiana counties. The Refuge consists of wetland, grassland and woodland communities. The Refuge provides habitat for many avian species including ducks, geese, non-game grassland and forest birds including many neo-tropical migrants, shorebirds, wading birds, birds of prey and Wild Turkey. A wide variety of reptiles and mammals including the copperbelly water snake, Kirtland's snake, river otter, and white-tailed deer, many fish species and a broad range of terrestrial and aquatic invertebrates also inhabit the Refuge. Included among the diverse assortment of wildlife and plants found on the Refuge are several federally listed species, including the federally listed endangered Indiana bat, and many more state-listed species. Species lists found in Appendix C note any state and federal designations.

The U.S. Fish and Wildlife Service

Muscatatuck NWR is administered by the U.S. Fish and Wildlife Service (Service). The Service is the primary federal agency responsible for conserving, protecting, and enhancing the nation's fish and wildlife populations and their habitats. It oversees the enforcement of federal wildlife laws, management and protection of migratory bird populations, restoration of nationally significant fisheries, administration of the Endangered Species Act, and the restoration of wildlife habitat such as wetlands. The Service also manages the National Wildlife Refuge System.

Great Blue Heron. Photo credit: U.S. Fish & Wildlife Service

The National Wildlife Refuge System

Refuge lands are part of the National Wildlife Refuge System, which was founded in 1903 when President Theodore Roosevelt designated Pelican Island in Florida as a sanctuary for Brown Pelicans. Today, the System is a network of about 550 refuges and 37 wetland management districts covering more than 96 million acres of public lands and waters. Most of these lands are in Alaska, with approximately 16 million acres located in the lower 48 states and several island territories.

The National Wildlife Refuge System is the world's largest collection of lands specifically managed for fish and wildlife. Overall, it provides habitat for more than 5,000 species of birds, mammals, fish, amphibians, reptiles, and insects. As a result of international treaties for migratory bird conservation and other legislation, such as the Migratory Bird Conservation Act of 1929, many refuges have been established to protect migratory waterfowl and their migratory flyways.

Refuges also play a crucial role in preserving endangered and threatened species. Among the most notable is Aransas NWR in Texas, which provides winter habitat for the highly endangered Whooping Crane. Likewise, the Florida Panther Refuge protects one of the nation's most

Figure 1: Location of Muscatatuck NWR

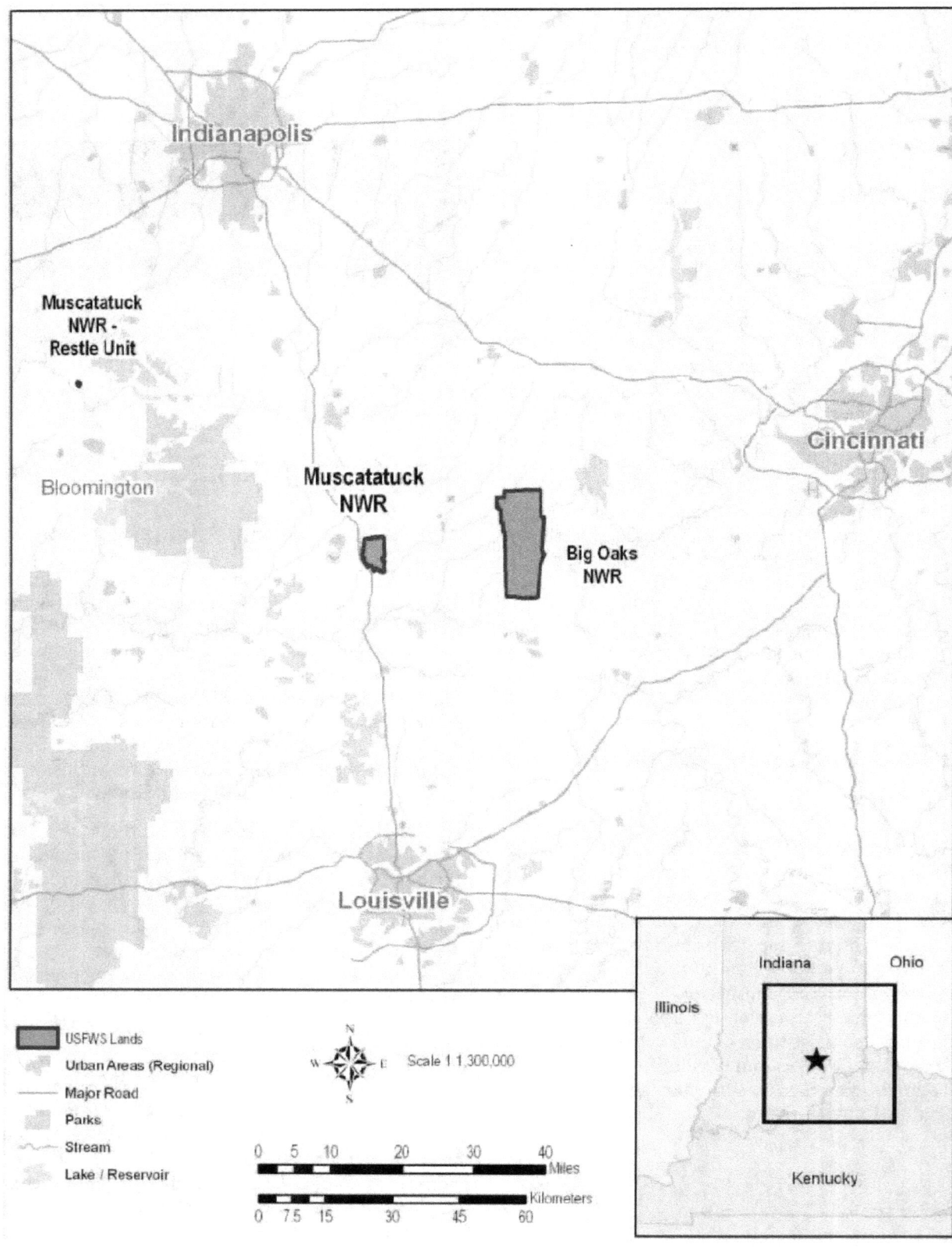

endangered predators. Refuges also provide unique recreational and educational opportunities for people.

When human activities are compatible with wildlife and habitat conservation, refuges are places where people can enjoy wildlife-dependent recreation such as hunting, fishing, wildlife observation, photography, environmental education, and environmental interpretation. Many refuges have visitor centers, wildlife trails, automobile tours, and environmental education programs. Nationwide, approximately 40 million people visit national wildlife refuges every year.

The National Wildlife Refuge System Improvement Act of 1997 established several important mandates aimed at making the management of national wildlife refuges more cohesive. The preparation of Comprehensive Conservation Plans (CCPs) is one of those mandates. The legislation directs the Secretary of the Interior to ensure that the mission of the National Wildlife Refuge System and purposes of the individual refuges are carried out. It also requires the Secretary to maintain the biological integrity, diversity, and environmental health of the National Wildlife Refuge System.

The goals of the National Wildlife Refuge System are to:

- Conserve a diversity of fish, wildlife, and plants and their habitats, including species that are endangered or threatened with becoming endangered.

- Develop and maintain a network of habitats for migratory birds, anadromous and interjurisdictional fish, and marine mammal populations that is strategically distributed and carefully managed to meet important life history needs of these species across their ranges.

- Conserve those ecosystems, plant communities, wetlands of national or international significance, and landscapes and seascapes that are unique, rare, declining, or underrepresented in existing protection efforts.

- Provide and enhance opportunities to participate in compatible wildlife-dependent recreation (hunting, fishing, wildlife observation and photography, and environmental education and interpretation).

Muscatatuck NWR. Photo Credit: Jon Kauffeld

- Foster understanding and instill appreciation of the diversity and interconnectedness of fish, wildlife, and plants and their habitats.

History and Establishment

In the early 1960s there was interest among the Indiana Department of Conservation, state-wide sportsmen and conservation organizations, and many business and civic leaders in southern Indiana for a national wildlife refuge in the area known as Mutton Creek Bottoms. Their interest was prompted by the recollection of past waterfowl use of the area, the reduction of waterfowl habitat throughout the area because of wetland drainage, an anticipated economic stimulus from tourists and sportsmen, and possible educational benefits derived from nature trails and wildlife observations.

With the approval of the Governor and support by local elected representatives, the Service presented the proposal for the Muscatatuck NWR to the Migratory Bird Conservation Commission on June 7, 1966. The Commission approved the acquisition of 7,922 acres to provide duck breeding and migration habitat. Lands for the Refuge were acquired under eminent domain. The Refuge was officially established by the acquisition of the first tracts on October 6, 1966. By April 24, 1973, acquisition was considered complete with 7,724 acres acquired; interest in a remaining in-holding had waned by 1979 because the asking price was too high. The 78-acre Restle Unit in Monroe County was acquired through a donation in 1991.

Refuge Purpose

The Refuge purpose "...for use as an inviolate sanctuary, or for any other management purpose, for migratory birds" derives from the Migratory

Bird Conservation Act. When proposed as a refuge to the Migratory Bird Conservation Commission in 1966, the area was identified as having good potential for waterfowl with expected increases in production and use during the spring and fall migrations. It was also noted that the Refuge would provide recreation facilities for the people of the vicinity.

The Refuge also manages nine conservation easement areas. The purpose of the easements, "... for conservation ... ", derives from the Consolidated Farm and Rural Development Act. The Service administers the easements as part of the National Wildlife Refuge System.

Refuge Vision

The Refuge staff considered past vision statements and emerging issues and drafted the following vision statement as the desired future state of the Refuge:

> As the land of winding waters, treasured for generations, Muscatatuck National Wildlife Refuge honors its heritage and connects visitors with the natural environment by conserving a rich mosaic of sustainable habitat for a diversity of wildlife and plants.

Purpose of the Plan

This CCP articulates the management direction for Muscatatuck NWR for the next 15 years. Through goals, objectives, and strategies, this CCP describes how the Refuge intends to fulfill its purpose and contribute to the overall mission of the National Wildlife Refuge System. Prior to the CCP, Refuge management was guided by a 1982 Master Plan, which is now dated, and other short-term plans of limited scope. There is a need for a broad, long-term look at management direction given changed conditions and scientific information, and over 40 years of on-the-ground experience by the Service managing the Refuge.

Several legislative mandates within the National Wildlife Refuge System Improvement Act of 1997 have guided the development of this plan. These mandates include:

- Wildlife has first priority in the management of refuges.

- Wildlife-dependent recreation activities, namely hunting, fishing, wildlife observation, wildlife photography, environmental education and interpretation, are priority public uses of refuges. We will facilitate these activities when they do not interfere with our ability to fulfill the refuges' purpose or the mission of the Refuge System.

- Other uses of the Refuge will only be allowed when determined appropriate and compatible with Refuge purposes and mission of the Refuge System.

The plan will guide the management of Muscatatuck NWR by:

- Providing a clear statement of direction for the future management.

- Making a strong connection between Refuge activities and conservation activities that occur in the surrounding area.

- Providing neighbors, visitors, and the general public with an understanding of the Service's management actions.

- Ensuring Refuge actions and programs are consistent with the mandates of the National Wildlife Refuge System.

- Ensuring that Refuge management considers federal, state, and county plans.

- Establishing long-term continuity in Refuge management.

- Providing a basis for the development of budget requests on the Refuge's operational, maintenance, and capital improvement needs.

Legal Context

In addition to the acquisition authorities of the Refuge, and the National Wildlife Refuge System Improvement Act of 1997, several federal laws, executive orders, and regulations govern its administration. Appendix E contains a partial list of the legal mandates that pertain to Refuge management and guided the preparation of this plan.

Chapter 2: The Planning Process

Meetings and Involvement

The planning process for this CCP began in March 2007. Initially, members of the regional planning staff and Muscatatuck NWR staff identified a list of issues and concerns that were associated with the management of the Refuge. These preliminary issues and concerns were based on staff knowledge of the area and contacts with citizens in the community.

Refuge staff and Service planners then asked Refuge neighbors, organizations, local government units, and interested citizens to share their thoughts in an open house and through written comments. In May 2007, people were invited to an open house at the Refuge's visitor center through local papers and a project update sent to the Refuge's mailing list of 1,067. Twenty-five people attended the open house. Comments were received from approximately 35 individuals during the comment period, which ended June 30, 2007. Following the public comment period, an additional meeting was held in the Fish and Wildlife Service Regional Office to review the public comments and identify concerns from subject specialists.

A Biological Program Review, which is an evaluation of the relevance and direction of the biological program through the collective inputs of professionals among the various fields of ecology and wildlife sciences, began with a 2-day meeting on June 20 and 21 of 2007. The Regional Refuge Biologist facilitated the event, which was attended by 17 individuals with various state, federal, and academic affiliations. Information was presented on the Refuge, the general ecology of the region, establishing legislation and policy directives, current issues facing the Refuge, prior program accomplishments, a report on the current biological inventory and monitoring program, and a draft vision for the future. The meeting was punctuated with field trips to specific sites to stimulate discussion and demonstrate issues of concern. The group discussed management alternatives and

Muscatatuck NWR. Photo Credit: U.S. Fish & Wildlife Service

potential strategies, identified potential biological program priorities, discussed the draft goals and objectives for the various program components and other ideas for the future of the program.

The planning team also considered the recommendations of a Visitors Services Review that was conducted June 19-22, 2006. The review evaluated the services of the Refuge against the minimum visitor services requirements in policy.

Issues

Issues play an important role in planning. Issues focus the planning effort on the most important topics and provide a base for considering alternative approaches to management and evaluating the consequences of managing under these alternative approaches. The issues, concerns, and opportunities expressed during the first phase of planning have been organized under the following headings.

■ Habitat and Wildlife

There is a need to prioritize wildlife species of management concern and their habitats and, within budget constraints and other limitations, manage according to those priorities. A strategic management direction is needed for wetlands, grasslands, forests, croplands, and the conversion of open lands to forests. Visitors see the current diversity of habitat as valuable, because it provides an opportunity to see a large number of bird and resident wildlife species.

■ Visitor Services

Visitors and staff recognize a tremendous potential in wildlife-dependent recreation, a popular and valued use of the Refuge. There is a need to weigh the delivery of visitor services within the wildlife mission of the Refuge and seek creative means for expanding wildlife-dependent recreation opportunities, outreach, and education.

■ Refuge Roads

The public recognizes the value of Refuge roads for access. There is a wide spectrum of opinion on how the roads should be maintained. Some like the roads as they are now; others would like to see improvements in the roads and associated facilities such as parking lots and wildlife overlooks.

■ Recreational Issues

Some individuals would like to see recreational opportunities expand on the Refuge to include dog training, an archery range, and horseback riding. These activities typically do not occur on refuges and many are not wildlife-dependent in nature. The planning process presents an opportunity to evaluate the requests and reach a decision on their appropriateness and compatibility.

■ External Impacts to the Refuge

Refuge habitats and waters are directly affected by land use on neighboring properties, surrounding area and upstream of the Refuge. Off-refuge factors such as water management, agricultural practices, transportation networks, industrial activities, and urban development influence many aspects of management at Muscatatuck NWR, including:

○ water quality and quantity on the Refuge;

○ sedimentation and contamination in streams, wetlands, and open waters;

○ wildlife disturbance from human activity and noise;

○ the severity of habitat fragmentation;

○ the diversity and pervasiveness of invasive species.

■ Support

There is wide support for the Refuge and its management among visitors. They note the value of the Friends Group, volunteer, and intern programs.

Wilderness Review

As part of the CCP process, lands within Muscatatuck NWR were reviewed for wilderness suitability. No lands were considered suitable for Congressional designation as wilderness as defined by the Wilderness Act of 1964. Muscatatuck NWR does not contain 5,000 contiguous acres of roadless, natural lands. Nor does the Refuge possess any units of sufficient size to make their preservation practicable as wilderness. Refuge lands and waters have been substantially altered by humans, especially by agriculture, drain construction, and road-building. Extensive modification of natural habitats and manipulation of natural processes has occurred. Adopting a "hands-off" approach to management at the Refuge would not facilitate the restoration of a pristine or pre-settlement condition, which is the goal of wilderness designation.

Preparation of the CCP

The CCP for Muscatatuck NWR was prepared by a team consisting of Refuge and Regional Office staff. The CCP was published in two phases and in accordance with the National Environmental Policy Act (NEPA). The Environmental Assessment, published as Appendix A in the Draft CCP, presented four alternatives for future management and identified a preferred alternative.

The Draft CCP/EA was released for public review and comment on April 6, 2009. A Draft CCP/EA or a summary of the document was sent to more than 1,000 individuals, organizations, and local, state, and federal agencies and elected officials. An open house was held on April 23, 2009, at the Muscatatuck NWR Visitor Center following release of the draft document. Twenty-five people attended the open house. We received a total of 40 comment letters and e-mails during the 33-day review period. Appendix K of the CCP summarizes these comments and our responses.

The preferred alternative was selected and has become the basis of the Final CCP, which will guide management over the next 15 years. It will guide the development of more detailed step-down management plans for specific resource areas and it will underpin the annual budgeting process through submissions to the Refuge Operating Needs System (RONS) and Service Asset Maintenance Management System (SAMMS). Most importantly, the CCP lays out the general approach to managing habitat, wildlife, and people at Muscatatuck NWR that will direct day-to-day decision-making and actions.

Chapter 3: Refuge Environment and Management

Introduction

Muscatatuck National Wildlife Refuge

Muscatatuck NWR manages lands in Jackson, Jennings, and Monroe Counties in south-central Indiana. Management responsibilities also include a 30-county Wildlife Management District, which involves management of U.S. Department of Agriculture's (USDA) Farm Service Agency Conservation Easements and team membership in the Wetland Reserve Program Wetland Evaluation Team with USDA – Natural Resource Conservation Service (NRCS) for the 22-county southeast Indiana area. Although formal management responsibility for the 30-county Partners for Fish and Wildlife private lands district was transferred by agreement to the Indiana State Private Lands Coordinator in 2004, Muscatatuck NWR still assists with past projects completed with Muscatatuck NWR partners, provides coordination and support in six counties, and makes referrals from other counties to the State Private Lands Coordinator.

Ecological Context

Historic Vegetation

Historically, the Refuge was a part of the expansive, contiguous deciduous hardwood forest that covered most of the central and southern part of the state. Lindsey (1997) listed oak-hickory and beech-maple as the dominant pre-settlement forest types. Prior to European settlement of the area, the Muscatatuck River Basin was an old lake basin. The forest community has been defined as "Bluegrass Till Plain Flatwoods" by the Indiana Invasive Plant Species Assessment Work Group (Jacquart et al. 2002) and "Southeastern Till Plain Beech-Maple

River otter. Photo credit: Dan Kaiser

Division" by IDNR Division of Nature Preserves (2005). This area is generally wet or moist most of the year.

Information gleaned from the General Land Office (GLO) survey notes from November 1806 is summarized in the following paragraphs. Names in bold are the names as found in the original survey notes and those within parentheses are current interpretations of the species represented (Homoya 2007).

In the Jennings County portion of the Refuge the area is mostly upland flats and moist slopes. The tree species mentioned the greatest number of times is **beech** (American beech; *Fagus grandifolia*). As with today, this species is characteristic of these communities. Three other species mentioned are **sugar** (sugar maple; *Acer saccharum*), **W. ash** (White ash; *Fraxinus americana*), and **cherry** (black cherry; *Prunus serotina*).

In the western portion of the Refuge (Jackson Co.) most of the same species listed above are mentioned; additional types occur, especially in the floodplains. The list includes: "**Ash;** (green ash; *Fraxinus pennsylvanica*), **maple** (red maple; *Acer rubrum* and/or silver maple; *Acer* *saccharinum*), **elm** (American elm; *Ulmus americana*) in the bottoms, **beech** (American beech; *Fagus grandifolia*) and **poplar** (tulip tree; *Liriodendron tulipifera*) on the Highland." These notes were describing a survey line between sections 25 and 26 T. 6 N. R. 6 E. Also mentioned for the floodplain in this region was **ironwood** (probably blue beech; *Carpinus caroliniana*, and not hop hornbeam; *Ostrya virginiana*).

W. oak (white oak; *Quercus alba*) and/or **swamp chestnut oak** (*Quercus michauxii*) and/or **swamp white oak** (*Quercus bicolor*), and **gum** (sweet gum; *Liquidambar styraciflua*) were mentioned in a floodplain just north of the Vernon Fork Muscatatuck River along the section line between sections 35 and 36, T. 6 N. R. 6 E. White oak is not a normal component of wet floodplain forests in Indiana, but does occur in slightly elevated portions of floodplains, (Homoya 2007). There are no references to any open areas or grasslands. There are references to a few swamps in the floodplain; they were forested and probably only ephemerally wet.

In addition to written descriptions of historic vegetation conditions, soil information can be used to understand the vegetation capacity of a landscape. The soils in any given locality are a result of the parent rock material, organisms,

Female Wood Duck and brood. Photo Credit: Mark Trabue

climate, and relief. These factors and the resulting soils limit what overlying native vegetation can inhabit an area. Soil survey data collected over the past century by the USDA's Natural Resource Conservation Service have included written descriptions of native vegetation, which can be tied to the soil unit and mapped. Figure 2 uses data from the Soil Survey Geographic (SSURGO) Database to display the potential natural vegetation found at Muscatatuck NWR. The dominance of a mixed deciduous forest covertype is consistent with other accounts of the region's native vegetation status.

The land of the future Refuge was cleared for farms in the mid 1800s as the state was settled by Europeans. When the Service purchased the land there were 116 private land ownerships, 4,100 acres being farmed, and most of the area had been altered from its original forest cover type. Since the Service has managed the land the cover has changed away from agriculture to managed wetlands and trees. Fire was likely a part of the forces shaping the forest prior to European settlement as indigenous populations used fire as a management tool in forested areas. Fire has been suppressed in the Muscatatuck NWR area for much of the last century, except for some areas of the Refuge that were treated with fire as a management tool in the 1990s.

Today the more common species in the bottomland hardwood forest are pin oak, swamp white oak, swamp chestnut oak, sweet gum, green ash, river birch, silver and red maple and shellbark hickory.

Land Use/Cover

The Refuge lies in a predominantly agricultural landscape. Farm land constitutes 63.5 percent of the land area in Jackson County and 59.1 percent in Jennings County (FedStats 2002). Within this predominantly agricultural landscape, the developed area of Seymour to the west of the Refuge is a notable exception (Figure 3). Forested lands and woodlots are scattered among the agricultural lands. Based on 2001 national land cover data developed by the Multi-Resolution Land Characteristics Consortium, the area within a 6-mile distance of the Refuge is 61.8 percent agricultural, 10.8 percent developed, and 26.4 percent forested (U.S. Geological Survey 2001).

Figure 2: Potential Natural Vegetation, Muscatatuck NWR

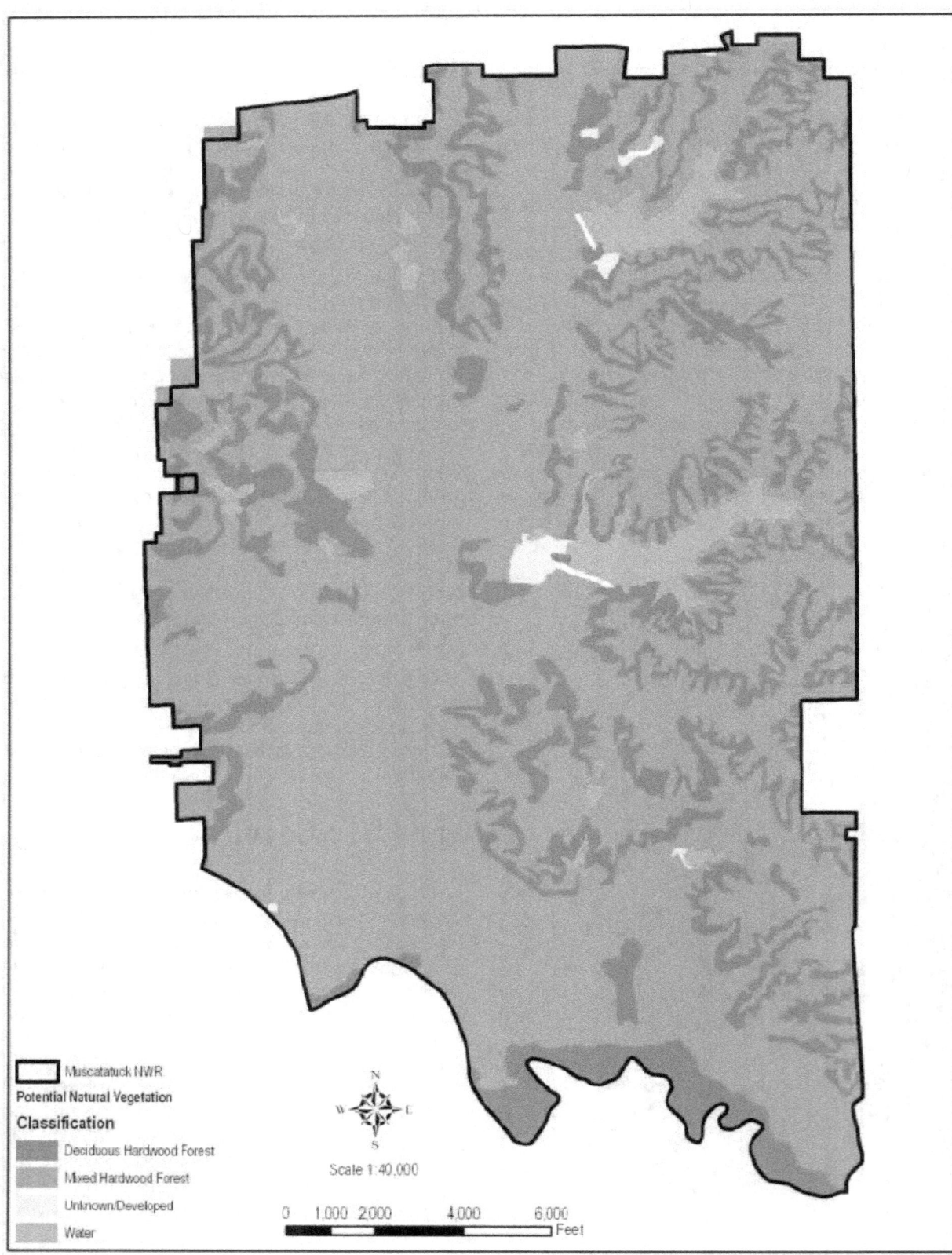

Figure 3: Land Use / Land Cover in the Vicinity of Muscatatuck NWR

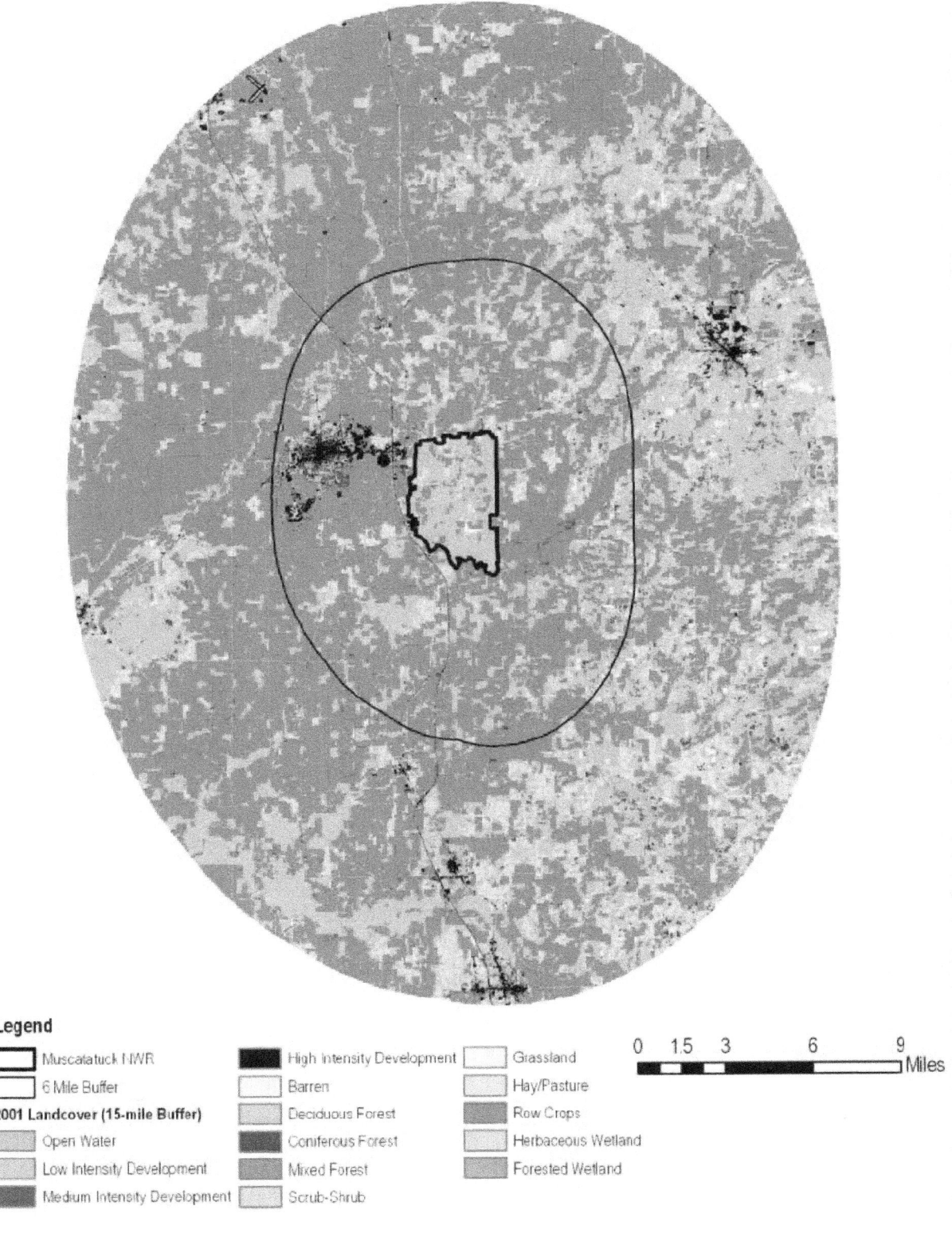

Legend

Muscatatuck NWR	High Intensity Development	Grassland
6 Mile Buffer	Barren	Hay/Pasture
2001 Landcover (15-mile Buffer)	Deciduous Forest	Row Crops
Open Water	Coniferous Forest	Herbaceous Wetland
Low Intensity Development	Mixed Forest	Forested Wetland
Medium Intensity Development	Scrub-Shrub	

0   1.5   3   6   9 Miles

Migratory Bird Conservation Initiatives

Several migratory bird conservation plans have been published over the last decade that can be used to help guide management decisions on refuges. Bird conservation planning efforts have evolved from a largely local, site-based orientation to a more regional, even inter-continental, landscape-oriented perspective. Several transnational migratory bird conservation initiatives have emerged to help guide the planning and implementation process. The regional plans relevant to Muscatatuck NWR are:

- The Central Hardwoods Joint Venture Concept Plan
- Upper Mississippi River and Great Lakes Region Joint Venture of the North American Waterfowl Management Plan
- The Upper Mississippi Valley/Great Lakes Regional Shorebird Conservation Plan
- The Upper Mississippi Valley/Great Lakes Regional Waterbird Conservation Plan

Each of the bird conservation initiatives has a process for designating priority species, modeled to a large extent on the Partners in Flight method of computing scores based on independent assessments of global relative abundance, breeding and wintering distribution, and vulnerability to threats, area importance, and population trends. These scores are often used by agencies in developing lists of priority bird species. The Service based its 2001 list of Non-game Birds of Conservation Concern primarily on the Partners in Flight shorebird and waterbird status assessment scores.

Region 3 Fish and Wildlife Conservation Priorities

Every species is important; however the number of species in need of attention exceeds the resources of the Service. To focus effort effectively, Region 3 of the Fish and Wildlife Service compiled a list of Resource Conservation Priorities (U.S. Fish & Wildlife Service 1999). The list includes:

- All federally listed threatened and endangered species and proposed and candidate species that occur in the Region.
- Migratory bird species derived from Service wide and international conservation planning efforts.

- Rare and declining terrestrial and aquatic plants and animals that represent an abbreviation of the Endangered Species program's preliminary draft "Species of Concern" list for the Region.

Appendix D lists 72 Regional Resource Conservation Priority species relevant to the Refuge.

Other Conservation and Recreation Lands in the Area

The state of Indiana, other federal agencies, and non-governmental conservation organizations own and manage lands and recreation access sites within a 50-mile radius of the Refuge (see Figure 4). The state areas include public access sites, fish and wildlife areas, recreation areas, forests, and nature preserves. The federal areas include Big Oaks National Wildlife Refuge, Hoosier National Forest, and Department of Defense lands. Among non-governmental organizations, The Nature Conservancy is a major land owner and manager. Local governments also own and manage community parks in the area. Conservation easements and other partners also own and manage a significant amount of land in the surrounding area.

Conservation Corridors

Increasing urbanization and widespread land use changes are greatly affecting natural landscapes and healthy ecological systems by fragmenting and degrading habitats. Traditional approaches to land conservation are often opportunistic, piecemeal, site specific, and narrowly focused.

However, increasing attention is being given to collaborative landscape conservation efforts that are proactive, strategic, comprehensive, and integrative. Regional analyses that consider larger geographic extents are helping to focus conservation efforts among a growing consortium of stakeholders and partners. Creating a series of ecological hubs and linkage corridors increases the connectivity, effectiveness, and resiliency of the biological systems that preserve biodiversity and essential ecological services.

Efforts are under way in Midwest Region of the U.S. Fish and Wildlife Service to create models that outline a basic conservation network throughout the Midwest. Recent emphasis on Strategic Habitat Conservation and the effects of global climate

Figure 4: Other Conservation and Recreation Lands in the Vicinity of Muscatatuck NWR

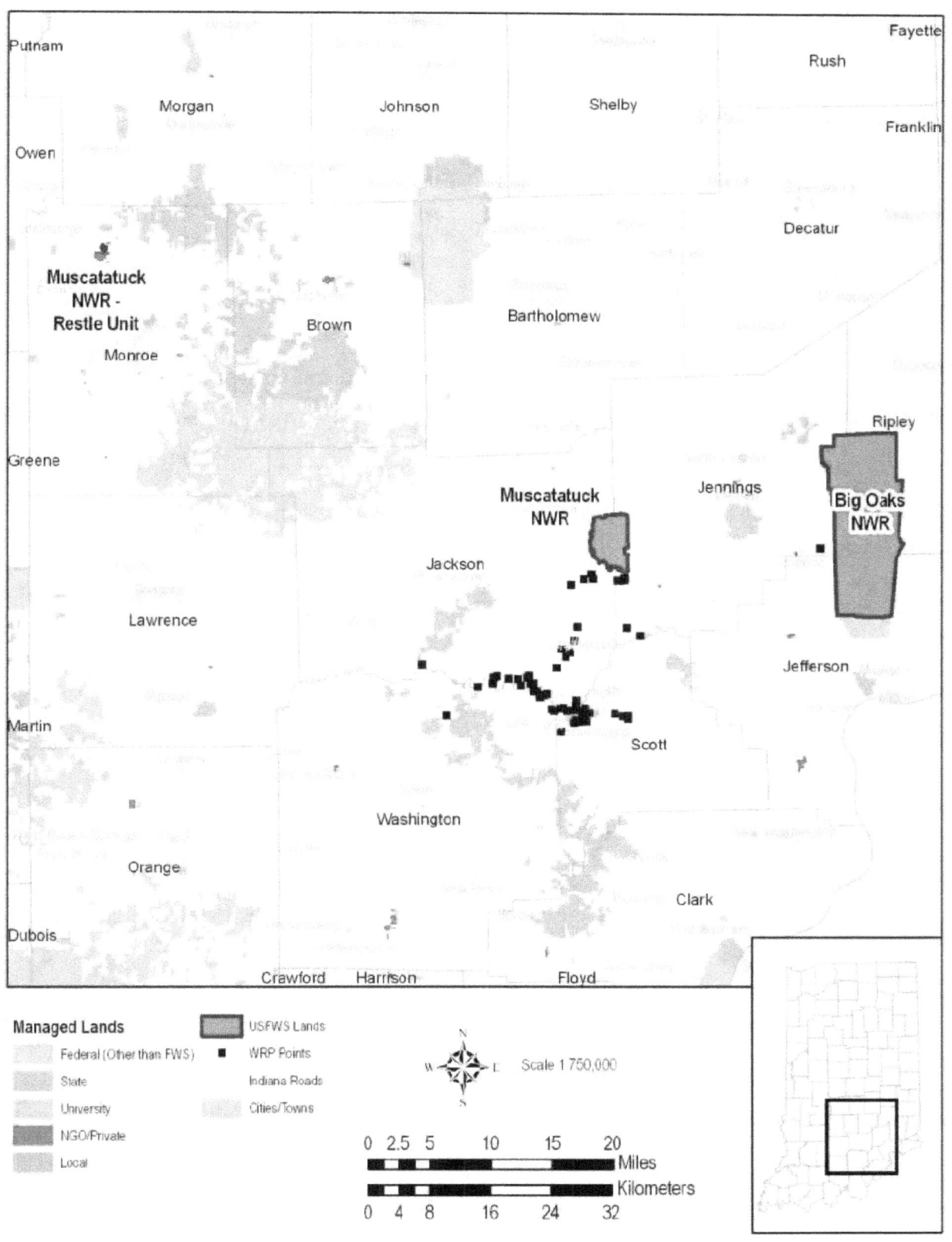

White-tailed deer. Photo credit: U.S. Fish and Wildlife Service

change have catalyzed these efforts in the Service. Using land cover (Figure 3 on page 11) and the existing conservation estate (Figure 4), it is possible to visualize the beginnings of a land conservation network with Muscatatuck NWR, Big Oaks NWR, and other major state and federal landholdings as major ecological hubs linked through private and public conservation efforts. The Refuge System is positioned well to play an integral role in the design and implementation of a regional conservation network.

The growing emphasis on landscape-level issues has demanded a shift in the scale at which environmental problems are approached. To continue providing the ecological services that sustain wildlife and human populations alike, the Service is looking outside Refuge boundaries and engaging in conversations with other members of the conservation community. It is only through collaborative efforts and partnerships – both public and private – that issues of this magnitude and scale can be effectively addressed.

Socioeconomic Context

Muscatatuck NWR is located in Jackson and Jennings Counties with a small satellite unit in Monroe County. Jackson and Jennings Counties are less racially and ethnically diverse than the state of Indiana as a whole. The population in the counties has a lower average income and a lower percentage of high school and college graduates than the state's population as a whole (U.S. Census Bureau 2008).

Population and Demographics

The population estimate for the two counties was 70,664 in 2005. The population increased 12.2 percent during the 1990s while the state's population increased 9.7 percent. Jennings County grew more at 16.5 percent, and Jackson County grew 9.6 percent. The two-county population was 98 percent white in 2005; the state population was 88.6 percent white. In Indiana, 6.4 percent of the people 5 years and older speak a language other than English at home; in Jackson County it is 4.3 percent; in Jennings County it is 2.5 percent. The population for Jackson County is projected to be 43,654 in 2025, a 3.4 percent increase from 2005; for Jennings County the projected population is 33,695 for 2025, an 18.5 percent increase from 2005. The largest community in Jackson County is Seymour with a 2005 population of 18,890. The largest community in Jennings County is North Vernon with a 2005 population of 6,433 (STATS Indiana, 2007).

Employment

In 2004 there were a total of 38,327 full- and part-time jobs in the two-county area. Manufacturing was the largest of the major economic sectors in both counties accounting for 25.8 percent of the jobs in Jackson County and 19.3 percent of the jobs in Jennings County. Retail trade, transportation, and warehousing were also notable sectors. Farm jobs made up 5 percent of employment (U.S. Census Bureau 2008).

Income and Education

Average per-capita income in the two counties was $25,885 in 2004; in Indiana it was $30,204. The median household income in 2003 for Jackson County was $41,502; for Jennings County $39,514; for Indiana and $43.323. In Jackson County, 11.5 percent of persons over 25 years of age hold a bachelor's degree or higher; in Jennings County 8.4 percent; in Indiana 19.4 percent of persons over 25 years hold a bachelor's degree or higher (U.S. Census Bureau 2008).

Table 1: Maximum Adult Audiences Within 30, 60, and 90 Miles of Muscatatuck NWR for Four Activities

Approximate Driving Distance to Refuge	Total Population	Birdwatching	Fishing	Hunting With Shotgun	Contribute to Environmental Organization
30 miles	285,584	15,674	44,988	14,619	3,095
60 miles	1,743,239	82,886	235,698	67,640	15,589
90 miles	5,164,171	235,928	657,836	181,566	41,891

Demand and Supply for Wildlife-Dependent Recreation

In order to estimate the potential market for visitors to the Refuge, we looked at 2007 consumer behavior data within approximately 30, 60, and 90-mile drives of the Refuge. The data were organized by zip areas. We used the three driving distances because we thought this was an approximation of reasonable maximum drives to the Refuge for an outing by different groups. From experience we know, for example, that visitors come from the nearby local area to view wildlife in the evening. We also know that people seeking interesting varieties of bird species drive from Cincinnati, Ohio to visit the Refuge. The 30-mile area extended beyond the communities of Bedford, Columbus, Greensburg, Madison, North Vernon, Salem, Scottsburg, and Seymour. The 60-mile area extended from the southern portion of the Indianapolis metropolitan area to the northern portion of the Louisville metropolitan area. The 90-mile area included the Cincinnati metropolitan area.

The consumer behavior data that we used in the analysis is derived from Mediamark Research Inc. data. The company collects and analyzes data on consumer demographics, product and brand usage, and exposure to all forms of advertising media. The consumer behavior data were projected by Tetrad Computer Applications Inc. to new populations using Mosaic data. Mosaic is a methodology that classifies neighborhoods into segments based on their demographic and socioeconomic composition. The basic assumption in the analysis is that people in demographically similar neighborhoods will tend to have similar consumption, ownership, and lifestyle preferences. Because of the assumptions

made in the analysis, the data should be considered as relative indicators of potential, not actual participation.

We looked at potential participants in birdwatching, fishing, and hunting with shotgun. In order to estimate the general environmental orientation of the population, we also looked at the number of people who might contribute to an environmental organization.

The consumer behavior data apply to persons greater than 18 years old. Table 1 displays the consumer behavior numbers for each of the three distances to the Refuge. The projections represent the maximum audience that we might expect to make a trip to the Refuge for approximate drives of half-hour, hour, and one and a half hours. Actual visitors will be fewer because the estimate is a maximum, and we expect only a fraction of these people will travel to the Refuge.

We also considered the maximum number of students that might potentially participate in environmental education offered by the Refuge by looking at the school populations in Jackson and Jennings Counties. For Jackson County the school enrollment in preschool through grade 12 was 8,142 according to the 2000 census. For Jennings County the equivalent enrollment was 5,828. The projected school age (5-19) population for the two counties for 2025 is 14,843.

Additional perspective on wildlife-dependent recreation was gained from Indiana's Statewide Comprehensive Outdoor Recreation Plan (SCORP) 2000-2004. In a survey of the population, recreation planners found that in the planning regions that contain the Refuge approximately 58 percent of the respondents participated in fishing regularly in the last year. Fishing was exceeded in participation only by the walking/hiking/jogging category. The approximate percentages of respondents for other activities were: nature observation/photography (36 percent), hunting (33 percent), and trapping (6 percent) (Indiana Department of Natural Resources 2000). Within the nature observation/photography category respondents reported participation in wildlife viewing, gathering (mushroom, berry etc.), viewing fall foliage, nature photography, and bird watching.

The SCORP identified the counties and regions that contain the Refuge as meeting or exceeding the regional recreation land standard of 35 acres per thousand population. The Indiana State Trails Plan (Indiana DNR 2006) reported 76 miles of trails in Jackson County and 17 miles of trails in Jennings County. The Refuge trails are included in these totals.

Climate

The Refuge experiences a continental climate of warm, humid summers and moderately cold winters. The area receives moisture from the Gulf of Mexico as air masses move up the Mississippi and Ohio River Valleys. January is the coldest month with a mean temperature of 28 degrees Fahrenheit. July is the warmest month with a mean temperature of 74.5 degrees Fahrenheit. April 20 and October 12 are the frost and freeze dates for 32 degrees Fahrenheit with a 50 percent probability. The average annual precipitation is about 46 total inches. Precipitation is distributed relatively evenly across the months of the year with a low average of 2.84 inches in February and a high average of 5.01 inches in May (Source: National Climatic Data Center).

Muscatatuck NWR. Photo Credit: U.S. Fish & Wildlife Service

Geology and Soils

The Refuge lies within the Scottsburg lowland physiographic division of Indiana. The lowland has resulted from a greater erosion of shales compared to the underlying limestones and siltstones of adjacent uplands. Thick glacial deposits that are older than Wisconsin glacial deposits cover the area with little variation in topography (Wayne 1956). More specifically, Muscatatuck NWR's geology includes the combination of underlying bedrock strata and the unconsolidated soils material deposited by glacial action.

The Refuge has upland and river valley areas, causing variations in depth of the unconsolidated soil material to bedrock. A well drilled in the northeast part of the Refuge encountered bedrock at a depth of 40 feet. The bedrock depths can vary quite widely depending on the amount of material deposited and subsequently removed by erosion. The glacial material is dominantly stratified sands and clays that have been blanketed with a mantle of wind blown silt (loess).

In the floodplain area, bedrock is typically less than 10 feet below the surface. (Marshall et al. 2007)

Hydric soils (Figure 5) cover 2,962 acres of the Refuge. Non-hydric soils cover the remaining 4,797 acres. Soils on the Refuge are grouped into five soil associations: Dubois-Peoga-Haubstadt, Stendal-Birds-Piopolis, Haymond-Wakeland-Wilbur, Bloomfield-Alvin, and a small amount of Ayrshire-Lyles (Marshall et al. 2007; Nagel et al. 1990; Nickell et al. 1976).

The Dubois-Peoga-Haubstadt association of soils are very deep, nearly level to strongly sloping, moderately well to poorly drained, medium textured soils that have formed in loess and the underlying stratified lacustrine sediments on terraces. The somewhat poorly drained Dubois soils are nearly level to gently sloping on narrow flats and upper side slopes. The moderately well drained Haubstadt soils are gently to strongly sloping on side slopes. Both Dubois and Haubstadt soils have very slowly permeable fragipans present in the soil profile. Peoga soils are nearly level, poorly drained, and are on broad flats. The moderately well-drained Otwell soils actually have a higher number of acres within the Refuge area, and are often intermixed with the Haubstadt soils. The minor soil in this association is the well-drained Negley soils on steep side slopes. Also included with this association is a small amount

Figure 5: Hydric Soils, Muscatatuck NWR

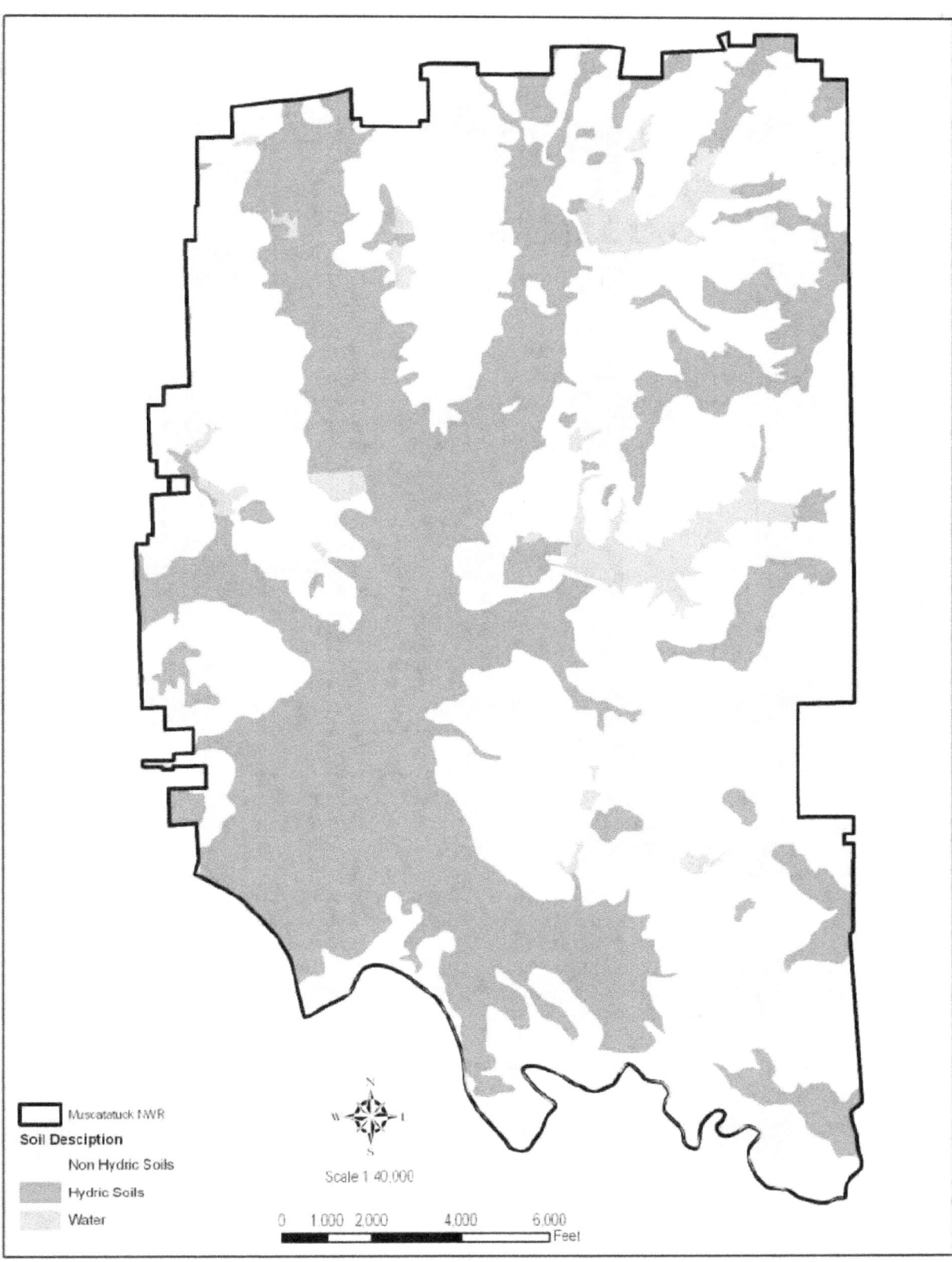

Muscatatuck NWR. Photo credit: U.S. Fish & Wildlife Service

of Illinoian till soils in the very eastern boundary of the Refuge. These soils are the somewhat poorly drained Avonburg, moderately well-drained Nabb and Cincinnati, which all have fragipans. The soils of this association comprise approximately 4,172 acres, or about 54 percent of the Refuge area.

The Stendal-Birds-Piopolis association of soils are very deep, nearly level, somewhat poorly to poorly drained, medium and moderately fine textured soils formed in fine-silty acid alluvium on floodplains. Within the Refuge area, Birds soil is the more dominant component of the association, with slightly more that 2,000 acres. Birds soils are poorly drained and are formed in non-acid silty alluvium over alluvium with a higher clay content, in slow backwater areas of floodplains. Stendal soils are somewhat poorly drained, are formed in silty acid alluvium and tend to occur on slightly elevated areas, which are called steps, of the floodplain. Piopolis soils are poorly and very poorly drained and are formed in clay alluvium on floodplains. There is currently no Piopolis mapped within the Refuge area. Minor soils in this association are the poorly drained Bonnie and moderately well-drained Steff soils. Bonnie soils are formed in silty acid alluvium and are found in similar positions as Birds soils. Steff soils are formed in silty acid alluvium and are found in positions similar to Stendal. These soils are found mainly in the watersheds of Mutton Creek Ditch, Storm Creek Ditch, and Sandy Branch. The soils of this association comprise approximately 2,367 acres, or about 30 percent of the Refuge area.

The Haymond-Wakeland-Wilbur association of soils are very deep, well to somewhat poorly drained, nearly level, formed in coarse-silty non-acid alluvium on floodplains. Within the Refuge area, Wakeland soils are the more dominant

component of the association, with slightly over 400 acres. Wakeland soils are somewhat poorly drained and are formed in silty non-acid alluvium on floodplains. Haymond soils are well-drained and are formed in silty non-acid alluvium on floodplains. Minor soil in this association is the well-drained, coarse loamy Wirt soils on natural levees of the floodplain adjacent to streams. These soils are found mainly in the Vernon Fork of the Muscatatuck River watershed. The soils of this association comprise approximately 600 acres, or about 7 percent of the Refuge area.

The Bloomfield-Alvin association of soils are very deep, nearly level to strongly sloping somewhat excessively to well-drained, coarse textured soils formed in eolian (windblown) sand deposits (dunes) on uplands. Bloomfield soils are nearly level to strongly sloping somewhat excessively drained on ridges and narrow side slopes of dunes. Alvin soils are well-drained and are intermixed with the Bloomfield soils on similar landforms. Minor soils in this association are the Bobtown and Medora soils. Bobtown soils are moderately well-drained and formed in moderately coarse textured eolian (windblown) sand deposits. Medora soils are moderately well-drained and are formed in loess and the underlying sandy outwash material, and have a fragipan. These soils are located mainly in the northwestern corner of the Refuge and comprise approximately 200 acres, or 3 percent of the Refuge area.

The Ayrshire-Lyles association of soils is very deep, nearly level, somewhat poorly and very poorly drained, moderately coarse textured coarse textured soils, formed in eolian (windblown) sand deposits (dunes) on uplands. Ayrshire soils are somewhat poorly drained and are on flats of uplands. Lyles soils are poorly drained, have very dark colored surface layers and are in slight depressions of uplands. These soils comprise about 43 total acres and are located mainly in the northwestern corner of the Refuge area.

Hydrology

The Refuge lies within a flat, relatively well drained portion of the Wabash River Basin (Figure 6). Water flows away from the Refuge down the Vernon Fork of the Muscatatuck River, into the Muscatatuck River, the White River, and on to the Wabash River. Three small streams, Sandy Branch, Mutton Creek, and Storm Creek, flow through the

Figure 6: Muscatatuck NWR and the Wabash River Basin Watershed

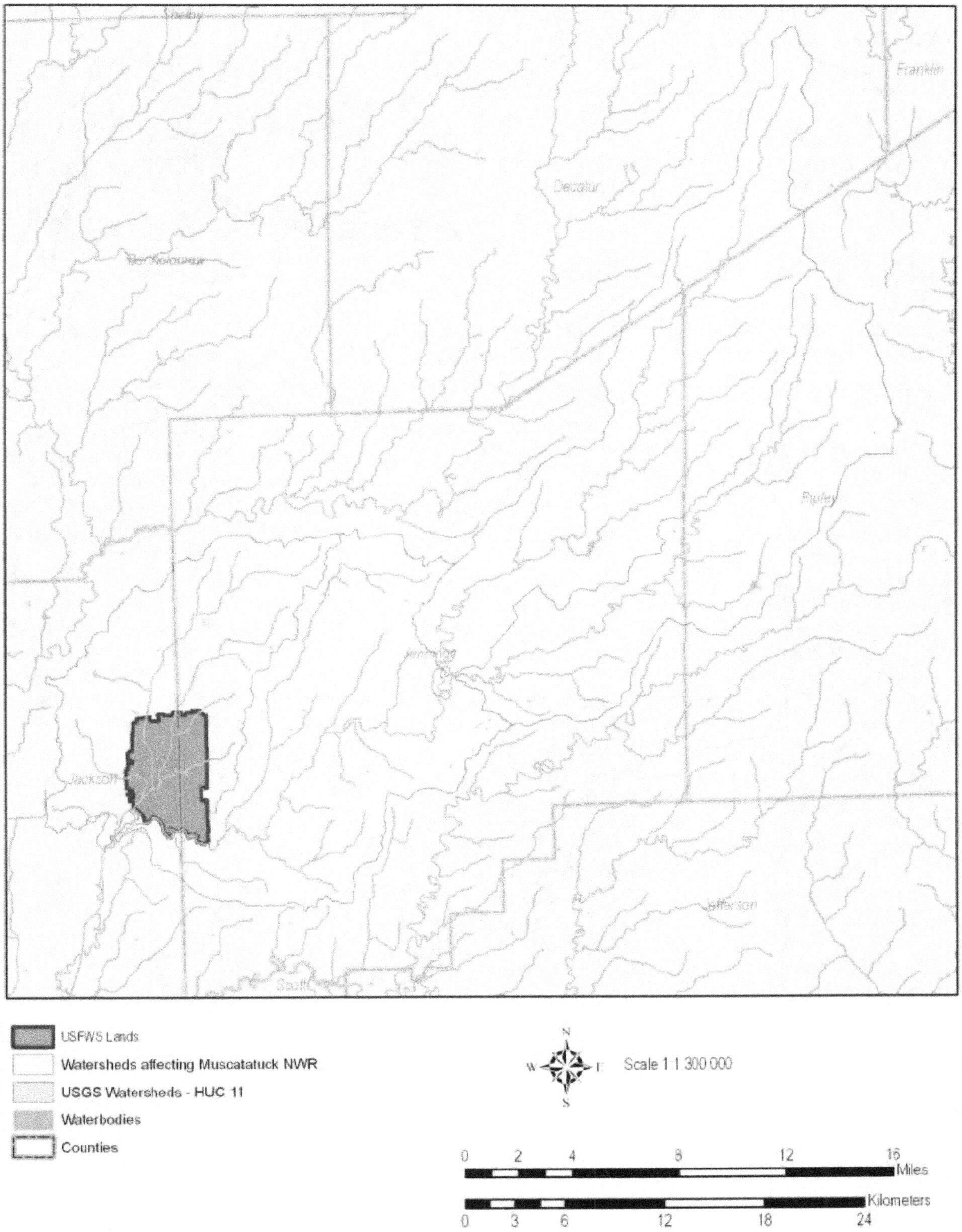
Decatur
Ripley
Jackson
Jefferson
Scott
USFWS Lands
Watersheds affecting Muscatatuck NWR
USGS Watersheds - HUC 11
Waterbodies
Counties
N
S
Scale 1:1 300 000
0 2 4 8 12 16
Miles
Kilometers
0 3 6 12 18 24

Refuge and enter the Vernon Fork soon after leaving the Refuge. The subwatersheds of Upper- and Lower- Mutton Creek and Upper- and Lower- Storm Creek, which cover 30,100 acres above the Refuge, flow into the Refuge. Approximately 8,525 acres of the Mutton Creek-Sandy Branch subwatershed, which includes the eastern portion of Seymour, also flows into the Refuge. The annual floodplain of the Vernon Fork extends 2,000 to 3,500 feet into the Refuge along its southern border. Annual floods inundate approximately 2,700 acres of the Refuge.

Refuge Habitats and Wildlife

Mini Marsh, Muscatatuck NWR. Photo credit: U.S. Fish & Wildlife Service

Acreages used to describe Refuge habitat in this section include the Restle Unit.

Wetlands

Wetlands cover roughly 70 percent of the Refuge and much of this land floods annually. (See Figure 7 for current Refuge land cover.)

The majority of wetland habitat is bottomland hardwood forest (4,180 acres), and managed water units that include moist soil units, brood marshes, greentree impoundments, and Stanfield, Moss and Richart Lakes (approximately 1,260 acres), which were built 1979-1982 with Bicentennial Land Heritage Program (BHLP) funds. The Refuge also has more than 70 other small ponds and wetland areas included in the 1,260 acres referenced above; these were constructed by former land owners to be stock ponds or ponds near residences and are utilized by migratory birds and wildlife. Several seeps exist on the Refuge, one of which is the Muscatatuck Seep Springs Research Natural Area. This wetland type is an acid seep spring that has only been documented in seven other locations in Indiana, one of which was destroyed, making it extremely rare in the state. Examples of wildlife that use these wetlands include Wood Ducks and Hooded Mergansers, which nest in the bottomland hardwoods, American Bald Eagle, copperbelly watersnake, river otter and many other species from all faunal assemblages.

Forests

Approximately 69 percent (about 5,400 acres) of the Refuge is covered by forests. Of this, about half of the Refuge, or approximately 78 percent of the forested area (about 4,180 acres), is classified as one of several types of bottomland hardwood forest. Bottomland hardwood forests are a type of cold-deciduous forest that are temporarily or seasonally flooded and occur on wet soils and in floodplains. American beech and a variety of maple and oak species dominate bottomland forests and ash, sweetgum, river birch and sycamore are also present. The remaining 15 percent of the forested area (approximately 1,210 acres) of the Refuge is classified as upland hardwood forest. Upland hardwood forest is also classified as a cold-deciduous forest type that primarily occurs in lowland or submontane habitats on soils that are unaffected by seasonal flooding. Varieties of oaks and maples dominate, and these forests can also include American beech and eastern red cedar along with other species (Sieracki et al. 2002).

Examples of trees commonly found on the Refuge include:

- pin oak
- swamp white oak
- swamp chestnut oak
- sweet gum
- green ash
- river birch
- silver maple
- red maple
- shellbark hickory
- white oak
- red oak
- white ash
- tuliptree

Figure 7: Current Land Cover, Muscatatuck NWR

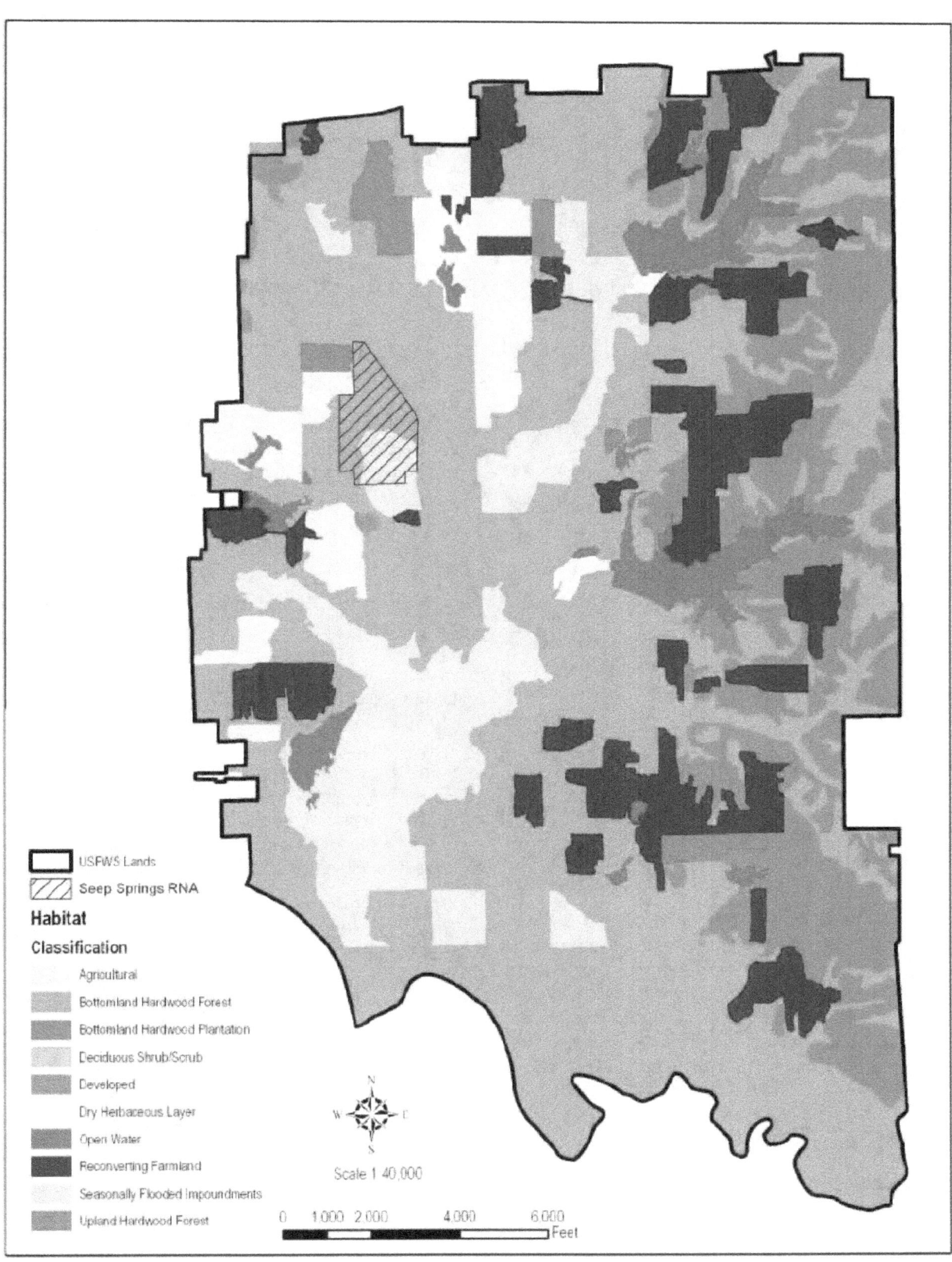

USFWS Lands
Seep Springs RNA

Habitat

Classification

Agricultural
Bottomland Hardwood Forest
Bottomland Hardwood Plantation
Deciduous Shrub/Scrub
Developed
Dry Herbaceous Layer
Open Water
Reconverting Farmland
Seasonally Flooded Impoundments
Upland Hardwood Forest

Scale 1 40,000

0   1,000 2,000   4,000   6,000
                                                Feet

■ American beech

Examples of wildlife that use the forests include white-tailed deer, eastern gray squirrel, eastern fox squirrel, southern flying squirrel, woodchuck, Indiana bat and forest birds such as:

- Wood Duck
- Hooded Merganser
- Red-shouldered Hawk
- Red-headed Woodpecker
- Northern Flicker
- Acadian Flycatcher
- Cerulean Warbler
- Prothonotary Warbler
- Worm-eating Warbler
- American Redstart
- Louisiana Waterthrush
- Kentucky Warbler
- Rusty Blackbird
- Yellow-billed Cuckoo
- Wood Thrush

Grasslands

Areas of grasslands totaling approximately 80 acres, including road edges, dam spillways and dikes, are mowed for maintenance purposes and, secondarily, for wildlife viewing along the auto tour route. The majority of these fields contain non-indigenous species such as fescue, timothy and orchard grass, and clover and the remaining dominant grassland vegetation includes native broadleaves, bluegrass, bluegrass-fescue, alfalfa-brome, and panic grass. Fescue is the dominant species over much of the non-cultivated open area.

A wide variety of wildlife utilize the grasslands including an abundance of small mammals, especially various mice and vole species, eastern cottontail rabbit, and larger mammals such as white-tailed deer and coyote, several snake species including black king snake, black rat snake, eastern garter snake, many raptor species including Red-tailed Hawk, and Northern Harrier, and a plethora of grassland birds such as:

- Sedge Wren
- Grasshopper Sparrow
- Henslow's Sparrow

Yellow Warbler, Muscatatuck NWR. Photo credit: Mark Trabue

- Song Sparrow
- Indigo Bunting
- Dickcissel
- Red-winged Blackbird
- Eastern Meadowlark
- Bobolink

Birds

More than 279 bird species have been reported on the Refuge and 120 of those are considered nesting species. A rich diversity of waterfowl, raptors, and songbirds are commonly observed on the Refuge. Wood Duck broods are common sightings in the spring and summer months. Waterfowl use days during the winter and spring migrations number in the hundred of thousands. A Bald Eagle nest has been active since 2002 and winter migrants are commonly seen. Muscatatuck NWR is also known for the spring and summer migration of songbirds, especially warblers, in May.

The Refuge was designated a Continentally Important Bird Area in June 1998. The designation was based on Christmas bird count data and the Refuge's wintering numbers of Canada Geese from the James Bay population. Between 2001 and 2007, the Refuge was a stopover site for the Whooping Crane Eastern Partnership (WCEP) ultra-light-led Whooping Crane migration every fall. A complete list of bird species and a general guide to their seasonal occurrence and status on the Refuge can be found in Appendix C.

Mammals

Thirty-seven species of mammals are known to occur on the Refuge. The mammals include the federally listed endangered Indiana bat and state-listed endangered evening bat, and the white-tailed deer, a species popular for hunting and wildlife viewing. Occurrence of the Indiana bat, including lactating females, on the Refuge was confirmed in 1995 and reaffirmed in 2007 by telemetry studies that found that the Indiana bat is a summer resident on the Refuge (Whitaker 1995; Carter 2007), and it may be more abundant than was generally thought. These bats are also known to form maternity colonies on the Refuge; one maternity roost was studied and its coordinates recorded in 2007, (Carter 2007).

Another notable mammal is the river otter, once extirpated from the state of Indiana. Reintroduction efforts for the state of Indiana were begun in January 1995 with 25 otters released at Muscatatuck NWR. This has resulted in numerous otters using the Refuge. Three confirmed otter litters were produced in 1996, and Refuge staff believe that they have produced litters annually ever since 1996. The reintroduction in Indiana has been successful and river otters are no longer considered endangered in the state (Johnson et al. 2007). A complete list of mammal species that occur on the Refuge can be found in Appendix C.

Amphibians and Reptiles

The wide diversity of habitats found on the Refuge makes it suitable for a broad range of amphibians and reptiles; 44 species of herpetofauna are known on the Refuge. They include three state-listed endangered species – the four-toed salamander, the copperbelly watersnake, and the Kirtland's snake – and the rough green snake, an Indiana Species of Special Concern.

As of November 1996, under the provisions of the Copperbelly Watersnake Conservation Agreement and Strategy, scientific investigation began to better understand the life history patterns of the copperbelly watersnake. The Refuge has been a stronghold for the species, allowing for intimate study (Kingsbury 1997). While many in the scientific community have commented on the ecology of the species, few have detailed aspects of its life history (Conant et al. 1991). Telemetry work at the Refuge has proven valuable in clarifying the ecological requirements of this species and observational data

collected since 1992 and tracking/locating data collected in 1997 through 2000 revealed this species' dependence on both the palustrine emergent habitat, as well as the floodplain forest habitat provided by the Refuge.

Indiana University Professor Dr. Meretsky discovered the state-listed endangered four-toed salamander during her work with the seep spring study. The salamander is associated with mature forests with wetlands with mossy edges and the young spend several months in the water before they come out on land. Records from central and southern Indiana appear to be based upon very small isolated colonies, some of which may no longer exist, making the Refuge population a significant find. A complete list of the amphibians and reptiles that occur on the Refuge is provided in Appendix C.

Fish

Fish species were collected and inventoried during a 2007 survey of waterbodies within the Refuge including tributary streams outside the Refuge. A total of 54 species were collected from within the Refuge, and more than 75 fish species are known to occur on the Refuge (Appendix C). The most diverse families represented were the minnow and darter families, which each included 11 species on the Refuge. Fishing for largemouth bass, bluegill, redear sunfish, crappie, and channel catfish is popular and draws an estimated 15,000 fishing visits per year at the Refuge.

In addition to the sites surveyed on the Refuge, 50 more sites were surveyed in the area surrounding the Refuge. New records for the Refuge included the finding of the eastern sand and harlequin darters in the Vernon Fork Muscatatuck

Red-eared Sliders. Photo credit: U.S. Fish & Wildlife Service

River. In addition, the flier was collected from Moss Lake and Mutton Creek, while the redspotted sunfish was collected from Mutton Creek. These records probably represent the northern and eastern records for these species.

Invertebrates

An intensive survey of aquatic macroinvertebrates was conducted concurrently with the fish survey during the spring of 2007. Fifty samples were collected from a variety of creeks, streams, and lake outlets. The results of this survey are still pending; however, five species of crayfish were collected including the paintedhand mudbug, Great Plains mudbug, northern crayfish, Sloan's crayfish, and rusty crayfish (Simon 2008).

Thirty three dragonfly species have been recorded on the Refuge including the beaverpond baskettail, eastern pondhawk, and shadow darner. The Refuge is known as a good location to observe dragonflies in the area (Curry 2001). With accompanying photographs taken at Muscatatuck NWR, many of these dragonfly species are highlighted in the book *Dragonflies of Indiana* (Curry 2001). The beaverpond baskettail dragonfly occurs on the Refuge and is considered a rare species in the state of Indiana. Butterfly surveys have been conducted since 2002 by volunteers using a protocol established by the North American Butterfly Association, and 60 species have been identified to date including the cabbage white, an exotic species. A complete listing of dragonfly and butterfly species documented on the Refuge can be found in Appendix C.

At least 24 species of mollusks have been documented as occurring on the Refuge (Harmon 1996, Fisher 2007) A follow-up investigation of several of the mussel survey sites used by Harmon (1996) was conducted in 2007 (Fisher 2007). A total of eight sites were sampled in 2007 for live, fresh dead, and weathered dead shells. Harmon's (1996) study documented 20 species present on the Refuge; the 2007 inquiry yielded three new species from the Vernon Fork that had never been documented on the Refuge, including elephantear, flutedshell, and deertoe. The little spectaclecase was found in both the 1996 and the 2007 surveys; however, only fresh dead specimens were encountered (Fisher 2007). This species is a species of special concern in Indiana and is listed as imperiled (S2) within the state. The Asiatic clam, a non-native invasive species, is markedly abundant on the Refuge,

Blue gill. Photo credit: U.S. Fish & Wildlife Service

especially within the Vernon Fork of the Muscatatuck River. A complete listing of mollusk species documented on the Refuge can be found in Appendix C.

Threatened and Endangered Species

State-listed/Candidate Species

A total of 61 state-listed endangered and special concern species have been documented on the Refuge with five more suspected to occur on the property. Examples of state-listed endangered species include:

- Indiana bat
- evening bat
- southern tubercled orchid
- climbing milkweed
- copperbelly water snake
- four-toed salamander
- Kirtland's snake
- Kirtland's Warbler
- Interior Least Tern
- Peregrine Falcon
- Bald Eagle
- Bewick's Wren
- Yellow-crowned Night-Heron
- Black-crowned Night-Heron
- Virginia Rail

- Common Moorhen
- King Rail
- Least Bittern
- Loggerhead Shrike
- Osprey
- Short-eared Owl
- Trumpeter Swan
- Northern Harrier
- American Bittern
- Upland Sandpiper
- Least Tern
- Black Tern
- Barn Owl
- Short-eared Owl
- Sedge Wren
- Golden-winged Warbler
- Marsh Wren
- Henslow's Sparrow
- Cerulean Warbler
- Black-and-white Warbler

State species of special concern on the Refuge include:

- least weasel
- little spectaclecase mussel
- Sharp-shinned Hawk
- Red-shouldered Hawk
- Great Egret
- Greater Yellowlegs
- Solitary Sandpiper
- Ruddy Turnstone
- Short-billed Dowitcher
- Wilson's Palarope
- Chuck-will's-widow
- Whip-poor-will
- Sandhill Crane
- Broad-winged Hawk
- Worm-eating Warbler
- Hooded Warbler
- rough green snake

Several other plant species are included on a state watch list. Those species are: American ginseng, bog bluegrass, Walter's St. John's-wort, smooth white violet, club spur orchid (also called small green woodland orchid), Loesel's twayblade and American lotus.

The Refuge species lists in Appendix C include each species' state and federal status.

Threatened/Endangered/Candidate Species (Fed Listed)

Least Tern, Whooping Crane, Indiana bat, and copperbelly watersnake use the Refuge.

Whooping Cranes from the "Operation Migration" project have used the Refuge as a stopover on their annual trip down to Florida. Free ranging/direct release cranes are routinely seen within 20 miles of the Refuge and one was spotted on the Refuge in 2008.

There is substantial documentation of the copperbelly watersnake's use of the Refuge. The copperbelly watersnake primarily inhabits shallow wetland systems consisting of sloughs, oxbows, river floodplains and buttonbush swamps, much of which have been lost or heavily fragmented (Pruitt and Szymanski 1997). In addition, the copperbelly watersnake is known to rely extensively on terrestrial habitat to traverse between spatially and temporally unpredictable wetland resources (Roe et al. 2003), offering an ideal system to investigate the role of terrestrial habitat on wetland connectivity. Presently, the copperbelly watersnake exists mainly as isolated, often small, populations separated by as much as 300 kilometers. Moreover, northern populations were listed as threatened by the Service and endangered by the states of Indiana, Michigan, and Ohio (Pruitt and Szymanski 1997). Genetic testing was done on the Muscatatuck NWR population in 2005 as part of a study that represented seven sampling sites located in Ohio/Michigan, Indiana, and Kentucky. The Indiana regional sampling site was conducted in a disjunct population along the Muscatatuck River, in the Muscatatuck NWR in Jackson County, Indiana, and at a wetland 29 river kilometers south of Muscatatuck NWR in Washington County, outside of Austin, Indiana. The two Indiana sites are as different from each other as they are from any of the other sampling sites, despite their geographic proximity. (Marshall et al. In Press)

Kudzu. Photo credit: U.S. Fish & Wildlife Service

The federally-listed endangered Indiana bat was confirmed on the Refuge in 1995 and reaffirmed in 2007 by telemetry studies that found that the Indiana bat is a summer breeding resident on the Refuge (Whitaker 1995; Carter 2007). These bats are also known to form maternity colonies on the Refuge; one maternity roost was studied and its coordinates recorded in 2007 (Carter 2007).

Several species that were previously considered candidate species occur at times on the Refuge. These include the Loggerhead Shrike and Cerulean Warbler, bog bluegrass, American ginseng, and the southern tubercled orchid.

Threats to Resources

Invasive Species

Invasive, exotic, and noxious weeds are common throughout most of the Refuge's habitat types. Although research on quality, distribution, and abundance estimates are lacking, it is evident to anyone passing through on Refuge roads that autumn olive, garlic mustard, reed canary grass, multiflora rose, crown vetch and many other species dominate certain portions of the landscape. Japanese stiltgrass, multiflora rose, tree-of-heaven, autumn olive and kudzu threaten the diversity and health of the bottomland and upland hardwoods while other species, such as reed canary grass, attempt to out-compete native vegetation along riparian corridors, in moist soil units and in other wetland types. Many of the invasive species encountered have the capability over time of producing solid monocultures that shade out native vegetation and reduce overall plant diversity and, consequently, overall animal diversity (Pimentel 2005).

Examples of invasives found on the Refuge include:

- purple loosestrife
- autumn olive
- Canada thistle
- Johnson grass
- multiflora rose
- moneywort
- common carp
- Asian clams
- Japanese stiltgrass
- oriental bittersweet
- garlic mustard
- kudzu
- reed canary grass
- Asian ambrosia beetle
- Asian ladybugs
- European Starling
- Brown-headed Cowbird
- House Sparrow
- mosquito fish
- gypsy moth

There has only been one account of a gypsy moth (1995) and subsequent traps have not revealed any moths. It is not considered a major problem.

Water Contamination

Water contamination affecting the Refuge includes surface runoff and National Pollutant Discharge Elimination System (NPDES) discharge from populated areas, crop and livestock runoff, septic system failures, accidental spills, as well as pollutants from power substations, petroleum refineries, and industrial parks in the area. Contaminants may be entering the Refuge via a number of surface and groundwater sources, including:

- Vernon Fork of the Muscatatuck River (VFMR) and its tributaries
- Mutton and Storm Creeks
- Sandy Branch Creek

- Numerous unnamed drainages that enter the system during flooding periods
- City of Seymour
- Adjacent highways, roads, and railroads including discharge from accidents
- Underground storage tanks

Agriculture is the primary land use in the watershed. Run-off from crop fields, pastureland, and feedlots contributes to non-point source pollution. Erosion, sedimentation, eutrophication, and contamination from application of pesticides, herbicides, and fertilizers all introduce contaminants into the watershed and Refuge system. Many of these substances, such as organochlorines and organo-phophates, are known to be toxic to fish and wildlife via direct exposure, bioaccumulation, and bio-magnification (Cox 1991). In addition to fluvial and riparian deposition, flooding occurs during high rainfall periods of the year in many areas of the Refuge. These flood waters carry debris, chemicals, and other contaminants to large otherwise terrestrial areas of the Refuge.

In addition to agriculture, rapid residential and transportation development in the areas surrounding the Refuge have had detrimental impacts on the watershed. As more land is cleared and paved, there are decreases in sediment interception, increased throughfall, and changes in roughness coefficients and slope, all of which contribute to increases in flow rates, erosion, and amount of particles, sediment, and other substances reaching the Refuge (Tang et al. 2005). The Refuge is within a mile or less of three major highways, all of which cross at least one of the three primary tributaries that enter the Refuge. This creates sources of run-off containing salts, fuel, and other petroleum products.

The construction of homes and businesses has put a strain on waste water treatment facilities and septic systems that could result in nutrient and bacterial problems within the watershed. There is also potential for accidental spills to occur. The Refuge is bordered on two sides by major highways (U.S. 31, U.S. 50 and I-65) and by a well-traveled county road (Jennings CR900W) on a third side. Two of the three roads encompassing the Refuge are hard surface roads. In addition, the CSX Railroad runs approximately three-quarters of a mile north of the Refuge, crossing both Mutton and Storm Creek ditches. Another railroad, the Madison

Railroad, crosses the VFMR upstream in North Vernon. In 1980, a derailed train spilled between 8,000 and 10,000 gallons of chlorobenzene directly into Storm Creek Ditch (McWilliams-Munson 1996).

Atmospheric deposition of heavy metals is a concern worldwide and the Refuge falls under the same general fish advisory as most of the waters in the state of Indiana. This advisory establishes recommendations for fish consumption based on elevated mercury levels in the fish in Indiana (Indiana Department of Natural Resources 2008). The problems associated with heavy metal contamination may be compounded at Muscatatuck NWR due to the impoundment of water and trapping of sediment, collection, and concentration of runoff from a large watershed, and the wetting and drying cycles that contribute to the methylation of mercury.

Urban Development

The city of Seymour is located just west of the Refuge, with Interstate 65 between the two as depicted in Figure 3 on page 11. U.S. Highway 50 passes across the northern boundary of the Refuge and continues west into downtown Seymour. Because of this crossroads, the development of businesses along the U.S. 50 corridor west of the Refuge has increased steadily, and the northern and western sides of the Refuge have seen an increase in residential development.

According to the U.S. Census, the population and number of housing units in both Jackson and Jennings Counties increased between 2000 and 2007. Both Jackson and Jennings Counties populations increased by just under 1,000 people, but the number of housing units in each increased by over 1,200 units in that same time period. These population and development increases bring additional concerns regarding impervious surfaces, increased traffic on roadways, additional water management needs, habitat loss and fragmentation, and increased visitation at the Refuge.

Military Activity

Areas adjacent to the Refuge have seen an increase in military activity in recent years. In addition to activity associated with Camp Atterbury and Jefferson Proving Grounds, in 2005 the Muscatatuck Urban Training Center (MUTC) was created in South Central Jennings County. The Indiana National Guard converted this 1,000-acre

Coyote. U.S. Fish and Wildlife Service photo.

site into an urban training center with 70 buildings and a mile of tunnels. Air traffic related to combat maneuvering and refueling, as well as training exercises and convoys, have increased the potential for wildlife disturbance and accidental discharges.

Atmospheric Concerns

In addition to the atmospheric deposition of heavy metals discussed in the water contamination section, ozone levels are a factor for the Refuge.

Ozone exposures in Indiana are the highest in the nation's north central region and are relatively high when compared with many states nationwide. The portion of Indiana that contains the Refuge, in particular, exhibits elevated ozone levels. The ozone exposure adversely affects trees and other plants. Ozone stress is expected to be less severe on some oaks and maples because they are relatively tolerant of ozone. Nevertheless, given the current ozone exposures and evidence of foliar injury, the potential exists for reduced tree growth and reduced forest health on the Refuge. (Woodall et al. 2005)

Climate Change Impacts

The U.S. Department of the Interior issued an order in January 2001 requiring federal agencies under its direction that have land management responsibilities to consider potential climate change impacts as part of long range planning endeavors.

The increase of carbon dioxide (CO_2) within the earth's atmosphere has been linked to the gradual rise in surface temperature commonly referred to as global warming. In relation to comprehensive conservation planning for national wildlife refuges, carbon sequestration constitutes the primary climate-related impact that refuges can affect in a small way. The U.S. Department of Energy's "Carbon Sequestration Research and Development" defines carbon sequestration as "...the capture and secure storage of carbon that would otherwise be emitted to or remain in the atmosphere."

Vegetated land is a tremendous factor in carbon sequestration. Terrestrial biomes of all sorts – grasslands, forests, wetlands, tundra, and desert – are effective both in preventing carbon emission and acting as a biological "scrubber" of atmospheric CO_2. The Department of Energy report's conclusions noted that ecosystem protection is important to carbon sequestration and may reduce or prevent loss of carbon currently stored in the terrestrial biosphere.

Conserving natural habitat for wildlife is the heart of any long-range plan for national wildlife refuges and management areas. The actions proposed in this CCP would conserve or restore land and habitat, and would thus retain existing carbon sequestration on the WMA. This in turn contributes positively to efforts to mitigate human-induced global climate change.

One Service activity in particular – prescribed burning – releases CO_2 directly to the atmosphere from the biomass consumed during combustion. However, there is actually no net loss of carbon, since new vegetation quickly germinates and sprouts to replace the burned-up biomass and sequesters or assimilates an approximately equal amount of carbon as was lost to the air (Boutton et al. 2006). Overall, there should be little or no net change in the amount of carbon sequestered at Kirtland's Warbler WMA from any of the proposed management alternatives.

Several impacts of climate change have been identified that may need to be considered and addressed in the future:

- Habitat available for cold water fish such as trout and salmon in lakes and streams could be reduced.

- Forests may change, with some species shifting their range northward or dying out, and other trees moving in to take their place.

- Ducks and other waterfowl could lose breeding habitat due to stronger and more frequent droughts.

- Changes in the timing of migration and nesting could put some birds out of sync with the life cycles of their prey species.

- Animal and insect species historically found farther south may colonize new areas to the north as winter climatic conditions moderate.

The managers and resource specialists responsible for the WMA need to be aware of the possibility of change due to global warming. When feasible, documenting long-term vegetation, species, and hydrologic changes should become a part of research and monitoring programs on the WMA. Adjustments in land management direction may be necessary over the course of time to adapt to a changing climate.

The following paragraphs are excerpts from the 2000 report: *Climate Change Impacts on the United States: The Potential Consequences of Climate Variability and Change*, produced by the National Assessment Synthesis Team, an advisory committee chartered under the Federal Advisory Committee Act to help the US Global Change Research Program fulfill its mandate under the Global Change Research Act of 1990. These excerpts are from the section of the report focused upon the eight-state Midwest Region.

Observed Climate Trends

Over the 20th century, the northern portion of the Midwest, including the upper Great Lakes, has warmed by almost 4 degrees Fahrenheit (2 degrees Celsius), while the southern portion, along the Ohio River valley, has cooled by about 1 degree Fahrenheit (0.5 degrees Celsius). Annual precipitation has increased, with many of the changes quite substantial, including as much as 10 to 20 percent increases over the 20th century. Much of the precipitation has resulted from an increased rise in the number of days with heavy and very heavy precipitation events. There have been moderate to very large increases in the number of days with excessive moisture in the eastern portion of the Great Lakes basin.

Scenarios of Future Climate

During the 21st century, models project that temperatures will increase throughout the Midwest, and at a greater rate than has been observed in the 20th century. Even over the northern portion of the region, where warming has been the largest, an accelerated warming trend is projected for the 21st century, with temperatures increasing by 5 to 10 degrees Fahrenheit (3 to 6 degrees Celsius). The average minimum temperature is likely to increase as much as 1 to 2 degrees Fahrenheit (0.5 to 1 degree Celsius) more than the maximum temperature. Precipitation is likely to continue its upward trend, at a slightly accelerated rate; 10 to 30 percent increases are projected across much of the region. Despite the increases in precipitation, increases in temperature and other meteorological factors are likely to lead to a substantial increase in evaporation, causing a soil moisture deficit, reduction in lake and river levels, and more drought-like conditions in much of the region. In addition, increases in the proportion of precipitation coming from heavy and extreme precipitation are very likely.

Midwest Key Issues:

1. Reduction in Lake and River Levels

Water levels, supply, quality, and water-based transportation and recreation are all climate-sensitive issues affecting the region. Despite the projected increase in precipitation, increased evaporation due to higher summer air temperatures is likely to lead to reduced levels in the Great Lakes. Of 12 models used to assess this question, 11 suggest significant decreases in lake levels while one suggests a small increase. The total range of the 11 models' projections is less than a 1-foot increase to more than a 5-foot decrease. A 5-foot (1.5- meter) reduction would lead to a 20 to 40 percent reduction in outflow to the St. Lawrence Seaway. Lower lake levels cause reduced hydropower generation downstream, with reductions of up to 15 percent by 2050. An increase in demand for water across the region at the same time as net flows decrease is of particular concern. There is a possibility of increased national and international tension related to increased pressure for water diversions from the Lakes as demands for water increase. For smaller lakes and rivers, reduced flows are likely to cause water quality issues to become more acute. In addition, the projected increase in very heavy precipitation events will likely lead to increased flash flooding and worsen agricultural and other non-point source pollution as more frequent heavy rains wash pollutants into rivers and lakes. Lower water levels are likely to make water-based transportation more difficult with increases in the costs of navigation of 5 to 40 percent. Some of this increase will likely be offset as reduced ice cover extends the navigation season. Shoreline damage due to high lake levels is likely to decrease 40 to 80 percent due to reduced water levels.

Adaptations: A reduction in lake and river levels would require adaptations such as re-engineering of ship docks and locks for transportation and recreation. If flows decrease while demand increases, international commissions focusing on Great Lakes water issues are likely to become even more important in the future. Improved forecasts and warnings of extreme precipitation events could help reduce some related impacts.

2. Agricultural Shifts

Agriculture is of vital importance to this region, the nation, and the world. It has exhibited a capacity to adapt to moderate differences in growing season climate, and it is likely that agriculture would be able to continue to adapt. With an increase in the length of the growing season, double cropping, the practice of planting a second crop after the first is harvested, is likely to become more prevalent. The CO_2 fertilization effect is likely to enhance plant growth and contribute to generally higher yields. The largest increases are projected to occur in the northern areas of the region, where crop yields are currently temperature limited. However, yields are not likely to increase in all parts of the region. For example, in the southern portions of Indiana and Illinois, corn yields are likely to decline, with 10-20 percent decreases projected in some locations. Consumers are likely to pay lower prices due to generally increased yields, while most producers are likely to suffer reduced profits due to declining prices. Increased use of pesticides and herbicides are very likely to be required and to present new challenges.

Adaptations: Plant breeding programs can use skilled climate predictions to aid in breeding new varieties for the new growing conditions. Farmers can then choose varieties that are better attuned to the expected climate. It is likely that plant breeders will need to use all the tools of plant breeding, including genetic engineering, in adapting to climate change. Changing planting and harvest dates and planting densities, and using integrated pest management, conservation tillage, and new farm technologies are additional options. There is also the potential for shifting or expanding the area where certain crops are grown if climate conditions become more favorable. Weather conditions during the growing season are the primary factor in year-to-year differences in corn and soybean yields. Droughts and floods result in large yield reductions; severe droughts, like the drought of 1988, cause yield reductions of over 30 percent. Reliable seasonal forecasts are likely to help farmers adjust their practices from year to year to respond to such events.

3. Changes in Semi-natural and Natural Ecosystems

The Upper Midwest has a unique combination of soil and climate that allows for abundant coniferous tree growth. Higher temperatures and increased evaporation will likely reduce boreal forest acreage, and make current forestlands more susceptible to pests and diseases. It is likely that the southern transition zone of the boreal forest will be susceptible to expansion of temperate forests, which in turn will have to compete with other land use pressures. However, warmer weather (coupled with beneficial effects of increased CO_2), are likely to lead to an increase in tree growth rates on marginal forestlands that are currently temperature-limited. Most climate models indicate that higher air temperatures will cause greater evaporation and hence reduced soil moisture, a situation conducive to forest fires. As the 21st century progresses, there will be an increased likelihood of greater environmental stress on both deciduous and coniferous trees, making them susceptible to disease and pest infestation, likely resulting in increased tree mortality.

As water temperatures in lakes increase, major changes in freshwater ecosystems will very likely occur, such as a shift from cold water fish species, such as trout, to warmer water species, such as bass and catfish. Warmer water is also likely to create an environment more susceptible to invasions by non-native species. Runoff of excess nutrients (such as nitrogen and phosphorus from fertilizer) into lakes and rivers is likely to increase due to the increase in heavy precipitation events. This, coupled with warmer lake temperatures, is likely to stimulate the growth of algae, depleting the water of oxygen to the detriment of other living things. Declining lake levels are likely to cause large impacts to the current distribution of wetlands. There is some chance that some wetlands could gradually migrate, but in areas where their migration is limited by the topography, they would disappear. Changes in bird populations and other native wildlife have already been linked to increasing temperatures and more changes are likely in the future. Wildlife populations are particularly susceptible to climate extremes due to the effects of drought on their food sources.

Administrative Facilities

The original portion of the Visitor Center (with restrooms) was constructed in the mid-1970s and featured a small office, lobby exhibit area, storage area, projection room, and auditorium/AV room separated by a breezeway from public restrooms. In 1989 the office was converted to a bookstore. Approximately 10 feet was added to the back of the original building in the early 1990s to create a bird viewing room, expanded bookstore, and additional storage areas. In 2003 a new wing, the Conservation Learning Center, was constructed using private funding obtained by one of the Refuge Friends groups, the Muscatatuck Wildlife Society Foundation. The new Conservation Learning center featured a large auditorium, exhibit area, and storage room. Numerous exhibits are located in the new wing. The two wings are connected by a breezeway with large glass windows. The Refuge office is situated in a remodeled ranch-style house across from the Visitor Center. Workshops, garages, storage buildings, and additional offices are located in the west-central area of the Refuge off of County Road 400 North.

The Muscatatuck Wildlife Society, our primary Friend's Group, operates a bookstore in our Visitor Center that is staffed by volunteers every afternoon and many mornings, and the building is closed when not staffed. Volunteers greet visitors, answer

Muscatatuck NWR Visitor Center. Photo credit: U.S. Fish & Wildlife Service

questions, and provide literature and information on Refuge hunting, fishing, and wildlife viewing opportunities. The Visitor Center has a paved, 16-car parking lot in front of the building, and a paved 33-car lot located across from the building off the loop road. A gravel overflow parking lot that can accommodate approximately 50 vehicles is located about 100 yards south of the Office, east of County Line Road.

Cultural Resources and Historic Preservation

The earliest generally accepted human culture in Indiana is known as the PaleoIndian, a small population of nomadic peoples who moved into the state about 14,000 years ago upon the retreat of the glaciers. Sites are rare, usually disturbed, and important. A PaleoIndian point has been found in Jackson County but none have been found on the Refuge.

The Service has conducted several archeological investigations on the Refuge, which have identified numerous Archaic culture sites in the period 10,500 to 3,000 years ago. During this period the people engaged in extensive trade of far distant exotic materials. They also adapted to major temperature and resulting environmental changes as the Pleistocene ended and the associated megafauna became extinct following the retreat of the glaciers. This was followed by the hot and dry altithermal, which ended during a climatic period much like the 20th century. The primary subsistence pattern of the Archaic period was hunting and gathering of a large range of animal and plant resources: "The ecotone between the swamp and the adjacent uplands [in the Refuge area] would have provided a unique blend of ecological resources for exploitation." (Myers 1979:11). Two cemeteries, the Barkman and Myers cemeteries, are also located on the Refuge.

Pottery, gardening, mounds (usually burial), and later the bow and arrow are indicative of the Woodland culture commencing about 3,000 years ago. Sites from this culture have been located on the Refuge. The Woodland culture was partially but not entirely displaced by the final prehistoric culture, the Mississippian, in the period 1,100 to 400 years ago. But by the time Western culture (Euro-American) arrived the area had been de-populated.

In the Refuge area neither the archeological nor the early documentary record provides any connection between prehistoric cultures and historic Indian tribes. The earliest written records indicate the Miami, Illinois, and Shawnee lived in the area, but the Iroquois from New York drove out those tribes in the early 1600s. Nevertheless, the Miami and Shawnee along with the Delaware were in Jackson and Jennings Counties until being displaced entirely by 1818.

Between the 1830s and the 1870s farmers settled on what is now the Refuge. Originally subsistence-based hog and corn farmers, the early settlers relied heavily on the abundant wildlife and plant resources. Later a network of rural graveled roads led to the introduction of manufactured goods, which improved rural life during the early 20th century. But concurrently, erosion caused by extensive deforestation from expanding farms stripped away the topsoil and some farmers abandoned the land. To create additional fertile farmland, Mutton and Storm Creeks were ditched for drainage between 1880 and 1900. "By 1870 most of the present refuge area was utilized for farming and this pattern of small farms continued essentially uninterrupted in the area until the creation of the Refuge in 1966." (Myers 1979:23)

Cultural resources are all an important part of the Nation's heritage. The Service is committed to protecting valuable evidence of human interactions with each other and the landscape. Protection is accomplished in conjunction with the Service's mandate to protect fish, wildlife, and plant resources.

As of March 1, 2008, the National Register of Historic Places listed 11 historic properties in Jackson County and five in Jennings County. This small number is surely not representative of the number of potential historic properties in the counties. Two of the National Register properties are archaeological sites that are are located on the Refuge, the listings resulting from Service-funded research: sites 12-J-62 and 12-J-87. Also as of March 1, the Refuge inventory of identified known and potential cultural resources based on Service-sponsored archeological investigations and maps resulted in a list of 140 sites of which 94 are on the National Register, have been determined eligible, or are considered eligible until determined otherwise. Archeological surveys have covered just 1,920 acres of the Refuge so many more sites are likely to occur on the Refuge. Of special note of the known sites is the Carl Myers farm (including log cabin, log barn, and persimmon orchard remnant) which should be nominated to the National Register.

The Refuge has a small number of Native American artifacts on exhibit in the Visitors Center. These artifacts were found on the Refuge and are on loan from the Glenn Black Museum of Indiana University in Bloomington. The display has several artifacts including lithic points, tools, and a pot. The Refuge is included in the Region-wide scope of collections statement dated October 31, 1994.

Muscatatuck NWR. Photo credit: U.S. Fish & Wildlife Service

Muscatatuck NWR. Photo credit: U.S. Fish & Wildlife Service

Visitation

Muscatatuck NWR is open from sunrise to sunset 365 days a year. There are two entrances to the Refuge and both have automatic gates that open at sunrise and close at sunset. Special extended hours are set during hunting seasons. The Conservation Learning Center is also regularly used for meetings and presentations by groups that have a wildlife conservation or management purpose or program, including evening hours by arrangement.

The Refuge annual visitation was estimated at approximately 174,000 in 2006. The number of visitors per year is obtained through estimates derived in large part from traffic counters at both entrances. Undetected malfunctions in the counters are believed to have led to reports of lower numbers of visitors in some recent years.

The Visitor Center is located on a loop off County Line Road (across from the Office) and is usually by-passed by repeat visitors. A counter at the main point of entry indicated approximately 13,000 visitors to the Visitor Center during the last year.

We do not have an accurate breakdown of visitor numbers per activity but we believe the largest segment of our visitors come for wildlife observation including bird watching, followed by fishing, interpretation/education, and hunting.

Current Management

Habitat Management

Acreages used to describe Refuge habitat in this section include the Restle Unit.

Wetland Management

A total of approximately 1,260 acres on the Refuge have water control structures, including moist soil units, greentree reservoirs, managed wetlands, and open water units (Figure 8). Annual water management plans have been followed since 1984 and these plans give management strategies for each unit that include specific water levels needed to create and maintain various habitat or to make food available and attractive to wildlife, particularly for Wood Duck production. Water management techniques include:

- Removing water to expose mudflats for shorebird use.
- Allowing seed germination of desirable moist soil plants.
- Allowing natural or mechanical rejuvenation of a permanent marsh or moist soil unit.
- Discouraging use of an area by muskrats.
- Adding water and maintaining different depths to stimulate invertebrate production.
- Creating and maintaining brood habitat and waterfowl migratory feeding areas (Smith and Kadlec 1983).

The primary goals of water management are to provide optimum conditions for food and cover for migrating birds, especially waterfowl, nesting and brood habitat for Wood Ducks and Hooded Mergansers, and habitat for other species that use wetland areas.

Moist Soil Units

Muscatatuck NWR actively manages 296 acres in 10 moist soil units through water and vegetation manipulation. Moist soil management on Muscatatuck NWR has been focused primarily on producing dense stands of perennial emergent vegetation on eight units to provide foraging and resting habitat for spring migrating waterfowl. Another objective on these eight units has been to provide brood habitat for resident Wood Ducks, Hooded Mergansers and Canada Geese. These objectives were achieved through water level

Figure 8: Water Management Infrastructure, Muscatatuck NWR

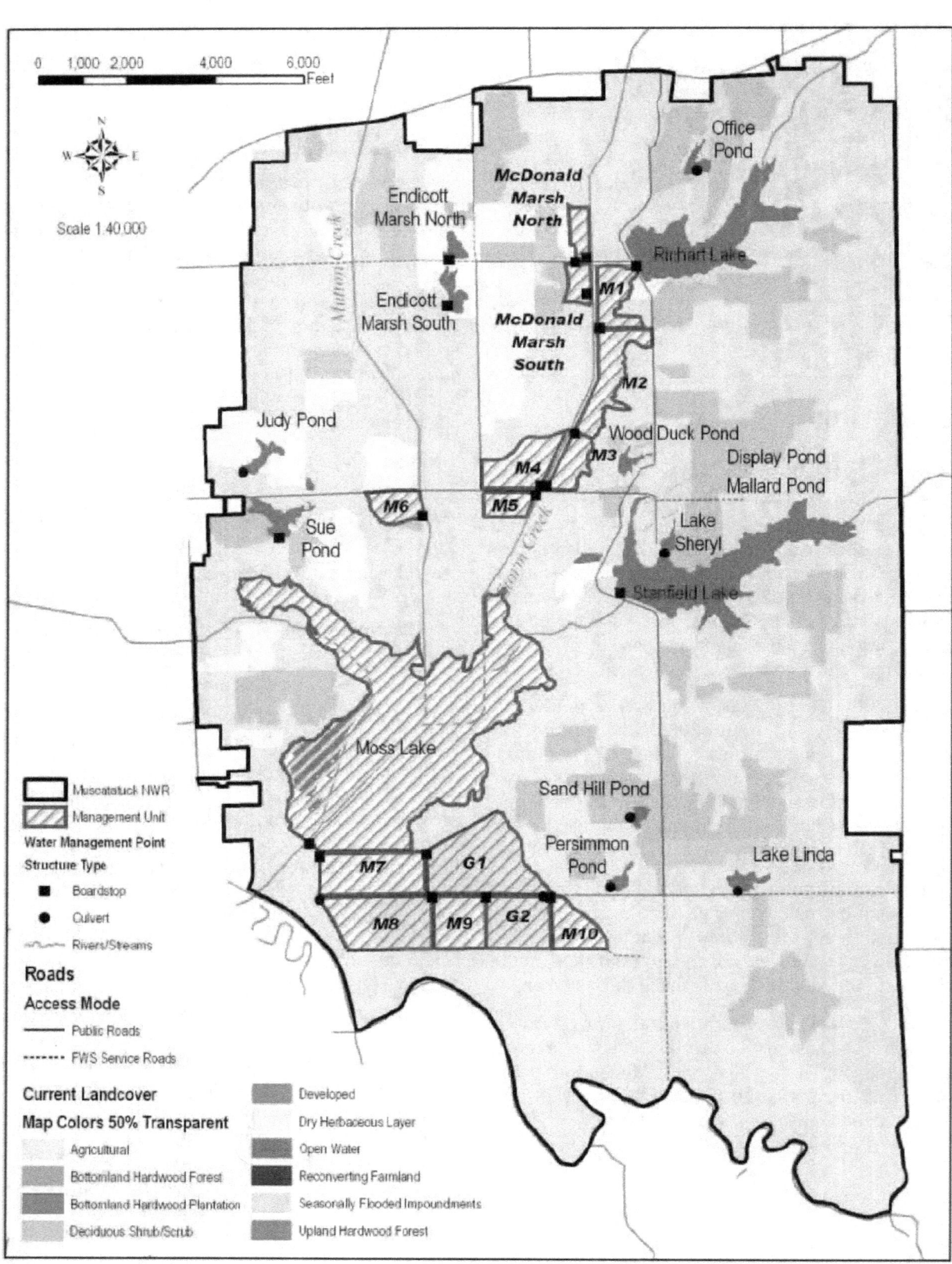

manipulations timed to coincide with providing optimum habitat conditions for germinating smartweed while also maintaining pool levels throughout the summer months for the broods. Seasonal flooding of these units has generally been planned to occur from September through April. However, proper hydrological manipulation in these units has proven difficult to achieve due to excessive flooding and/or beaver activity combined with a lack of personnel. The remaining two units have been managed to provide sparse perennial emergent vegetation combined with drawdowns timed to coincide with southward migrating shorebird arrival to provide optimum mudflat habitat, a critical need for this avifaunal group (Smith and Kadlec 1983). Water manipulations are generally conducted so that flooding occurs between September and March, although these units have been subjected to the same limitations outlined above.

Regular maintenance of moist soil units is a necessary phase in any management scheme due to the eventual invasion of these areas by more persistent or woody vegetation, i.e. buttonbush, willows, and Eastern cottonwood. The preferred means of maintaining a particular unit generally involves methods of mechanical disturbance, mowing or disking, to set back succession (Gray et al. 1999). Most units are scheduled to undergo treatment approximately once every 3 to 5 years. However, due to a shortage of staff and impediments to drawdown such as beaver activity and inclement weather, the achievement of many desired management activities are not realized as scheduled. In a normal year, plans call for the maintenance of one to three of the moist soil units. During this process, drawdown may begin earlier than "normal" to facilitate entry into the units with the necessary equipment. Following vegetation manipulation the units are reflooded and enter back into the "normal" cycle of drawdown and floodup until another maintenance cycle is necessary.

Grasslands

Grassland management is extremely limited, with only 80 acres currently in this kind of habitat. Active management of grasslands in the past entailed mowing, burning, and haying; however, these activities have been abandoned largely due to lack of staff and funds, increasing costs of active management, and changes in objectives. The current objective for many areas that were previously farmed (approximately 870 acres) is to allow them to revert to hardwood forest to reduce

Muscatatuck NWR. Photo credit: Jon Kauffeld

forest fragmentation. Once that process begins, those areas are considered in the context of forest management.

Control of invasive species is at the forefront of management goals at the Refuge, and exotic species found in grassland areas are addressed on a case-by-case basis. It is currently considered desirable to control invasives throughout all habitat types because of their threat to the biological integrity and diversity of every habitat as native species are out-competed for space and resources. Often these shifts in the floral community structure and composition are followed by shifts in the faunal community, which in some instances could be detrimental to rare or endangered species and reduce overall diversity.

Forests

With approximately 4,180 acres in bottomland hardwood forest (including 48 acres on the Restle Unit) and approximately 1,210 acres in upland hardwood forest, these areas comprise the dominant cover type on the Refuge. Forest restoration is primarily accomplished through natural succession. Currently, approximately 870 acres of Refuge land are in the process of reverting back to upland and bottomland forest from previous agricultural use. Most fields are small and are surrounded by excellent seed sources for deciduous trees, although some tree planting of oaks (mast producing trees) has occurred and will continue to occur and increase as funding permits. The U.S. Forest Service has seven permanent inventory points located on Muscatatuck NWR as part of its national Forest Inventory and Analysis (FIA) Program. The FIA is a national program of the USDA Forest Service that conducts and maintains comprehensive inventories of the forest resources in the United States (Forest Service 2007). This provides forest/landscape level assessments.

Tree planting has occurred sporadically since the Refuge was established. From establishment in 1966 to 2000, approximately 82 acres were planted in selected fields that had been retired from farming (Sieracki et al. 2002). The fields selected were chosen because of their location near existing forested tracts and to help repair forest fragmentation. Since 2000, 30 additional acres were planted in 2004, 15 acres in 2007, and 19 acres in 2008. The Refuge plans to plant 28 acres in 2009. The Refuge requests planting plans from the local area IDNR Forester prior to undertaking any new planting projects. The plans include native species of a diversity of tree species (mostly oaks) at a rate of 500 trees per acre. Planting has been done by a consulting forester. The Refuge Friends Group, the Muscatatuck Wildlife Society, and the National Wild Turkey Federation have helped fund projects.

Cropland

Food crops of corn and soybeans with wheat as a cover are planted annually on 267 acres of cropland under a cooperative farm agreement with a local farmer. According to the 2007 vegetation map, the Refuge retains approximately 330 acres of land associated with agriculture. The Refuge's share of the crops is left in the field for wildlife. This maintains open habitat and adds diversity to a mostly forested Refuge (Donalty et al. 2003). Canada Geese, waterfowl, Sandhill Cranes, and resident species forage on the Refuge's share of the crop. Wintering raptors prey upon small mammals feeding in these fields. Farmed acres also create good wildlife viewing along Refuge roads and the auto tour route.

Monitoring

A number of surveys, censuses, studies, and investigations are conducted on the Refuge that help to monitor the status of its wildlife and plant populations (see Table 2). Birds, mammals, herptofauna, and habitat are monitored on regular schedules. The surveys are conducted by Refuge staff, volunteers and in partnership with IDNR. Weekly waterfowl surveys, mid-winter waterfowl and Bald Eagle counts, and a few other surveys are requested by the state on an annual basis and the survey data upon completion is sent to IDNR. Staff with IDNR summarize and analyze the information

and provide the Refuge copies of the analyses. The purpose of monitoring is, in general, to determine the presence or absence and estimate the numbers of fish and wildlife present and to aid in making management decisions, and to respond to information requests from state agencies, the public and other partners.

Public Use

The National Wildlife Refuge System Improvement Act of 1997 established six priority uses of the Refuge System. These priority uses all depend on the presence of wildlife or expectation of the presence of wildlife, and are thus called wildlife-dependent uses. These uses are:

- hunting
- fishing
- wildlife observation
- photography
- environmental education
- environmental interpretation

Muscatatuck NWR provides opportunities for all six priority uses of the Refuge System.

Hunting

Hunting is permitted for white-tailed deer, rabbit, squirrel, turkey, and quail in certain locations on the Refuge during most of the established state seasons. Hunting leaflets are updated annually and hunters are required to sign the front of the leaflet and carry it with them while hunting. The Refuge also keeps the state of Indiana Hunting and Trapping Guide with all state rules and regulations in stock as a service to hunters. Deer and turkey hunting are allowed on a large portion of the Refuge during their respective seasons, while squirrel, rabbit, and quail hunting are only allowed in a small portion of the deer and turkey hunting area. No hunting is allowed in the Refuge closed area, in a large section in the northeast corner of the Refuge where the Visitor Center and most of the hiking trails are located, or within 100 yards of any building (Figure 9 on page 38).

Special deer hunts are held for archery and muzzleloading gun hunters during certain periods and approximately 3,000 hunters participate annually. The deer hunt drawings are done by the state. Bowhunters hunt in a different time period from the muzzleloading hunters. A late "open" archery season, open to all hunters with a valid state

Table 2: Monitoring History, Muscatatuck NWR

Study/Survey	Priority (10 high, 1 low)	Scales	FWS R3 RCP	No. Runs	No. Routes
Water Level Monitoring, MSU Hydrology	10	Refuge		26+	1
Invasive Species Mapping and Monitoring	10	Refuge, State, National		N/A	N/A
MSU Vegetation Cover Survey	9	Refuge		1	N/A
Water Quality Monitoring	8	Refuge, State		4	5
Waterfowl Brood Survey	8	Refuge	✓	10	1
Species Lists	7	Refuge	✓	N/A	N/A
Tubercled Orchid Survey	7	Refuge, State		1	2
Migratory Waterfowl Surveys	6	Refuge, State, National	✓	52	1
Fish Survey	6	Refuge, State	✓	N/A	N/A
FWS Eastern Greater Sandhill Crane Survey	5	Refuge, Region	✓	1	1
Audubon Christmas Bird Count	4	Refuge, State, National	✓	1	?
Audubon May Day Count	4	Refuge, State, National	✓	1	?
Bald Eagle Count	3	Refuge, State		1	1
NoAm Amphibian Monitoring Program	3	Refuge, State, National		3	1
Great Blue Heron Rookery Count	3	Refuge, State		1	1
Aquatic Invertebrate Survey	3	Refuge, State	✓	N/A	N/A
Abnormal Amphibian Monitoring	3	Refuge, Region, National		N/A	N/A
Butterfly Abundance and Diversity	2	Refuge		1	?

hunting license and available tag, is held on the Refuge after the muzzleloader season is over. Only handicapped hunters are permitted to use crossbows during Refuge deer hunts. The deer hunting area is the same as the turkey area – approximately three-quarters of the land area of the Refuge.

The turkey hunt requires a special permit during the spring season and involves 10-15 hunters per day over approximately three-fourths of the land area of the Refuge. Special permit drawings are done by the state. Rabbit hunting is open to members of the public with a valid state hunting license and involves a small percentage of Refuge visitors. Rabbit and quail hunting are the only hunting activities on the Refuge where dogs may be used and be off-leash. Squirrel hunting is a new,

small, but growing activity. The rabbit, quail, and squirrel hunting area covers the southeast quarter of the Refuge and is the area east of County Line Road and south of Barn Road. Very few visitors hunt quail here as the quail population is marginal and most of the hunting area is reverting to brush.

The Refuge remains open to non-hunting activities throughout the hunting season. Refuge visitors and hunters scouting for a future hunt day may enter hunting areas for any otherwise allowed purpose. All Refuge public use roads also remain open during all hunts as do all public fishing sites.

Hunters park on the Refuge only in designated hunting areas to access all parts of the Refuge that are open to hunting. Additionally, many hunters park on adjacent public roads, including CR 900 W.,

Figure 9: Public Use, Hunting, at Muscatatuck NWR

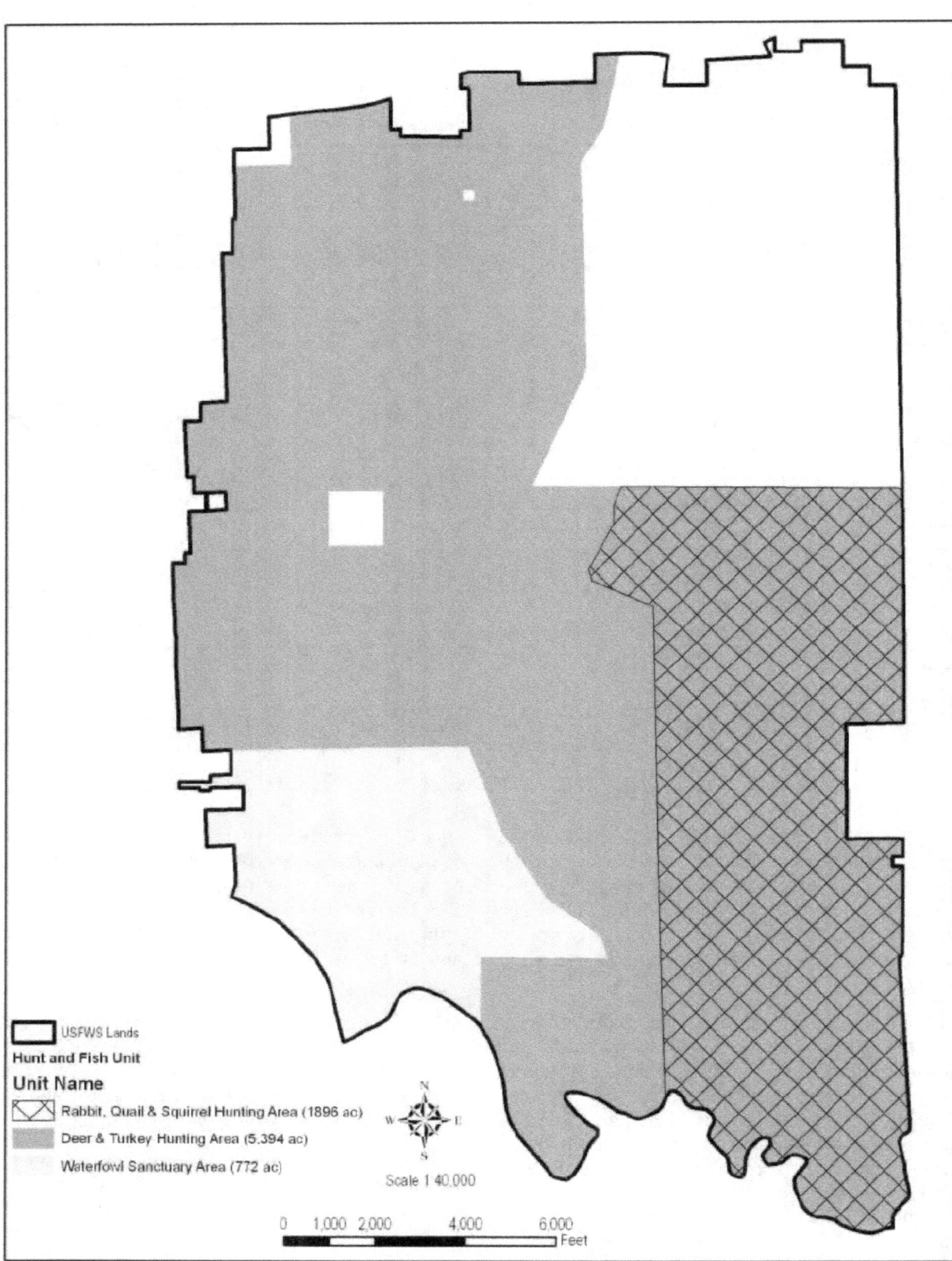

USFWS Lands

Hunt and Fish Unit

Unit Name

Rabbit, Quail & Squirrel Hunting Area (1896 ac)

Deer & Turkey Hunting Area (5,394 ac)

Waterfowl Sanctuary Area (772 ac)

Scale 1:40,000

0   1,000 2,000   4,000   6,000
Feet

Turkey hunting on Muscatatuck NWR. Photo credit: U.S. Fish & Wildlife Service

Hwy. 31, and CR 500 N., outside the Refuge and walk in to their hunting areas, but most park along the Refuge roads. Refuge staff have little contact with hunters aside from answering questions prior to and during the hunt. Self-service deer registration boxes are located at each entrance gate where hunters are required to register their kill before taking it to a state-authorized check station. Turkey hunters are asked to report the location of their takes, and successful deer hunters are asked to fill out a harvest card.

Fishing

Fishing is provided year-round at two large lakes, Stanfield and Richart, two small lakes, Linda and Sheryl, and at Display, Mallard, Sand Hill, and Persimmon Ponds. A fishing leaflet is available and is updated annually as needed. The Refuge also keeps the state of Indiana Fishing Guide with all state rules and regulations in stock as a service to anglers. Fishing structures and paved paths provide accessibility to handicapped anglers at three sites – Stanfield Lake and Lake Linda, which have

accessible floating ramps and platforms, and Sand Hill Pond, which has a paved walkway. Stanfield Lake has a concrete boat ramp and non-motorized boats may be launched and used on this lake. Parking lots and single-panel kiosks with regulations and leaflets are located at each fishing area except for Richart Lake, Display Pond, Mallard Pond, and Lake Sheryl. Concrete outhouse facilities are located at the Stanfield Lake and Persimmon Pond parking lots for the convenience of all visitors. Regular bathroom facilities with running water are located at the Visitors Center. A map of all Refuge fishing areas is provided in the fishing leaflet.

Fishing in the creeks and the seasonal drainages that enter and cross the Refuge is not allowed in an effort to provide relatively undisturbed habitat to Wood Ducks and their broods, which make extensive use of these habitats. Fishing is also not allowed in any of the Refuge's constructed moist soil units or marshes. Fishing is permitted from the banks of the Muscatatuck River except from the shoreline in the waterfowl sanctuary closed area.

Refuge fishing areas are generally shallow. Aquatic weed growth makes bank fishing difficult in the warm months and some Refuge visitors use "float tubes" or "belly-boats" – inner-tube type aides for wading (or floating) across the water. Fishing is permitted by hook and line only, and generally state regulations apply. Sought-after fish species include largemouth bass, bluegill, crappie, and channel catfish.

Interpretation, Observation, and Photography

Nine miles of roads are open for wildlife observation from autos, buses, motorcycles, or bicycles, plus an approximately 4-mile auto tour route with numbered posts and an interpretive leaflet. There are two observation structures, the Hackman Overlook on Richart Lake and the Endicott Observation Deck on the Auto Tour Route. The Hackman Overlook is located approximately one-half mile from the Richart Trail parking lot and overlooks Richart Lake. Recently, this structure has attracted vandals who have been marking it with graffiti and carvings, and the structure has been identified by staff as a maintenance problem. The Endicott Viewing Platform is an accessible raised wooden structure that overlooks both the North and South Endicott Marshes, has two fixed public use spotting scopes, and provides good opportunities to view marsh, wading, and waterbirds (Figure 10).

Figure 10: Visitor Services Facilities, Muscatatuck NWR

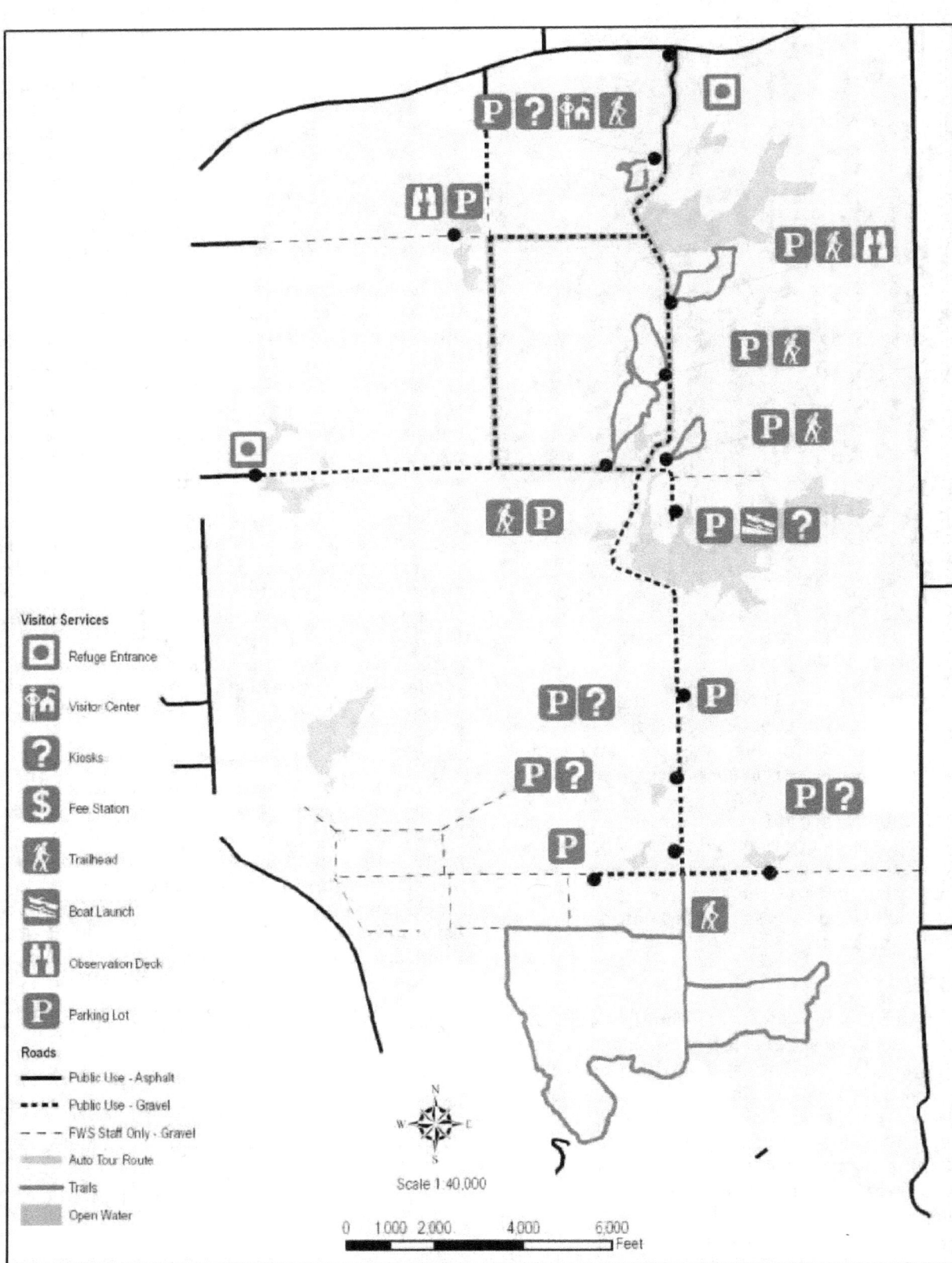

There are seven hiking trails of various lengths on the Refuge including the 0.4-mile (paved) Chestnut Ridge Interpretive Trail near the Visitor Center that features numbered posts with a leaflet. Most hiking trails are about a mile long except for the East and West River trails in the floodplain of the Muscatatuck River, which between them provide a 7-mile route for wildlife observation and hunter access along the river.

A self-service audiovisual program that presents an overview of the Refuge is available at the Conservation Learning Center. There are interpretive exhibits in both wings of the building and the Indiana Junior Duck Stamp Contest entries are on display in the CLC auditorium. New exhibits were recently built and installed in the old wing of the Visitor Center by a contractor and were opened to the public in the summer of 2008. A two-panel kiosk is located in the Visitor Center parking lot.

Large Refuge special events include a migratory bird festival in May, kids fishing event in June, and a friends' group Refuge Week "Log Cabin Day" festival in October. The "Wings Over Muscatatuck" bird festival held on International Migratory Bird Day is the Refuge's major annual event and attracts a growing audience of approximately 1,000 visitors when the weather is good. The Jackson County Visitor Bureau and the Muscatatuck Wildlife Society are major sponsors of this event, which features day-long guided birding tours of the Refuge, bird walks, bird banding demonstrations, bird and wildlife interpretive programs, live birds of prey/Bald Eagle programs, exhibits by conservation groups, vendors, and kids' birding activities.

The "Take a Kid Fishing" event at Muscatatuck NWR has been funded by the Muscatatuck Wildlife Society for many years. The 1-day event features special fishing for "kids and friends" in a pond normally closed to fishing, fishing and casting contests, fish art contests, loaner fishing poles, free bait, fishing lessons on request, and lots of door prizes. Trophies are awarded to event winners. Attendance varies between 400-600 people.

With the help of the Service's National Conservation Training Center, Muscatatuck NWR staff operate two booths at the National Future Farmers of America (FFA) Convention in Indianapolis for 3 days each October. The focus of the outreach effort is on providing career and background information on the Fish and Wildlife Service and wildlife conservation issues. Between

Visitors at Muscatatuck NWR. Photo credit: U.S. Fish & Wildlife Service

40,000-50,000 young people and several thousand teachers attend the convention annually, and this event is considered the largest gathering of students anywhere in the United States.

The "Log Cabin Day" festival in October celebrates the end of National Wildlife Refuge Week and is a project of the Muscatatuck Wildlife Society. The friends group provides a free ham and bean lunch at Myers Cabin during the event and there are old-time crafts, music, blacksmiths, a storyteller, horse-drawn wagon rides into the adjacent closed area (which is open that week), wildlife exhibits and information, and a volunteer set-up with a spotting scope on the Refuge Bald Eagle nest. "Wetland Day" programs have been held in mid-March for several years and feature guided waterfowl tours.

Wildlife photographers visit the Refuge on a regular basis but exact numbers are unknown. Annual wildlife photography contests are held in conjunction with bird festival and Refuge Week events and the Refuge hosts the monthly meetings of the Muscatatuck Photography Club.

Environmental Education

Many school groups visit the Refuge during the spring and fall, and primarily use the Refuge for self-directed activities. Unfortunately, with transportation funding cuts to public schools, numbers have been decreasing over the last few years. Refuge staff assist teachers prior to their visits whenever possible but do not usually work with students directly. Staff work with Girl Scouts on badge-work and "linking girls to the land" activities.

Four "Conservation Field Day" programs are held for third-graders from Jackson and Jennings Counties in May and October with about 300 youngsters involved each day, and as such provides Refuge contact with most of the third-graders in each of these counties each year. The interagency effort features programs on wildlife, forestry, soils, wetlands, and recycling. Instructors usually include educators from the Indiana Department of Natural Resources, local Soil and Water Conservation Districts, Purdue Extension, Indiana Department of Environmental Management, Solid Waste Management Districts and the Refuge. The programs feature hands-on activities for the youngsters and are well received by area teachers.

Muscatatuck NWR manages the Indiana Junior Duck Stamp art contest with over 450 entries each year. Refuge volunteers do much of the work in administering the program and the Muscatatuck Wildlife Society provides a substantial amount of the award funding. Other partners in the program include the Indiana Department of Natural Resources, Ducks Unlimited, and Bass Pro Shops. An awards ceremony is held at the Refuge during the May migratory bird festival. The original art of the Junior Duck Stamp Contest winners is kept on display in the Visitor Center Auditorium for one year before being returned to the students.

A "Junior Birder" kids program is administered during the summer months and is being expanded with volunteers. An "Invasive Species" patch program is available and has been used by Scouts and other youth groups. Master Naturalist classes and teacher workshops are held on the Refuge periodically. Songbird, Prairie, and Wetland Trunks are available on loan from the Refuge as are other educational materials. Kids' activities are an important part of the migratory bird festival held annually in May, and "skins and bones" are featured at the Refuge Week festival.

The "Refuge Rangers," an elementary school group of about 30 students from Hayden School, has spent considerable time learning about the Refuge and helping with projects under the leadership of their teacher, a Refuge volunteer. This group has

recently published a field guide to Muscatatuck NWR written by and for children, and with the assistance of the National Fish and Wildlife Foundation and the Muscatatuck Wildlife Society, this guide is being made available to all students who visit the Refuge as part of a school-based field trip.

Non-wildlife Dependent Recreation

Collecting mushrooms, nuts, and berries is permitted along with collecting shed deer antlers. Large numbers of people collect mushroom species at the Refuge in the spring.

Some jogging and bicycling occurs on the Refuge. Jennings County High School regularly brings their physical education and cross-country teams out for practice runs on Refuge trails.

Predator, Pest, and Invasive Species Management

Animal Species

Currently two mammalian aquatic nuisance species exist at the Refuge, the North American beaver and muskrat. Beaver create serious problems on the Refuge by constructing dams that impede water flow and cause flooding, which has proven to be detrimental to bottomland hardwood stands and has resulted in less than desirable conditions in moist soil units and green tree units. This also creates an enormous workload for Refuge staff who spend countless hours removing mud and debris from water control structures and tearing out dams from waterways. These animals also damage stands of timber by girdling trees, causing either mortality or stunting growth due to the loss of cambium tissue.

Beaver and muskrat will both burrow into dike banks, reducing overall structural integrity. These burrows reduce functionality of the dikes in two ways, both of which are costly to repair. First, over time these burrows cave in, causing surface damage that may encumber travel of vehicles or equipment, thus slowing down or preventing maintenance efforts. Second, these burrows can either directly cause seepage or leaks in dikes or do so indirectly by creating open sites that erode, leading to leaks and seepage. Refuge staff have begun to address these issues by removing problematic animals.

Three other species are targeted for control on the Refuge: feral dogs, feral cats, and Mute Swans. Feral dogs and cats are hand trapped or live trapped when evidence of their presence is detected. These animals are then turned over to a county animal control officer. Mute Swans are an invasive species targeted for control because their aggressive territorial behavior discourages use of wetlands by other waterfowl.

Plant Species

Invasive plant species management requires a multi-faceted approach that involves inventory, control, and monitoring. Preliminary mapping surveys of invasive plant species began in 2003 and are an ongoing project. Japanese stiltgrass, kudzu, garlic mustard, Japanese knotweed, oriental bittersweet, tree-of-heaven, and purple loosestrife have all been mapped, at least partially, with only kudzu and the loosestrife believed to have been fully mapped. A final report from a Challenge Cost Share research grant was submitted in November of 2007 and included information on many of these species and their distributions.

Invasive plant control is a species-specific and site-specific endeavor, and a list of all control methods for every species occurring on the Refuge is beyond the scope of this plan. However, most of the control efforts at Muscatatuck NWR involve chemical application, usually a glyphosate based product, although this is not always the case. Chemical applications may be foliar, basal bark, or cut stump treatments and may be used in combination with mechanical treatments. Mechanical means are employed when such methods are feasible and judicious. These methods

Myers Cabin, Muscatatuck NWR. Photo credit: U.S. Fish & Wildlife Service

may include hand-pulling, cutting (with weedeaters, brush cutters, or mowers), and disking (Blossey 2004). Fire, although not currently used on the Refuge, is also a viable option for the control of many species and may be considered for use in the future. Currently biological and mechanical control methods are in use at the Refuge. Recently, the Refuge has focused on attacking stiltgrass, loosestrife, knotweed, kudzu, garlic mustard, and tree-of-heaven as part of an early detection rapid response approach. Work has begun to create "weed free" areas starting with an area surrounding the Visitor Center. Creating an Integrated Pest Management Plan (IPM) is a high priority for the Refuge and will be essential in establishing long-term objectives, strategies, and priorities for invasive plant management.

Treatments are often conducted by volunteers and interns, or through partnerships with local groups and organizations. With a limited staff, these associations help the Refuge to accomplish an otherwise impossible task. Partnering and sharing resources is an integral part of the management of invasives at Muscatatuck NWR and will continue to be into the future. Currently, a multi-agency/partner project is under way to establish a Southern Indiana Cooperative Weed Management Area (CWMA). The Refuge has taken a role in the project and expects to work closely with partners as establishment progresses.

Archaeological and Cultural Resources

The Myers Cabin is a restored family log cabin at the south end of the Refuge that was built between 1870-1890 by Louis Myers. The barn behind the cabin was built in 1900 and is an excellent example of "hand-pegged" construction. Carl Myers, a son of Louis, was in the plant nursery business and developed (or found) some seedless persimmon trees, which he sold commercially from his house adjacent to Myers Cabin. A small grove of the seedless persimmon trees still remains close to the cabin. The cabin was continuously occupied by the Myers family and the barn was in use until it was purchased by the Fish and Wildlife Service around 1966. Both structures are in very good condition and have been restored and maintained by the Muscatatuck Wildlife Society.

The Barkman Cemetery is located along County Line Road and was in use at the time of the Refuge establishment. A path to the cemetery is maintained for ease of access from a small parking lot. There are more than 30 headstones, and many have been repaired by volunteers. The cemetery is maintained by Refuge and volunteer staff and is regularly visited by family members.

The Myers Cemetery is a small site located along the East River Hiking Trail, and has only about seven headstones. It is in the woods and does not require mowing. A marker for an unknown civil war soldier was apparently stolen from the cemetery in the early 1980s.

The Refuge has two national register archaeological sites, the Low Spur site and the Sand Hill site. The Sand Hill site and most of the Refuge area was scoured by collectors long-before the Refuge was purchased. Over 73 archaeological sites have been documented on the Refuge by professional archaeologists. Recovered artifacts indicate the Refuge area was intensively occupied in the Archaic (10,000-1,000 B.C.) and Woodland (1,000 B.C.-A.D. 1200) time periods with Late Archaic and Woodland components particularly well represented. Early Archaic sites were found on upland ridge and bluff tops and both Early and Late Archaic sites were found on ridge spurs and lowland terraces. Large multi-component sites were located on a variety of landforms. Many of the sites have been interpreted as short-term, temporary campsites, perhaps seasonal extractive camps (like hickory-nut processing) or sites occupied for part of the year. Fire-cracked rock, chert flakes, projectile points, and pieces of pottery were commonly found during excavations and are curated at the Glenn Black Museum at the University of Indiana in Bloomington, Indiana.

Law Enforcement

Until 2003, the Muscatatuck NWR law enforcement staff consisted of one or more collateral duty officers assisted by state conservation officers and State Police when needed and as available. From 2003 to 2006 no station staff did law enforcement work and collateral duty officers from Big Oaks NWR worked during deer hunts on a limited basis. In 2006, a full-time Refuge Officer assigned to Big Oaks NWR was responsible for all of the law enforcement work at both Big Oaks NWR and Muscatatuck NWR. That position was vacated in 2007. The full-time law enforcement position at Big Oaks NWR was tranferred to Muscatatuck NWR in late 2007 and the Refuge has filled the position. This position continues to be a shared position between both Refuges, and also

provides limited assistance to Patoka River NWR in southwestern Indiana. Law enforcement support is also provided by our zone officer, state conservation officers, and the State Police.

Historically, the Refuge had a reputation as a "trophy" deer hunting area and was known to local Conservation Officers as an active deer poaching area. In the past, while operating on a part-time basis as a collateral duty, Refuge officers focused on resource-oriented violations: fishing in areas closed to fishing, deer poaching, marijuana growing, and ginseng collecting. More recent efforts undertaken by full-time officers have expanded to include a larger number of violations associated with public use including: after-hours trespass, illegal vehicle operation, driving without a license, and illegal substance possession offenses, in addition to wildlife resource based violations.

The Refuge receives excellent but limited support from state conservation officers from two counties. The Seymour State Police Post is within 4 miles of Muscatatuck NWR and responds when called for serious problems. County Sheriff deputies are sometimes seen on the Refuge, and have been helpful. The State Police frequently have been called to let locked-in visitors out of the Refuge at night. This is a burden for the post and an issue that requires attention. Law Enforcement personnel from Crab Orchard NWR and Cypress Creek NWR provide assistance by working on larger operations.

Existing Partnerships

The Refuge has partnerships with local, state, and national organizations. These partnerships benefit the Refuge in many ways, including fostering good community relations and enhancing habitats and wildlife populations. Examples of partnerships include the following:

- The Refuge is a host agency for Experience Works (formerly Green Thumb), a senior work training program that supplies enrollees that work on the Refuge an average of 20 hours per week.

- A curatorial cooperative agreement between the Service and the Glenn A. Black Laboratory of Archaeology, University of Indiana, provides for the curation and storage of the 10 Refuge archeological collections containing a total of 23,635 artifacts. Artifacts are owned by the Federal Government and can be recalled by the

Regional Historic Preservation Officer for exhibits and other Refuge and Service purposes.

■ Muscatatuck NWR has been fortunate to have many partners in the local area, including:

  ○ Muscatatuck Wildlife Society

  ○ local Soil and Water Conservation Districts

  ○ Natural Resource Conservation Service

  ○ Purdue Extension

  ○ local Ducks Unlimited Chapters

  ○ local Wild Turkey Federation

  ○ Indiana Department of Natural Resources

  ○ local Resource Conservation and Development Councils

  ○ area conservation and birding clubs

  ○ sporting good stores

  ○ scouting and civic groups

  ○ local Visitor Bureaus

  ○ U.S. Forest Service

  ○ Hayden School Refuge Rangers

  ○ local universities

Other Management Areas

Research Natural Area

The Muscatatuck Seep Springs Research Natural Area (MSS-RNA) occupies a 97-acre portion of the Refuge (Figure 13 on page 50). It is one of only seven acid seep springs documented in Indiana. The cold, acidic groundwater yields a unique assemblage of plant species. Many of the plants that occur here are restricted to these exact environmental conditions. These conditions are extremely uncommon in the landscape, especially in southern Indiana. This community is also ranked G3 (Globally Rare) in the Natural Heritage system, an international database of biological and conservation sites coordinated by the Nature Conservancy. State-listed plant species found here are: American ginseng, club spur orchid, southern tubercled orchid, bog bluegrass, Walter's St. Johnswort, and smooth white violet. Also found here are the state-listed endangered four-toed salamander and the state-listed endangered copperbelly watersnake.

Figure 11: The Restle Unit of Muscatatuck NWR

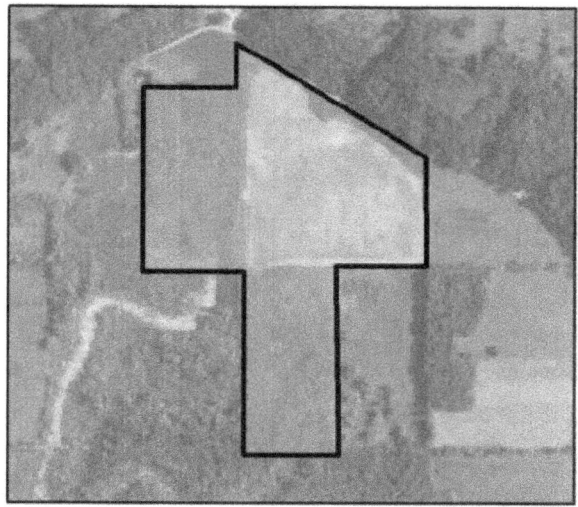

☐ Restle Unit

Current Habitat

▨ Bottomland Hardwood Forest

▨ Seasonally Flooded Impoundments

Scale 1:16,000

Restle Unit

The Restle Unit of Muscatatuck NWR is a 78-acre parcel in Monroe County, northwest of Bloomington, Indiana, that was donated to the National Wildlife Refuge System in 1990 (see Figure 11). It has a 30-acre emergent wetland that was repaired by a Maintenance Action Team in September 2005. The rest of the remaining acreage is bottomland hardwoods. It is a palustrine floodplain forest with swamp white oak, pin oak, swamp cottonwood, sycamore and silver maple.

Historically the area was a part of a large forested area called the Central Hardwood Region. The GLO original survey notes of 1811 and 1815 refer to forests comprised of beech, burr oak, maple, water oak, poplar, hickory, elm, and ash (Slusher and Welch 2001). The land was cleared for agriculture in the mid-1800s as the state was settled and tile drainage began in the late 1800s. An extensive system of ditches was put in place in order to control the hydrology for farming.

The Restle Unit lies within the outer margin of the floodplain on the north side of Bean Blossom Creek. Steep uplands with intermittent streams form a border north of the property. The Unit is relatively flat, has a low gradient, and is seasonally flooded. It is located in the south central part of the state, in a region known as the Mitchell Karst Plain Section of the Highland Rim Natural Region, as classified by the Indiana Natural Heritage program. The major soil types are Zipp, silty clay loam that is frequently flooded, and Burnside silt loam, which is occasionally flooded (Thomas 1981).

The Restle Unit provides habitat for a diversity of wildlife including Wood Ducks, Canada Geese, Hooded Mergansers, Mallards, and other waterfowl. At least 80 bird species have been identified using the unit including Bald Eagle, Osprey, Northern Harrier, Black-crowned Night-Heron, Great Egret, and Great Blue Heron. Beaver, muskrats, white-tailed deer, eastern fox squirrel, raccoon, red fox, opossum, and eastern mole are mammals that have been seen on the Unit. Some of the amphibians and reptiles seen in the Unit include cricket frog, green frog, spring peeper, southern leopard frog, painted turtle, snapping turtle, northern banded water snake, and ribbon snake. The federally-listed endangered Indiana bat has not been confirmed on the Unit, but is suspected to be present because the habitat provided matches its requirements. No studies have been conducted to find them. An IDNR radio collared bobcat was tracked using the Restle Unit in June and July 2002.

The Restle Unit is surrounded by a complex of protected land called the Bean Blossom Bottoms that includes acreage owned by Sycamore Land Trust and Wetland Reserve Program land. A total of 708 acres are protected. At least 109 bird species, including Prothonotary Warbler, Wood Thrush, Cerulean Warbler, Red-headed Woodpecker, American Woodcock, Willow Flycatcher, Prairie Warbler, Henslow's Sparrow, Virginia Rail, and King Rail, all have been reported from the Bean Blossom Bottoms area and the area is recognized as an Indiana Important Bird Area (IBA) by the Audubon Society. These lands support a Bald Eagle nest, a Great Blue Heron rookery, the state-listed endangered Kirtland's snake and northern crayfish frog (last confirmed in 1998).

The Unit is included in the Audubon designated Beanblossom Bottoms Important Bird Area (IBA). State-listed species seen include the Bald Eagle, Northern Harrier, Barn Owl, Osprey, Black-crowned Night-Heron, and Black Tern. State species of concern include the Great Egret, Red-

shouldered Hawk, and Sandhill Crane. Twenty-three bird species of Conservation Concern were listed on the IBA nomination form (Cole 2007).

Invasive, exotic species and noxious weeds seen at the Unit include reed canary grass, Asian bush honeysuckle and European starling. Thorough inventory work has not yet been done.

Management of the Unit as stated in the Restle donation document is: "grantee shall perpetually manage the real estate as a wetland habitat for native wildlife and plant enhancement and protection." Deed restrictions to the management of the property include the prohibition of timbering, burning, hunting, trapping, fishing, use of herbicides or insecticides, construction of buildings, general public access, and commercial sale of any resources. The restrictions have exceptions for the protection of wetlands, protection of native plant and animal habitat, and construction of observation blinds.

The 30-acre wetland area will be managed for migrant and nesting waterfowl and, when appropriate, mudflats may be exposed for shorebird use. The bottomland hardwood forest will continue to grow without active management.

The Restle Unit was donated with the restriction that "no general access of the public to the area shall be permitted." An observation deck overlooking the unit with a parking area on Bottom Road was constructed in 1998 and is available for the public to use.

Farm Service Agency Conservation Easements

The Refuge manages nine conservation easement areas totaling 130.5 acres located within the Wildlife Management District, a 30-county area in Indiana (Figure 12). On these Farm Service Agency (FSA) easements, the FWS is authorized to protect and manage important natural resource interests including wetlands, floodplains, riparian corridors, and endangered species habitat. Ownership of the easement land is retained by private individuals, but with restrictions related to conservation management. Service employees are responsible for habitat management and are granted access for maintenance, monitoring, enforcement, and other management activities.

Most FSA conservation easements are visually checked for boundary signs, trespass, and various other infractions every 2 years.

Figure 12: FSA Easements Administrated by Muscatatuck NWR

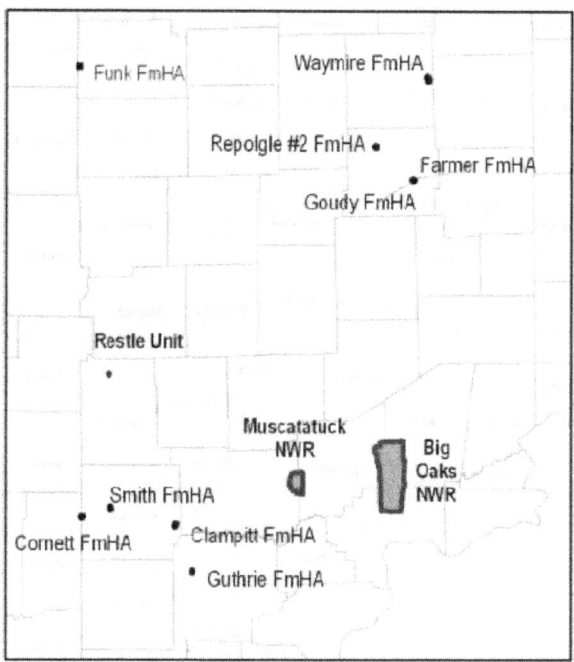

Table 3: Six-year Operating and Maintenance Budget

FY 2002	FY 2003	FY 2004	FY 2005	FY 2006	FY 2007
$1,339,425	$805,000	$570,343	$682,920	$662,410	$546,139

Current Staff and Budget

Staff

The Refuge's staffing, as of September 2007, includes eight full-time equivalent positions:

- Refuge Manager
- Wildlife Refuge Specialist
- Wildlife Biologist
- Maintenance Mechanic
- Tractor Operator (vacant)
- Park Ranger (law enforcement)
- Outdoor Recreation Planner
- Administrative Technician

Budget

A 6-year history of the operating and maintenance budget for the Refuge is shown in Table 3.

Chapter 4: Management Direction

Goals and Objectives

This chapter presents the goals, objectives and strategies that will guide management and administration of the Refuge over the next 15 years. This management direction represents the plan for the Refuge and mirrors Alternative C in the Environmental Assessment that was prepared as part of the planning process (Appendix A of the Draft CCP).

The Refuge has three goals:

- *Goal 1: Habitat* – A dynamic mosaic of vegetation that includes an expanse of upland and floodplain deciduous forest similar to that historically present along with lakes, marshes, and moist soil units.

- *Goal 2: Wildlife* – Support the maximum sustainable breeding and post-breeding populations of cavity-nesting waterfowl, neotropical migratory birds, Indiana bats, and a diversity of migratory, rare wetland, and resident species.

- *Goal 3: People* – Visitors understand and appreciate the natural environment and its processes through participation in high-quality, wildlife-dependent recreation and educational opportunities.

The goals are general statements of future desired conditions on the Refuge. The objectives under each goal are specific statements of what will be accomplished to help achieve the goal. Strategies listed under each objective specify the activities that will be pursued to realize an objective. The strategies may be refined or amended as specific tasks are completed or new research and information come to light. Some strategies are linked to the duties of an employee position, which indicates that the strategy will be accomplished with the help of a new staff position. When a time in number of years is noted in an objective or strategy, it refers to the number of years from approval of

Wood Duck drake. Photo credit: Mark Trabue

this CCP. If no time is given, the objective is to be accomplished within the 15 years of the life of the plan.

Goal 1: Habitat

Maintain a dynamic mosaic of vegetation that includes an expanse of upland and floodplain deciduous forest similar to that historically present along with lakes, marshes, and moist soil units.

Objective 1.1: Upland Hardwood Forest

Over the long-term (100-200 years), on areas dominated by upland flats and moist slopes, achieve an approximately 1,520-acre mosaic of upland hardwood stands of different age and structural classes dominated by poplar, oak, hickory, white ash, black cherry, maple, and beech. Within 15 years, restore approximately 310 additional acres of reconverting farmland to upland hardwood and maintain the existing approximately 1,210 acres of upland forest. Also within 15 years enhance 150 acres of upland forest by removing invasive species and employing various improvement techniques to ensure proper understory development, regeneration, and age class and species compositions.

Rationale: Land use practices, invasive plant introduction, and modifications to the hydrology of the landscape over the past century have drastically altered the vegetative communities on the Refuge and led to increased fragmentation of the habitat. Studies have shown that forest fragmentation reduces nesting success of migratory birds because of increased nest predation and parasitism. Area-sensitive forest bird species generally require large, contiguous blocks of forested habitat and are also negatively impacted when fragmentation results in smaller contiguous acreages (Robinson et al. 1995).

Historically, the Refuge was a part of the expansive, contiguous hardwood forest that covered most of the central and southern part of Indiana (Jackson 1997). Of the identified upland soils within the Refuge boundary, approximately 1,210 acres are currently in upland forest. An additional 310 acres (approximately) of potential upland forest have been identified that are currently in various cover types considered reconverting farmland. This acreage will be both allowed to naturally convert to upland hardwoods and planted to trees of species that were historically present. This will help reduce forest fragmentation and provide habitat for migratory birds, Wood Ducks and the Indiana bat.

The Refuge has carried out reforestation activities in recent years to reduce fragmentation of forested habitats and retire former agricultural fields and pastures. The intent is to manage native forest land for structural and plant species diversity and ensure healthy soil and water resources. Closed canopy forests often result in poor regeneration of shade intolerant species, especially oak species, and often result in poor understory development. However, natural openings caused by death or wind throw of one or more trees create open habitats that are quickly colonized by herbaceous plants, shrubs, and tree seedlings, and these temporary openings are desirable because they provide diversity within the otherwise forested matrix and are important habitat for wildlife (Collins and Battaglia 2002). To replicate these natural openings, openings 1 acre or less in size will be artificially created as part of forest management.

Invasive species such as autumn olive, Japanese honeysuckle, bush honeysuckle, multiflora rose, Japanese stiltgrass, and garlic mustard have invaded a large percentage of the Refuge's forested habitats. These species outcompete and shade out native vegetation, resulting in the development of monotypic stands of non-native vegetation, thus reducing vegetative diversity, inhibiting regeneration, and threatening rare and endangered plant populations (Pimentel et al. 2005). This

Muscatatuck NWR. Photo credit: Jon Kauffeld

objective represents the Refuge's intent to more actively manage and restore upland forest habitat to benefit forest-dependent wildlife, especially certain species of migratory waterfowl, neotropical migratory birds, and mammals (e.g. Indiana bat, southern flying squirrel).

Large contiguous blocks of native upland forests are expected to provide breeding and nesting habitat for the Wood Thrush, Chestnut-sided Warbler, Yellow-billed Cuckoo, Pileated Woodpecker, and Cerulean Warbler, as well as habitat for the Indiana bat, waterfowl and other migratory birds, and upland game species.

Strategies:

1. Conversion of approximately 310 acres of former cropland to upland hardwood forest (Figure 13). This may include site preparation, planting a cover crop, planting tree seedlings, and weed control treatments. Some areas may be allowed to naturally revert to forested habitat through natural succession.

2. Tree planting of white and red oaks, black cherry, persimmon, and black walnut taking soil types and native trees into consideration will occur on 160 acres. It is believed that hickory, beech, and maple trees will be restored through natural regeneration. Planting plans will be written in cooperation with the IDNR District Forester.

3. Complete a forest management (habitat management) step-down plan in 5 years.

4. Removal of invasive plant species within upland forested habitats through integrated pest management (IPM) strategies outlined in an approved IPM plan.

Figure 13: Future Land Cover, Muscatatuck NWR

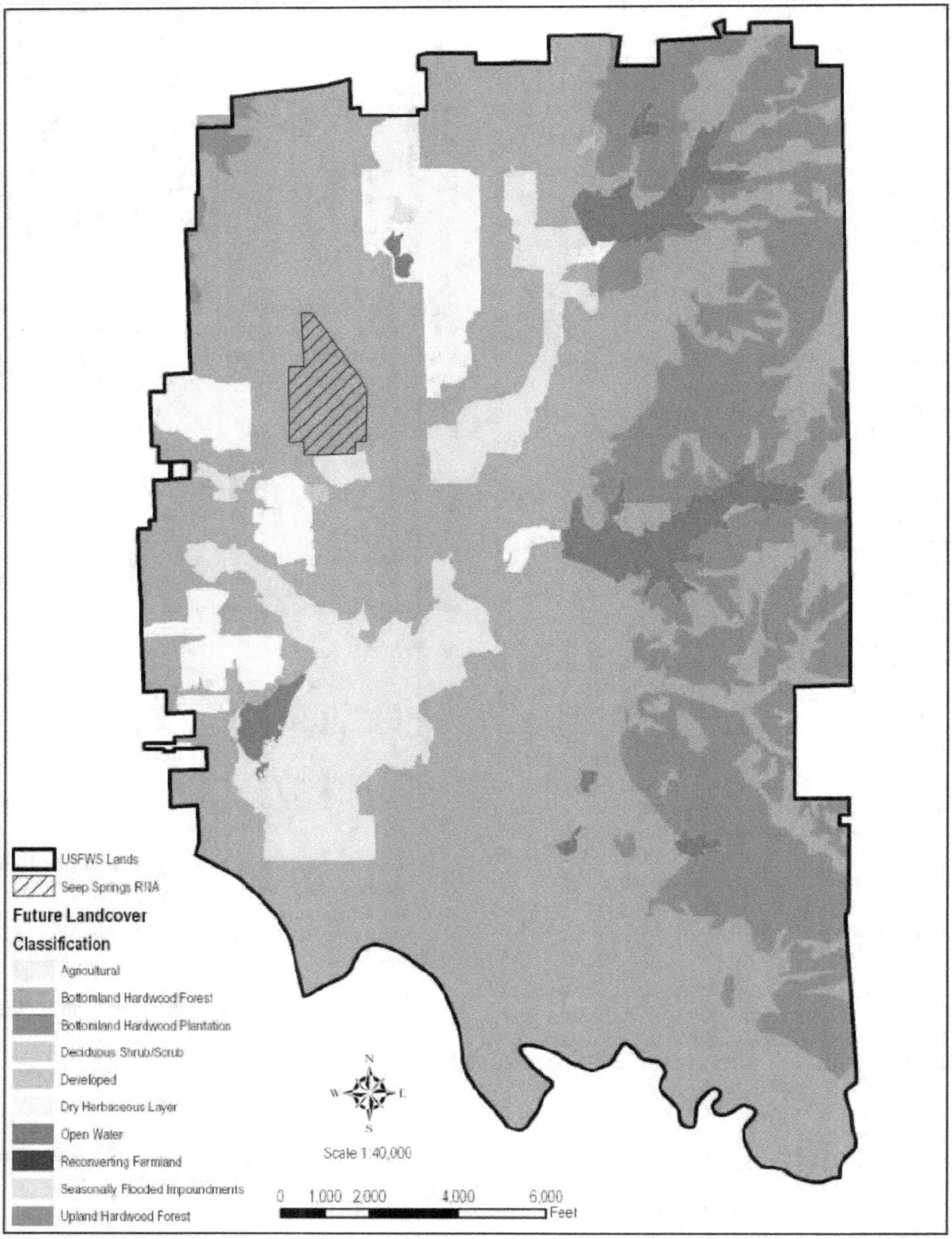

USFWS Lands
Seep Springs RNA

Future Landcover Classification

Agricultural
Bottomland Hardwood Forest
Bottomland Hardwood Plantation
Deciduous Shrub/Scrub
Developed
Dry Herbaceous Layer
Open Water
Reconverting Farmland
Seasonally Flooded Impoundments
Upland Hardwood Forest

Scale 1:40,000

0   1,000 2,000   4,000   6,000 Feet

5. Decrease undesirable tree basal area through selective cutting to promote establishment and growth of more desirable native hardwoods. Silvicultural treatments may be conducted under contract by commercial timber harvesting firms.

6. Timber stand improvement to include thinning dense stands, and deadening cull trees that are competing with more valuable wildlife trees, and selective harvest on a small scale to allow for habitat diversity and opening of canopy to stimulate plant growth, regeneration and recruitment on forest floor. Apply appropriate silvicultural treatments to manage forest health, species composition, and age structure. Treatments may include non-commercial forest stand improvement treatments (girdling, cutting, and/or applying herbicide to individual stems), and commercial timber cutting (thinning, improvement cuttings, and regeneration cuttings). Thin young stands of trees (pre-commercial) using appropriate methods to reduce competition for resources and allow residual trees to develop into healthy mature stands.

7. Artificially replicate the small openings in the forest (1 acre or less) that would have occurred naturally to provide the natural diversity of habitat that should be present within the forest matrix.

8. Fill the existing (vacant) tractor operator position and add a biological science technician to assist with reforestation efforts, eradication of non-native tree species, and timber stand improvement efforts.

Objective 1.2: Bottomland Hardwood Forest

Over the long-term (100-200 years) achieve approximately 4,790 acres in large blocks (greater than 500 acres) of mature bottomland forest (12-30 inch average dbh) with a canopy cover of 60-80 percent consisting of mixed sycamore, oak, beech, green ash, sweetgum and maple. In addition to maintaining the approximately 4,135 acres of bottomland hardwoods, 650 additional acres will come from:

■ Reconverting farmland (approximately 500 acres).

■ Current farmland (approximately 15 acres).

■ Water management units 8, 9 and 10.

■ Inundated portions of the Seep Springs RNA and Mutton Creek (approximately 135 acres).

(The Restle Unit is considered separately in Objective 1.7.)

Within 15 years, restore natural hydrology in the area of the current greentree reservoirs, moist soil units 8, 9, 10, and Moss Lake greentree area to allow flooding and ebbing with the natural changes in the river. Stop maintaining Mallard and Display Ponds and allow them to revert to bottomland hardwood forest. Vary water levels in the shallow northeastern portion of Richart Lake, closely monitoring effects and habitat changes. The area of the current lower moist soil units, with the exception of M7, will have started reverting back to bottomland hardwood forests with an oak component. Sheet flow through these areas will be restored to allow more natural movement of runoff, dead timber areas within greentree reservoirs will be restored to live stands through the natural regeneration of oaks, if possible, and through seeding or planting, if necessary.

Rationale: Historically the Refuge was a part of the expansive, contiguous hardwood forest that covered most of the central and southern part of Indiana (Jackson 1997). The Muscatatuck Flats and lowlands area is in the Bluegrass Natural Region of southeast Indiana. The bottomland is characterized by relatively level plain poorly drained flats. The Muscatatuck River floodplain is one of the most extensive areas of bottomland hardwood forest remaining in the Midwest. The floodplain forest along the Muscatatuck River is characterized by sweetgum, swamp white oak, and shellbark hickory (Sieracki et al. 2002).

Increasing, the bottomland hardwood areas at Muscatatuck NWR along the Muscatatuck River and smaller streams will provide important breeding habitat for Wood Duck, Acadian Flycatcher, and Cerulean Warbler as well as summer habitat for the federally-listed endangered Indiana Bat and habitat for the state-listed endangered copperbelly watersnake (Sallabanks et al. 2000; Kingsbury 1997).

Land use practices, development of roads, beaver dams, and modifications to the hydrology of the Refuge have impeded drainage, causing seasonal flooding to persist for longer than had occurred historically. The prolonged flooding helped shift composition of bottomland hardwood forests towards tree species with greater water tolerances, and largely eliminated regeneration, resulting in single-aged mature stands. In some areas semi-permanent flooding resulted in complete tree mortality and shifts in habitat type from forested wetland to open water or marsh (Kozlowski 2002).

Planned modifications to the drainage system will allow for water management that more closely resembles historical conditions and the restoration of species associated with those conditions. This objective represents the Refuge's intent to more actively manage bottomland forest habitat to benefit forest-dependent wildlife, especially certain species of migratory waterfowl, neotropical migratory birds, resident cavity nesting species, and mammals (e.g. Indiana bat, southern flying squirrel). The Refuge's intent is to actively manage the return of the forested landscape to conditions that allow passive hydrological management that resembles the historic hydrological regime to benefit and protect the wide array of plant and animal species that flourish in such environments.

One measure of the biological integrity of bottomland hardwood forests is whether the timing and frequency of events such as flooding correspond to historical conditions.

Strategies for Green Tree Reservoirs (G1, G2, and Moss Lake acres):

1. Discontinue prescription flooding of the Green Tree Reservoirs(GTR) and allow them to fluctuate naturally from the creeks and river influences and from precipitation and resulting runoff. The units will no longer be purposely flooded via management intervention.

2. Actively pursue draining excess water prior to the growing season to encourage regeneration and avoid killing trees. The stoplogs within the structure at Moss Lake will not be set higher than 540.0 at any time to protect the forested systems that are struggling to survive along the borders of the unit; it may be determined from bathymetry/forestry investigations that the maximum elevation for stoplogs should be 539.5 or 539.0, and thus the maximum elevation may be further reduced.

3. A bathymetric investigation of Moss Lake will be completed by 2012 to determine the maximum stoplog elevation for the Moss Lake

water control structure to prevent impounding water in the forested areas of Moss Lake.

4. Modifications will be made on the Moss Lake Water control structure by 2013 to increase the discharge capabilities of the structure. Screw gates or other comparable designs will be installed in several if not all of the six bays within the structure to increase discharge and reduce the buildup of sediment within the impoundment. Moss Lake GTR areas will no longer serve as a greentree reservoir, but will function as a floodplain forest whose hydrology will attempt to mimic the natural influence of the Muscatatuck River without dikes and structures.

5. Acquire the machinery necessary (i.e. small amphibious backhoe) to access and remove the beaver dams and other impediments to water flows on the creeks, at the various water control structures, and in other areas where drainage is impeded.

Strategies for Bottomland Hardwoods (includes Green Tree Reservoirs):

1. Allow natural regeneration of trees to occur when possible and augment natural processes with planting seeds or seedlings when necessary. Manage timber to promote regeneration of mast producing tree species.

2. Conduct forest surveys or inventories every 5 years to monitor changes in health, composition, and structure of bottomland forests

3. Develop and implement short- and long-term forest management plans within 5 years of CCP completion as a component of habitat management planning efforts.

4. Conduct forest management activities such as thinning dense stands or midstory and selective harvest on a small scale to allow for habitat diversity and opening of canopy to stimulate plant growth, regeneration and recruitment on forest floor.

5. Provide vernal pools where feasible.

6. Conduct a study to learn more about the hydrology and geomorphology of the Refuge.

7. Remove portions of the dikes forming the greentree reservoirs and moist soil units 8, 9, and 10 after completing a hydrological study, unless contradicted by the study.

Eastern Bluebird. Photo credit: Mark Trabue

8. Timber stand improvement to include thinning dense stands, selective harvest on a small scale and deadening cull trees that are competing with more valuable wildlife trees to allow for habitat diversity and opening of canopy to stimulate plant growth, regeneration and recruitment on forest floor. Apply appropriate silvicultural treatments to manage forest health, species composition, and age structure. Treatments may include non-commercial forest stand improvement treatments (girdling, cutting, and/or applying herbicide to individual stems), and commercial timber cutting (thinning, improvement cuttings, and regeneration cuttings). Thin young stands of trees (pre-commercial) using appropriate methods to reduce competition for resources and allow residual trees to develop into healthy advanced stands.

9. Restore hydrology and micro/macrotopography based on current knowledge and future recommendations from hydrogeomorphological investigations. Attempt to replicate historic conditions that included hydrologic features such as depressions, oxbows, and swale topography. Also, to replicate permanent, semi-permanent and seasonally flooded wetlands that were historically present in the Muscatatuck River Basin.

Objective 1.3: Grassland

Maintain approximately 470 acres of open grassland to benefit wildlife viewing and to provide high-quality nesting and forage habitat for grassland bird species. These areas should be capable of providing high-quality breeding habitat for listed species (e.g., Henslow's Sparrow), waterbirds (e.g. Great Blue Heron) and other migratory birds (e.g. , Bobolink, Dickcissel, Loggerhead Shrike, Grasshopper Sparrow and Sandhill Crane), and contributing to the native biological diversity of the Refuge. In addition to 80 acres of existing grassland areas, approximately 310 acres of currently agricultural land and approximately 85 acres of formerly cropped but now reconverting lands will be managed for grassland habitat.

Rationale: Pre-European settlement vegetation within the current boundaries of the Refuge was dominated by deciduous forest with little to no open grasslands occurring except small openings where natural events (i.e. wind throws, tornadoes, or beaver) created gaps in the forest (Jackson 1997). Small temporary and permanent forest openings are part of the historic vegetative condition of the Refuge. Furthermore, the diversity of birds present at the Refuge can be attributed to the diverse habitat types and many wildlife enthusiasts, observers, and bird watchers are drawn to the Refuge because of the diversity of species and habitats. The diversity provides Refuge visitors with quality wildlife-dependent recreation opportunities. Even though historically larger grasslands were not prominent on the Refuge, benefits to grassland bird species may still be derived from the retention and/or expansion of grassland habitat in strategic locations. Populations of many grassland bird species are declining, in part because of loss of habitat (Herkert 1994). These grasslands can serve as habitat for Grasshopper Sparrow, Henslow's Sparrow, Eastern Meadowlark and Sandhill Crane. They will also provide habitat for Kirtland's snake (Conant and Collins 1991).

Strategies:

1. Protect, restore, or enhance the blocks of grassland habitat and ensure they are comprised of short, medium, and tall height-density patches containing diverse structure (e.g., bare soil, stiff-stemmed forbs, and sparse woody vegetation) with a 75 percent grass and 25 percent forbs mix with a minimum of six grass species and a minimum of 30 herb

species. The Refuge will focus on creating blocks of grassland habitat that are structurally open and free of major linear woody edges. In most cases, woody cover will represent less than 5 percent of the grasslands habitat. Maintain Refuge grasslands through periodic burning and/or mowing with some grasslands (25-50 percent of the total grassland landscape) remaining free from burning or mowing, between 3 and 6 years to provide habitat for Henslow's Sparrow, Northern Bobwhite Quail, Field Sparrow, and other species that prefer a well-developed duff layer and the presence of some shrubs. Some thicket areas and isolated trees will be allowed to persist to provide breeding habitat for Loggerhead Shrike, Bell's Vireo, Yellow-breasted Chat, and other species in some of the grassland areas.

2. Place grassland openings along the perimeter of the Refuge and along the wildlife auto tour route to minimize fragmentation, promote habitat diversity, and promote wildlife observation.

3. Periodically inventory grasslands to determine species composition and stem density and to detect invasive species.

4. Under the guidance of an integrated pest management plan, work toward removing and preventing the establishment of non-native invasive species within Refuge grasslands with special emphasis placed on autumn olive, multiflora rose, Johnson grass, and non-native thistles.

Objective 1.4: Moist Soil Units and Emergent Marsh Units

Maintain 175 acres in Units 1-7 under moist soil management to provide annual food crops and resting habitat for migratory waterbirds, Wood Duck habitat and mudflats for shorebirds. Also, maintain an additional 238-634 acres (depending on Moss Lake water levels) of emergent marsh in McDonald and Endicott Marshes, Moss Lake, and Sue Pond to provide feeding, resting, and nesting habitat for all waterbirds including secretive marsh birds, waterfowl, wading birds, and shorebirds. (See Table 4) (The Restle Unit is considered separately in Objective 1.7.)

Table 4: Water Management Units Under the CCP, Muscatatuck NWR

Water Management Unit	Approximate Acres
Moist Soil Units	
Moist Soil 1	22
Moist Soil 2	20
Moist Soil 3	17
Moist Soil 4	37
Moist Soil 5	13
Moist Soil 6	14
Moist Soil 7	52
Total	175
Emergent Marsh Areas	
McDonald Marsh North	14.5
McDonald Marsh South	13
Endicott Marsh North	6
Endicott Marsh South	11.5
Moss Lake (min - max)	180 - 576
Sue Pond	13
Total	238 - 634

Rationale: Moist soil management is a widespread practice for producing a diverse mixture of native herbaceous plant foods and invertebrates. It partially mimics seasonal flooding that has long occurred in the Muscatatuck NWR lowlands, but moist soil units – areas impounded by dikes, and structures that permit precise control of water levels – allow managers to produce conditions favorable to growth of native plants such as millets and sedges (Haukos and Smith 1993). Seeds produced by these plants provide balanced nutrition for migrating waterfowl, and also provide food and habitat for other migratory birds and wildlife. The diverse mixture of native plants also creates conditions that produce abundant invertebrates, a high protein wildlife food source.

Emergent marshes are some of the most productive natural systems in the world (Waide et al. 1999). The productivity, however, is derived from the dynamic nature of hydrological events and the resulting vegetative responses (Haukos and Smith 1993). Cyclical management of marsh units, including periodic full and partial drawdowns need to be incorporated into the water management regime. Changes in these systems could drastically increase use of the units and the Refuge by waterbirds, increase amphibian and macroinvertebrate production, and increase the overall plant diversity of the marshes and the Refuge.

Strategies for Moist Soil Units:

1. Disturb (through mowing, disking, fire, etc.) an average of one-third of the moist soil unit acreage annually to set back succession.

2. Moist soil units will be maintained in early successional native plant communities for the production of annual seed crops.

3. Limit public access to moist soil units during peak duck use periods by closing the levees to hiking, bird watching, etc.

4. Maintain most moist soil units dry throughout much of the growing season (April through September) to produce food for migratory birds except where shallow irrigation will aid in beneficial moist soil plant production, or when managing a unit for a late summer/fall drawdown to benefit fall migrant shorebirds.

5. Maintain dikes and water control structures in good working order controlling muskrats and beaver to prevent excessive damage (i.e. honeycombing) and disruption of water management capability.

6. Provide additional fall-flooded, shallow-water habitat for shorebirds when feasible.

7. Begin draining some moist soil units in March when feasible to expose mudflats by April to benefit migrating shorebirds that can feed on invertebrates.

8. Manage water levels within moist soil units to provide optimum depths for dabbling ducks, shorebirds, and wading birds.

9. Ensure that water management regimes between and within years incorporates variation in depth, duration, and in the timing of drawdown and reflooding. The seasonal and annual shifts in hydrologic condition set the stage for vegetation development within the various impoundments.

Osprey. Photo credit: Dan Kaiser

10. Remove trees, stumps, fallen logs, and other woody debris from Units M1-M6 via bulldozer or other means, yet ensure that topsoil is retained. This will facilitate proper management of these units especially during maintenance/disturbance operations and will help to prevent the establishment of willows and other undesirable woody vegetation within the units.

11. Remove debris piles from previous rehabilitation work to allow disturbance throughout the units via disking or mowing and to prevent establishment and continued issues with the proliferation of willows within the units.

12. Control exotic and invasive plant and animal species.

13. Conduct annual vegetation monitoring to gather data necessary to make management decisions and to evaluate and document management actions and corresponding responses.

Strategies for Emergent Marsh Units:

1. Ensure proper water levels to promote the development of diverse complex vegetative structure within the units and to provide water depths suitable for waterbird use.

2. Increase the distribution and interspersion of cattail and other emergent vegetation.

3. Ensure that water management regimes between and within years incorporates variation in depth, duration, and in the timing of drawdown and reflooding. The seasonal and

annual shifts in hydrologic condition set the stage for vegetation development within the various impoundments.

4. Conduct periodic drawdowns to consolidate sediment, increase plant germination, and reduce fish populations.

5. Control exotic and invasive plant and animal species.

6. Within 2 years of CCP approval, identify and adopt marsh management strategies conducive to meeting emergent marsh objectives.

7. Conduct periodic marsh monitoring using established rapid assessment protocols for wetlands including vegetative, amphibian, and macroinvertebrate indices of biotic integrity and secretive marsh bird surveys.

Objective 1.5: Invasive Plant Species

Inventory all Refuge lands for invasive plant species within 5 years of plan approval. Identify, monitor, control, and eliminate exotic and invasive species found on the Refuge and rapidly respond to new invasive species.

Rationale: Invasive species are detrimental to native plant and animal populations. Invasive species are considered to be one of the greatest threats to the National Wildlife Refuge System.

Autumn olive, garlic mustard, reed canary grass, Canada thistle, crown vetch and many other species dominate certain portions of the Refuge landscape. Japanese stiltgrass, multiflora rose, Japanese honeysuckle, tree-of-heaven, and kudzu threaten the diversity and health of the bottomland and upland hardwoods while other species, such as reed canary grass and purple loosestrife, compete with native vegetation along riparian corridors, in moist soil units, and in other wetland types.

Many of the invasive species encountered have the capability over time of producing solid monocultures, shading out native vegetation and reducing overall plant diversity and consequently overall animal diversity (Blossey 2004). Many of the same natural disturbances, such as drought, flood and wildfire, that maintain productivity of natural systems also provide opportunities for invasive species to multiply and spread.

Human activities and disturbances on the landscape also create conditions conducive to the spread of invasive species. It is very important that the Refuge staff is able to inventory and monitor the spread of invasive species and take actions to minimize the distribution of a species or control its abundance on the landscape.

Though unlikely that invasives will be completely eradicated from the landscape, targeted chemical, mechanical, manual, and biological controls or prescribed fire can reduce their impact on native species. Success will be based on reducing the spread and size of infestations, complete eradication, or stabilization of infestations. The Refuge will employ a strategy of early detection, rapid assessment, and rapid response (ED/RA/RR). ED/RA/RR amplifies the probability that invasions will be managed effectively while populations are confined to a small area and eradication is feasible. Populations, once well established, are rarely completely eradicated; mitigation of their negative impacts is a reasonable expectation (Blossey 2004). Furthermore, overall costs of ED/RA/RR are inevitably much lower than costs associated with long-term reduction and control of well established populations.

Strategies:

1. Develop an integrated pest management (IPM) plan.

2. Inventory and map the distribution of invasive species.

3. Using IPM strategies, identify treatment protocols for all known invasive plants inhabiting the Refuge and for the plants most likely to invade in the near future.

4. Prioritize species and locations for treatment. Use a diverse array of control tools and techniques individually or in combination, including but not limited to mowing, biological controls, herbicides, prescribed fire, and revegetation.

5. Evaluate all ground-disturbing management actions for their potential to facilitate the spread of invasive plants. Establish and implement a survey design that monitors invasive species and allows comparison of different management regimes.

6. Develop an annual monitoring and mapping strategy for invasive species.

7. Implement early detection, rapid assessment, and rapid response strategies for 'new' invaders.

8. Increase training for staff members on invasive species identification.

9. Increase public awareness of the invasive species issues facing the Refuge and encourage public involvement through workshops, presentations, work days, special events, and other stewardship opportunities.

10. Cooperate with state and federal agencies, non-government organizations, and neighboring landowners to strategize, inventory, monitor, and treat invasive species on a larger landscape level scale.

11. Fill the existing (vacant) full-time tractor operator position to assist with invasive species eradication. Also add one wildlife biologist to oversee and manage field efforts and two full-time biological science technicians to help with controlling invasives, forestry, and grassland management.

12. Develop and enhance relationships with universities, colleges, schools, and other organizations such as the Boy Scouts, Girl Scouts, Wildlife Society, Audubon Society etc. and encourage participation in the fight against invasive species on the Refuge.

Objective 1.6: Seep Springs Research Natural Area

Restore the hydrology and vegetative community of the Seep Springs Research Natural Area to a condition that approximates an undisturbed seep springs site.

Rationale: The Seep Springs is one of only seven acid seep springs documented in Indiana.

The cold, acidic groundwater yields a unique assemblage of plant species, and many of the plants that occur here are restricted to these exact environmental conditions. These conditions are extremely uncommon in the landscape, especially in southern Indiana. This community is also ranked as Globally Rare in the Natural Heritage system, a ranking system developed by The Nature Conservancy.

State-listed plant species found here are: American ginseng, club spur orchid, southern tubercled orchid, bog bluegrass, Walter's St. Johns wort, and smooth white violet. The state-listed

endangered four-toed salamander and the state-listed endangered copperbelly watersnake are also found in the Seep Springs Research Natural Area.

Refuge staff and partners have recognized that the condition of the Seep Springs vegetative community is in poor condition, needs immediate attention, and that changes to several current management practices are required. The following issues have been identified as problems that have caused poor drainage conditions to exist, the persistence of high water levels, and the degradation of the Seep Springs vegetative community over the several decades:

■ County road 400 S, immediately to the south of the Seep Springs, was raised in the early 1980s and a drainage culvert under this road was removed.

■ Beaver populations and activity have increased in the area and contributed to consistently higher water levels in Mutton Creek and throughout the Refuge

■ Log jams have accumulated in the Mutton Creek system, contributing to poor drainage. Jams are difficult to remove because of limited access for equipment

■ Moss Lake has been maintained at a level of 541 msl - a level where water begins to have an impact on the Seep Springs and increases the time required for drainage during periods of heavy inflow and flooding.

All of these factors and others have contributed to higher water levels and altered the flow regimes in the area. The changed conditions in the area have led to an observable change in the vegetation, severe tree mortality, and a shift in the habitat type from a seasonally flooded forested wetland to a permanently flooded marsh.

In order to preserve and restore the special characteristics of the Seep Springs Area, it is necessary to better understand the current and historical conditions at the site and then formulate approaches to returning the site to a less disturbed condition. The key to maintaining the health of the Seep Springs community is to understand how water flows into and out of the site, and the nature of the historical hydrologic regime that led to the development of the seep. This information can be most effectively obtained through a hydrogeomorphological study, and management solutions devised. However, some immediate steps are needed to improve the drainage of the area and reduce long-term retention of water on the community.

The site is also threatened by a number of invasive species including garlic mustard, moneywort, reed canary grass, and Japanese stiltgrass. Control of these invasive species will need to be addressed.

All of these issues will have to be addressed to facilitate the recovery of the Research Natural Area. Even with implementation of the proposed strategies, continued degradation and tree mortality at the site is likely for a period of several years to a decade as the full impacts of extended flooding are realized. Funding is a limiting factor in the rate of response to these problems, as several issues that must be addressed will require additional maintenance dollars.

Immediate Strategies

1. Reduce the impact of Moss Lake and Mutton Creek on the Seep Springs Area during the growing season, March-November, by reducing water levels and increasing discharge rates of the Moss Lake water control structure

Red fox. Photo credit: U.S. Fish & Wildlife Service

(WCS) during high flow periods. Two of the six bays in the Moss Lake WCS will be modified immediately, with modification of additional bays as necessary to allow the Refuge the ability to mimic a natural short duration pulsing flood regime.

2. Construct access routes for equipment and personnel along Mutton Creek between County 500 North and Moss Lake to facilitate access for beaver dam, log jam, and sediment removal, to allow for population control of nuisance species, and to allow for consistent monitoring.

3. Control the beaver population on the Refuge and reduce the number of creek obstructions.

4. Restore the full drainage capability of Moist Soil Unit 6 (M6) through removal of silt from channels and borrow ditches.

5. Remove the berm and beaver dams that restrict discharge flows along the primary drain for the Seep Springs area into Mutton Creek – the southeastern drainage ditch north of County Road 400 North, and southeast of the Seep Springs.

6. Install a backflow preventer on the M6 outflow culvert to reduce flooding and maintain a lower water table.

7. Install water level gauges to allow water level monitoring of the RNA.

Long-term Strategies:

8. Form a working group of qualified professionals and stakeholders to collaboratively assist in the implementation of these strategies and to make recommendations on water levels, management practices, and modification of existing or construction of new water control, drainage, and moist soil unit infrastructure (particularly M6 and its outlet structure) needed to provide the best possible conditions for the Seep Springs community.

9. Conduct a hydrogeomorphologic investigation to determine historic water regimes and to determine realistic recommendations for restoring the hydrology and, in particular, to reduce the influence of Mutton Creek on the Seep Springs during the growing season, March-November.

10. Determine best management practices for restoring the forested habitat that has been degraded, ensuring proper species composition and preventing establishment or release of invasive species into the Seep Springs.

11. Inventory, monitor, map, and control invasive species in and near the Seep Springs.

12. Develop a monitoring plan/protocol to monitor the overall health of the Seep Springs and to watch for changes in plant communities, sedimentation, and hydrology.

13. Determine if the Seep Springs area should be protected from all public entry and, if so, sign the area and develop and make available informational material to educate the public.

Objective 1.7: Restle Unit

Maintain 48 acres of bottomland forest and manage a 30-acre moist soil unit to support water bird feeding, resting, and breeding.

Rationale: The Refuge must "perpetually manage the real estate as a wetland habitat for native wildlife and plant enhancement and protection." To best fulfill its commitment, the Refuge will manage the constructed unit on the Restle Unit as a moist soil unit because this follows the establishing direction for the Refuge. The Refuge purpose "...for use as an inviolate sanctuary, or for any other management purpose, for migratory birds" derives from the Migratory Bird Conservation Act.

The forest will be maintained, but not managed. The donation document for the Restle Unit states:

"No timbering, burning, hunting, trapping, or fishing shall be permitted, except that plant harvesting or controlled burning for the protection of the wetland or research into the protection of wetlands are permitted."

The donation document also states:

"Wildlife harvesting within the levee constructed by the Fish and Wildlife Service in 1990 is also permitted for the protection of the wetland within the levee. The permitted activities specified in this paragraph are to be conducted only by personnel of the grantee or their designees for that specific purpose."

Bald Eagles at Muscatatuck NWR. Photo credit: Mark Trabue

Strategies:

1. Develop a water management plan within 2 years of plan approval to guide management of the impoundment.

2. Maintain dike and water control structure in good working order.

3. Use mechanical, chemical and biological controls to check the spread of invasive plant species.

4. Communicate with other state and federal resource agencies, as well as non-governmental organizations, to stay current on emerging threats and effective management and control techniques related to invasive species.

Objective 1.8: Conservation Easements

Meet Service monitoring guidelines for FSA over next 15 years.

Rationale: The Refuge is responsible for managing FSA easements (formerly Farmers Home Administration easements, or FmHA) within a 30-county Wildlife Management District. These easements were placed on the properties when landowners defaulted on their Farmers Home Administration loans. Properties were then resold to the original landowner or to another individual at a discounted price due to the easement. FSA easements are an agreement between the FSA and the FWS, authorizing the Service to protect important natural resource interests on easement properties such as wetlands, floodplains, riparian corridors, and endangered species habitat.

Ownership of the easement land is retained by private individuals, but with certain restrictions on altering important natural resources on the easement lands. Service employees are granted access for management, maintenance, monitoring, and enforcement purposes. There is no public access to these easement properties unless explicitly stated in the individual easement document.

Strategies:

1. Bi-annually inspect each FSA easement and follow-up with landowner contact.

2. Send letters to new landowners informing them of existing easements on their property, along with the associated regulations

3. Follow protocols within the Service's easement manual to handle all potential violations.

Objective 1.9: Landscape Conservation

In collaboration with internal and external partners, identify priority areas and begin implementing strategies for watershed improvement and regional land conservation within three years of CCP approval.

Rationale: The scale at which environmental problems, and their solutions, are addressed has begun to evolve from traditionally site-specific or locality-based approaches to a broader, more regional approach. It is not possible for a national wildlife refuge to work only within refuge boundaries and expect to meet its ideals for the long-term conservation and protection of wildlife, habitats, and ecological services.

The trend toward this landscape-level perspective has been catalyzed by new environmental research, expanded computing and technological capabilities, changing communication forums, and an increased understanding of landscape-level environmental issues and constraints. In addition, a number of initiatives within the Fish and Wildlife Service have resulted in the agency beginning to shift its emphasis toward a broader and more integrated approach to conservation, including the adoption of Strategic Habitat Conservation (SHC) and increased focus on global climate change.

As a part of the conservation landscape, Refuge lands and Service personnel will play an active role in efforts directed at understanding and mitigating these new environmental challenges. Furthermore, it is only by working with partners – both public and private – that threats such as habitat loss, fragmentation and degradation, water quality and quantity concerns, interrupted or altered natural processes, global climate change, biotechnology, declines in native biodiversity, growing numbers of invasive species, and other such issues can be addressed.

Strategies:

1. Gather and review existing literature and data relevant to landscape and watershed conservation in the region.

2. Meet with partners and stakeholders to discuss the range of issues and interests in landscape conservation and watershed planning.

3. Involve the public in Service planning related to landscape conservation and watershed planning.

4. Coordinate across Service divisions to leverage expertise, programs, and services for landscape conservation and watershed planning initiatives.

5. Conduct a science-based landscape assessment that incorporates the interests of partner agencies, organizations, stakeholders, and the public in its analyses.

6. Identify target areas for conservation efforts, including land acquisition, conservation easements, work on private lands, and other tools available for land conservation and watershed improvement.

7. Share results with partners and stakeholders.

8. Work with partners, stakeholders, and willing private landowners to protect, enhance, or restore conservation targets identified by the analysis.

9. Seek additional funding for landscape conservation and watershed improvement efforts.

10. Participate in local discussions, meetings, and projects related to landscape-level issues.

11. Raise local awareness of the Service's role in landscape conservation and watershed improvement.

12. Work with partners and stakeholders to increase the collective awareness of landscape and watershed conservation issues, opportunities, and benefits through environmental education, outreach, and technical assistance.

13. Encourage local communities to use the science-based assessments in their planning.

Goal 2: Wildlife

Support the maximum sustainable breeding and post-breeding populations of cavity-nesting waterfowl, neotropical migratory birds, Indiana bats, and a diversity of migratory, rare wetland, and resident species.

Objective 2.1: Monitoring

Over the long-term, document the effect of reforestation and management on wildlife species diversity and abundance. Surveys will identify the presence/absence of species and abundance of select high priority species as well as surveying key indicator species to monitor the overall health of the local environment and impacts of management actions.

Rationale: The Refuge purpose "...for use as an inviolate sanctuary, or for any other management purpose, for migratory birds" derives from the Migratory Bird Conservation Act. Approximately

Wild Turkey at Muscatatuck NWR. Photo credit: Mark Trabue

280 species of birds have been documented as using the Refuge. Most of the birds that use the Refuge are migrants either passing through during spring and fall, or wintering on the Refuge. However, the Refuge also supports an abundance of breeding bird species with 121 species confirmed as breeding at the Refuge. Among these breeding species are Wood Duck, Canada Geese, Least Bittern, and Sora Rail, as well as many passerine species, and a colony of Great Blue Heron. Water and moist soil management efforts focus on providing suitable resting, nesting, and foraging habitat for all waterbirds, and monitoring populations can give indications of whether the Refuge is effective in its management actions.

The Refuge is home to a diversity of reptile and amphibian species attributable to the abundance of wetlands and diversity of habitats. Many of these species are invaluable assets as a food supply to the myriad of species that prey on them. More than 40 species have been documented, including frogs, toads, salamanders, skinks, turtles, and snakes. Among the snakes are the state-listed endangered Kirtland's snake and copperbelly watersnake. Several other species of reptiles and amphibians that occur on Muscatatuck NWR are listed as endangered or threatened at the state level, including the four-toed salamander. Amphibians are especially sensitive to changes in their environment and their populations are declining worldwide (Houlahan et al. 2000; Wake 1991; Blaustein et al. 1994). Monitoring the health of reptile and amphibian populations at Muscatatuck NWR may help detect other environmental problems such as contaminants or impacts due to global climate change. Baseline data on reptiles and amphibians that occur at the Refuge are incomplete, outdated, and possibly unreliable.

With ample water year-round and the influence of the Vernon Fork, Storm, Mutton, and Sandy Branch Creeks, a wide variety of fish species flourish at Muscatatuck NWR (Patrick and Palavage 1994). A total of 85 species have been documented on the Refuge. The most diverse are the minnow (22 species) and darter (13 species) families. Anglers fish for largemouth bass, bluegill, redear sunfish, black crappie, and catfish. The eastern sand darter and harlequin darter have been found in the Vernon Fork of the Muscatatuck River at the south end of the Refuge. In addition, a flier was collected from Moss Lake and Mutton Creek in 2007 and a redspotted sunfish was collected from Mutton Creek the same year; these occurrences are perhaps the furthest north and east for these species on record. Monitoring fish assemblages can serve numerous purposes. Several species of fish can be surveyed as indicator species for water quality and environmental health (i.e. darter spp) (Patrick and Palavage 1994). Fishing pressure, if too great or too little, can have serious implications to the health of a fisheries system and therefore periodic evaluation will allow for recommendations necessary for regulation of sport fishing.

The Refuge supports several resident game species that attract visitors for hunting and wildlife observation. White-tailed deer and Wild Turkey are abundant in southern Indiana and on the Refuge. Food and cover are available in plentiful supply. The Northern Bob-white Quail and eastern cottontail rabbit populations are relatively small and will likely diminish with the reduction in Refuge grasslands and fragmentation of the forest (Twedt et al. 2007; Harper 2007). Squirrel populations are healthy and these species will likely experience a positive effect from forest reforestation efforts (Fisher and Wilkinson 2005).

Deer monitoring on Muscatatuck NWR is lacking. Spotlight surveys, deer exclosures, and/or indicator plant surveys should be utilized and interpreted to determine population sizes and make management recommendations. Emigration and immigration can greatly alter population size and density and can be extremely variable from year to year. Food availability, mainly mast production, is largely responsible for these variations in deer demographics. Damage to surrounding landowners' property can occur during years of poor mast production. Overpopulation of deer can lead to the damage of seedlings, especially oaks, which can impede regeneration success in the hardwood areas of the Refuge. Overgrazing can lead and contribute to changes in species composition, which in turn can result in negative effects on other plant and animal species (Rooney and Waller 2003). A firm understanding of population size and management decisions based on regular monitoring is necessary to prevent these negative effects, while sustaining a viable population.

Reforestation of the open, fallow, and retired farm fields and other grassy openings may result in significant changes in the faunal assemblages currently present at the Refuge. It is believed that closing in the forests and reducing fragmentation will result in increases to forest interior bird species. However, this will be to the detriment of grassland bird species. It is imperative that Refuge staff be able to monitor the bird response to such large scale changes to verify changes at the Refuge following reforestation.

Strategies:

1. Develop a monitoring plan within 5 years and incorporate when possible the recommendations from the Biological Review and Inventory and Monitoring Review.

2. Conduct weekly waterfowl surveys to monitor use, production, and effectiveness/impacts of management actions; send this data to cooperating state partners.

3. Conduct secretive marsh bird surveys every 5 years using an established protocol to monitor use and response to management actions.

4. Work with partners, the Biological Monitoring Team, and other professionals to develop a method to correlate vegetation surveys, water level monitoring, and waterbird response to enhance existing knowledge and provide data necessary for management.

5. Conduct pre- and post-bird monitoring in conjunction with habitat management efforts including conversions and restoration/regeneration efforts.

6. Conduct heron rookery surveys annually to monitor the health of the colony; send this data to cooperating state partners.

7. Annually monitor Bald Eagle nest production and conduct annual nest searches for this species.

8. Conduct shorebird surveys using the International Shorebird Survey Protocol to track occurrence, relative abundance, and response to management regimes.

9. Conduct a thorough baseline inventory of herpetofauna occurring on Refuge.

10. Establish surveying and monitoring for several herptile species as indicators of environmental health and water quality as well as monitoring the impacts of global climate change.

11. Conduct annual frog call surveys in accordance with the North American Amphibian Monitoring Program protocols; send this data to cooperating state partners.

12. Conduct fisheries surveys every 5 years to monitor populations, environmental health, water quality, and to allow for recommendations necessary for regulation of sport fishing.

13. Monitor deer populations to protect regenerating trees, prevent depredation issues on adjacent lands, ensure viable populations, and to generate data necessary for establishing annual hunting regulations.

14. Partner with conservation and private organizations to assist with monitoring inventory and educational efforts.

15. Monitor Region 3 Regional Conservation Priority (RCP) species every 5 years through nationally recognized protocols and link results to regional and national databases.

16. Ensuring high-quality, scientifically based monitoring will require the addition of one wildlife biologist and two full-time biological science technicians.

Objective 2.2: Federally Listed Threatened and Endangered Species

Protect federally listed species and their habitats.

Rationale: Whooping Cranes, Indiana bats, and Least Terns use the Refuge. Least Terns and Whooping Cranes use the Refuge during migration. Indiana bats are resident species. The Refuge population of copperbelly watersnakes is not included in the federal listing, which addresses populations north of Indianapolis. However, ongoing research indicates that the Muscatatuck NWR population may be important because it is thriving while many populations are declining and may be attributable to various habitat components. A population of bog bluegrass is located in the seep spring area. This plant is apparently flourishing in that area.

Strategies:

1. Maintain close coordination with the Ecological Services office on any habitat alteration that may affect Indiana bat habitat.

2. Facilitate continued research and monitoring of Indiana bats on the Refuge.

3. Facilitate continued research and monitoring of copperbelly watersnakes on the Refuge.

Refuge sign. Photo credit: U.S. Fish & Wildlife Service

4. Facilitate inventory, mapping, monitoring, and research as necessary on federally-listed or candidate species that are found at the Refuge within the life of this plan.

5. Consider federally-listed species when making management decisions and actions.

6. Protect, as necessary, areas and habitats known to benefit or support federally-listed species.

Objective 2.3: State T&E Species and Species of Concern

Consider known populations of state-listed species in management actions.

Rationale: Species on the state endangered list that occur on the Refuge include:

- Indiana bat
- southern rein orchid
- climbing hempvine
- copperbelly water snake
- four-toed salamander
- Kirtland's snake
- eastern mud turtle
- Kirtland's Warbler

- Peregrine Falcon
- Bald Eagle
- Yellow-crowned Night-Heron
- Black-crowned Night-Heron
- Virginia Rail
- Common Moorhen
- King Rail
- Least Bittern
- Loggerhead Shrike
- Osprey
- Trumpeter Swan
- Northern Harrier
- American Bittern
- Upland Sandpiper
- Least Tern
- Black Tern
- Barn Owl
- Short-eared Owl
- Sedge Wren
- Golden-winged Warbler
- Cerulean Warbler
- Marsh Wren
- Henslow's Sparrow

The following state species of special concern occur on the Refuge:

- least weasel
- little spectaclecase mussel
- rough green snake.
- Sharp-shinned Hawk
- Red-shouldered Hawk
- Great Egret
- Sandhill Crane
- Broad-winged Hawk
- Black-and-white Warbler
- Worm-eating Warbler
- Hooded Warbler
- Greater Yellowlegs
- Solitary Sandpiper
- Ruddy Turnstone
- Short-billed Dowitcher

- Wilson's Phalarope
- Chuck-will's-widow
- Whip-poor-will

Several other plant species are included on a state watch list. Those species are: American ginseng, bog bluegrass, Walter's St. John's-wort, smooth white violet, and club spur orchid. The Refuge is within the range of several other state-listed species. Surveys need to be conducted to document the presence of these species on Refuge lands. A monitoring plan will be developed and surveys will be conducted to confirm species presence. State-listed threatened and endangered species will be considered in management actions on the Refuge.

Strategies:

1. Facilitate inventory, mapping, monitoring, and research as necessary of state-listed or candidate species that are found at the Refuge within the life of this plan.

2. Protect, as necessary, areas and habitats known to benefit or support state-listed species.

3. Consider state-listed species when making management decisions and actions.

Goal 3: People

Visitors understand and appreciate the Refuge and the natural environment and its processes through participation in high-quality, wildlife-dependent, interpretive recreational and educational opportunities.

Introduction: "Quality," as used in the following objectives, is defined by the criteria for developing and evaluating wildlife-dependent recreation programs in the Service Manual (605 FW 1). Quality incorporates elements of safety, minimal conflict, accessibility, resource stewardship, understanding, appreciation, and satisfaction. Quality also incorporates the reasonable opportunity to experience wildlife. The Improvement Act of 1997 also directs refuges to promote opportunities for families to experience wildlife-dependent recreation, which will be considered in visitor services planning.

Muscatatuck NWR. Photo credit: U.S. Fish & Wildlife Service

Objective 3.1: Hunting

Refuge hunters will experience quality hunting opportunities for deer, Wild Turkey, squirrel, and rabbit. An opportunity to hunt quail will continue to be provided.

Rationale: As one of the six priority wildlife-dependent recreational uses identified in the National Wildlife Refuge System Improvement Act of 1997, hunting provides a traditional recreational activity on the Refuge with no definable adverse impacts to the biological integrity or habitat sustainability of Refuge resources.

For safety, hunters will need to wear hunter orange on all hunts with the exception of turkey hunts. To minimize conflict with the purposes of the Refuge there will be no waterfowl hunting and no hunting of any kind in the waterfowl sanctuary or the northeast portion of the Refuge (currently a no-hunting area). Interpretive and informational programs delivered through brochures and special events will be developed to promote resource stewardship, understanding, and appreciation among hunters. Hunting times for squirrel, rabbit, and quail will be consistent with the state season. Archery deer hunting will extend, except for a break during the muzzleloader season, from after National Wildlife Refuge Week in October through the end of the state season. A muzzleloader hunt for deer will occur by special permit drawing during the state season. A hunt for turkey will occur by special permit drawing during the state spring season. To expand opportunities for youth and family participation, state youth hunts will be offered with

the help of cooperators. Partners will also be solicited to help recruit under-represented populations to participate in the hunting programs. (See Figure 9 on page 38.)

Strategies:

1. Develop a Visitor Services step-down plan within 2 years.

2. Update Refuge-specific hunting regulations.

3. Recruit cooperators to assist with hunts by youth and under-represented populations.

Objective 3.2: Fishing

Refuge anglers will experience quality boat, shore and float-tube fishing on Stanfield Lake and quality bank, pier, or platform fishing opportunities on Stanfield and Richart Lakes, Lakes Sheryl and Linda, and Persimmon and the Sand Hill Ponds.

Rationale: As one of the six priority wildlife-dependent recreational uses identified in the National Wildlife Refuge System Improvement Act of 1997, fishing provides a traditional recreational activity on the Refuge with no definable adverse impacts to the biological integrity or habitat sustainability of Refuge resources.

To better fulfill the quality criteria, modifications will be made to the current fishing program. To improve accessibility, electric trolling motors will be allowed on Stanfield Lake after several years of monitoring to develop a baseline understanding of fish populations, and additional accessible fishing sites will be developed on Lake Sheryl and Persimmon Pond. Shoreline improvements (deepening) to existing fishing areas will be made in select areas to improve bank fishing. Interpretive and informational programs delivered through brochures, kiosks, and special events will be developed to promote resource stewardship, understanding, and appreciation. To improve the reasonable opportunity to experience wildlife, the take of fish will be more closely monitored and managed through regulation, which will insure sustainable, healthy populations. Spawning and nursery habitat will also be improved when feasible. To promote opportunities for children to fish, a pond will be designated as a "kids only" fishing pond with the possible restriction of catch and release.

To evaluate improvements in the fishing program and summarize progress, the Refuge will use the evaluation standards of RAPP (Refuge Annual Performance Plan). RAPP measures act as a general indicator of how successful management is in satisfying the criteria for quality of recreation use as described in the Service Manual. As the visitor services program of the Refuge matures and more details are specified in a visitor services plan, the Refuge will be able to move to more direct and specific measures of recreation quality. These direct measures will include a survey of visitors.

Strategies:

1. Develop a Visitor Services Step-down plan within 2 years.

2. Develop a fishery management plan in cooperation with the Service's Carterville Fisheries Office.

3. Update Refuge-specific regulations to permit electric motors on Stanfield Lake and designate a "kids only" fishing area.

4. Construct additional accessible fishing sites and modify existing sites.

5. Continue annual kids' fishing event.

6. Improve banks and shoreline to enhance fishing opportunities in select areas.

7. Withdraw Mallard and Display Ponds from the fishing program and allow these areas to revert to bottomland hardwood forest.

Objective 3.3: Wildlife Observation and Photography

Refuge visitors will experience quality wildlife observation and photography opportunities.

Rationale: Wildlife observation and photography are both priority wildlife-dependent recreation activities listed in the National Wildlife Refuge System Improvement Act of 1997. These activities occur, for the most part, along or near Refuge roads and trails (Figure 14).

To promote safety and improve the experience of visitors, the west entrance to the Refuge will be closed. Closing the entrance will eliminate the use of Refuge roads as a short-cut for highway traffic and ensure that motorists using Refuge roads are there to visit the Refuge. The reduced traffic flow will contribute to a reduction in the conflicts between commuters and people viewing wildlife.

Bicycling is permitted on paved or gravel roads and would likely increase with less vehicle traffic and paving of the auto tour route. Trails will remain closed to bicycles to minimize conflict among visitors on narrow trail treads.

To minimize maintenance work load and expense, the East and West River Trails will not be maintained and will be allowed to revert back to forest. To improve accessibility and reduce dust, efforts will be made to obtain funding to asphalt the auto tour route and improve the surface of trails. A wildlife observation structure will be built near the Shop area to facilitate viewing of wildlife using the open area. Species that are expected to be seen from the structure include deer, Wild Turkey, Sandhill Cranes, and Canada Geese. The Hackman Overlook structure will be evaluated in a visitor services step-down plan for potential modification or removal. The observation platform at the Restle Unit will be maintained and interpretation provided. Two annual photo contests and annual migratory bird day activities will be held to promote public understanding and increase appreciation of natural resources and the Refuge's role in managing and conserving them.

Strategies:

1. Develop a Visitor Services step-down plan within 2 years.

2. Define and enter construction needs in the appropriate databases.

3. Within 15 years, survey visitors to determine the quality of their Refuge experience.

4. Close West Entrance Road.

5. Extend Refuge hours to 1 hour before sunrise and 1 hour after sunset.

Objective 3.4: Interpretation and Environmental Education

Participants will experience quality interpretive and environmental education opportunities at or above the 2008 level.

Rationale: Interpretation and environmental education are both priority wildlife-dependent recreational uses listed in the National Wildlife Refuge System Improvement Act of 1997. Interpretation will be delivered through visitor center exhibits, programs, brochures, a website, and

Figure 14: Future Visitor Facilities, Muscatatuck NWR

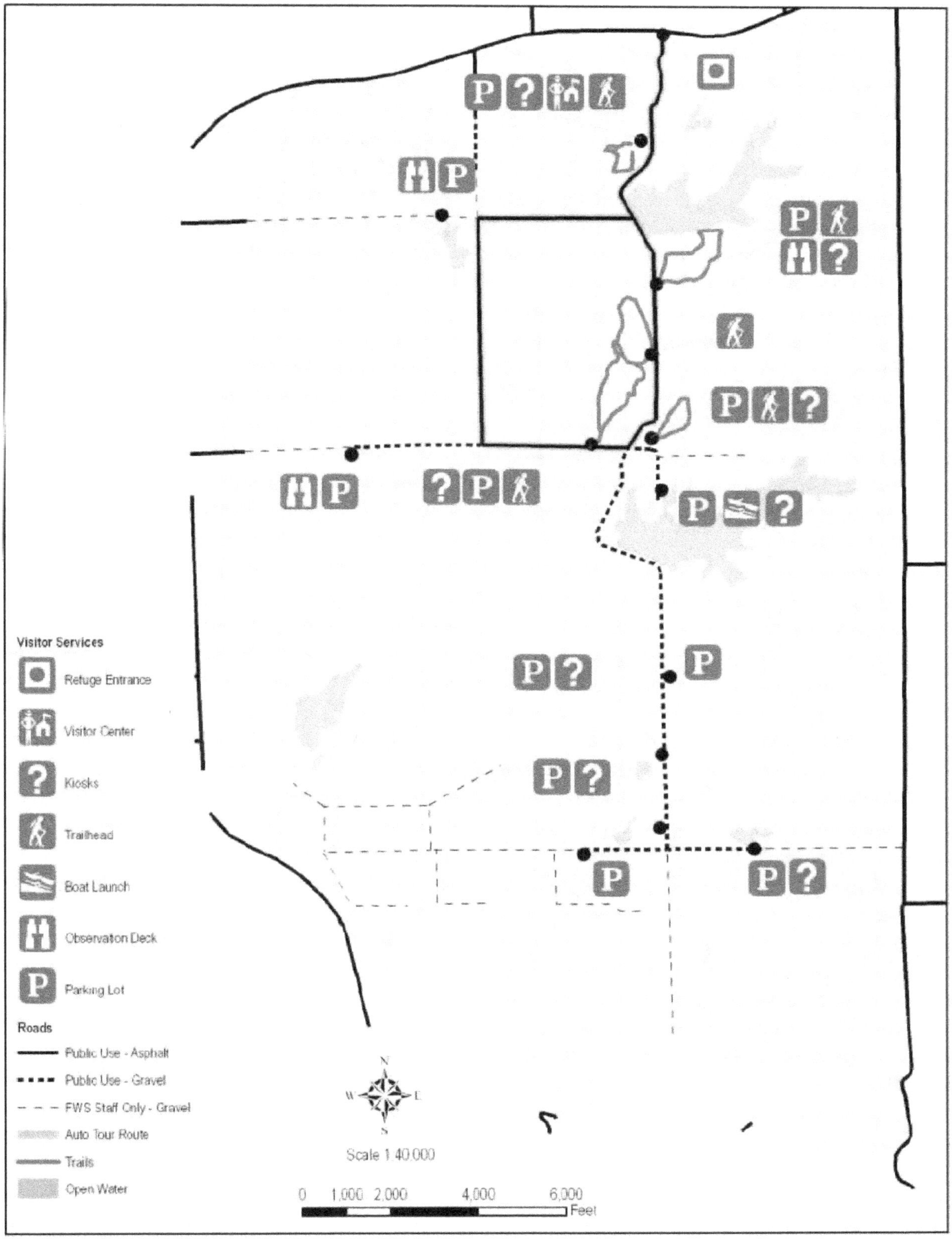

Visitor Services

- ⊡ Refuge Entrance
- 🏛 Visitor Center
- ? Kiosks
- 🚶 Trailhead
- 〰 Boat Launch
- 🏠 Observation Deck
- P Parking Lot

Roads

- —— Public Use - Asphalt
- ▪▪▪▪ Public Use - Gravel
- – – – FWS Staff Only - Gravel
- ▒▒▒ Auto Tour Route
- ═══ Trails
- ▒ Open Water

Scale 1 40,000

0   1,000 2,000   4,000   6,000
Feet

signs along the auto tour route, Chestnut Ridge Trail, trailhead and fishing area kiosks, and at the Myers Cabin.

The Refuge will continue to host the annual Conservation Field Days for Jackson and Jennings County third-graders as part of the interpretive program. The Refuge will also continue to host the annual Indiana Junior Duck Stamp Program and contest.

Interpretive activities will continue to be designed to promote resource stewardship, conservation, understanding, and appreciation of America's natural resources and the Refuge's role in managing those resources.

Environmental education programs will be developed and administered to satisfy the Service's description of environmental education as specified in current policy. Following the principle of allowing program participants to demonstrate learning through Refuge-specific stewardship tasks and projects that they can carry over into their everyday lives (605 FW 6.4.B), the Refuge will continue to work with Hayden School and others on Refuge activities.

Strategies:

1. Develop a Visitor Services step-down plan within 2 years.

2. Continue interpretive programs and visitor center exhibits at 2008 level or higher.

3. Improve Refuge brochures and website.

4. Continue activities with the Hayden School group and the Junior Birder program.

5. Continue the Conservation Field Day events.

6. Improve interpretive signs on the Auto Tour Route, Chestnut Ridge Interpretive Trail, trailheads, and fishing sites.

7. Hire one full-time park ranger to organize and augment the interpretation and environmental education program, including oversight of the visitor services step-down plan, increasing Refuge programming, and ongoing coordination with local schools. (Position will also serve to enhance volunteer coordination.)

The Refuge Bookstore, Muscatatuck NWR. Photo credit: U.S. Fish & Wildlife Service

Objective 3.5: Volunteers

The 3-year moving average of annual hours contributed by volunteers will increase throughout the life of the plan.

Rationale: The Refuge has received strong support from volunteers and interns. Opportunities for enhancing the wildlife and visitor services programs will likely always exceed the Refuge's budget. Therefore, all Refuge activities will continue to benefit from volunteer participation, and certain activities will require volunteer participation to be successful. A coordinated and efficiently run volunteer program will be essential to achieving many Refuge goals. A continuously expanding program is desirable, but unforeseen circumstances may affect the level of participation in a particular year. Therefore, a 3-year moving average will be used to monitor the participation in the volunteer program, which will permit some variation from year to year but document long-term growth.

Strategies:

1. Recruit new volunteers to assist with resource management and visitor services.

2. Recognize and supervise volunteers as adjunct staff.

3. Continue to staff the Visitor Center with volunteers.

4. Add one full-time park ranger with split responsibilities between volunteer coordination, environmental education, and interpretation.

Objective 3.6: Partnerships

Increase and improve partnerships over the level of the 2007 program.

Rationale: Partnerships greatly expand the range of conservation activities. Muscatatuck NWR has been fortunate to have many partners in the local area including the Refuge Friends group (the Muscatatuck Wildlife Society), the local Soil and Water Conservation Districts, USDA's Natural Resources Conservation Service, Purdue Extension, local Ducks Unlimited Chapters, the local Wild Turkey Federation, the Indiana Department of Natural Resources, local Resource Conservation and Development Councils, area Conservation and Birding Clubs, sporting good stores, scouting and civic groups, local Visitor Bureaus, the U.S. Forest Service, the Hayden School Refuge Rangers, local universities, and many others.

Strategies:

1. Maintain existing partnerships by committing staff time to work with partners on Service priority conservation activities.

2. Identify, establish regular communication, and coordinate local efforts with partners involved in landscape conservation, watershed planning, and other off-Refuge conservation issues.

3. Contact at least one new potential partner each year.

Objective 3.7: Community Outreach

Promote public understanding and appreciation of Muscatatuck National Wildlife Refuge to traditional and under-represented populations through off-site events, programs, newsletters and the website at levels at least as great as 2008.

Rationale: The Refuge values its visitors, neighbors, and the local community. The Refuge is an asset to the community and has received strong support in the past.

Continued support is essential for the success of the Refuge. It is important that the Refuge continues efforts to build and maintain open communication with neighbors and the broader community to let them know the successes, challenges, and opportunities in conservation and wildlife-dependent recreation. In an ideal setting, the objective would be to achieve an appreciation of the value and need for fish and wildlife conservation among a larger percentage of the population living around the Refuge. The success in achieving the objective would be determined through a survey of the general population.

However, for an objective to be useful it must be measurable in both a conceptual and practical sense. It is not practical to propose that the Refuge will conduct a survey of the general population anytime in the next few years, because the approvals and costs are beyond the likely resources of the Refuge. As an alternative, the objective reflects the assumption that providing neighbors and community members with written and oral information will lead to positive conservation attitudes and action. Public understanding of the purpose of Refuge lands, including appropriate and compatible uses, may lead to a reduction in illegal activities such as dumping, littering, and speeding on Refuge roads.

Strategies:

1. Upgrade the Refuge website with basic, time-sensitive, and newsworthy information about Muscatatuck NWR.

2. Maintain a Refuge mailing list and Refuge newsletter.

3. Review and update the station outreach plan.

Objective 3.8: Law Enforcement

People feel safe on Muscatatuck NWR and the resource is protected.

Rationale: The Refuge is responsible for protecting Refuge resources and providing a safe environment for employees and visitors. The Refuge's law enforcement program is a critical tool in protecting trust resources, habitat, public facilities, employees, and the visiting public. To provide this essential service, the Refuge will share regional resources and cooperate with other law enforcement authorities to meet its responsibilities.

Strategies:

1. Share regional law enforcement resources.

2. Partner with Indiana DNR Conservation Officers and other state and local law enforcement officers.

The Muscatatuck Wildlife Society was instrumental in preserving the Myers Barn. Photo credit: U.S. Fish & Wildlife Service

Objective 3.9: Cultural Resources

Over the life of the plan, avoid and protect against disturbance all known Refuge cultural, historic, or archeological sites.

Rationale: Cultural resources are an important facet of the country's heritage. Muscatatuck NWR, like all national wildlife refuges and wetland management districts, remains committed to preserving archeological and historic sites against degradation, looting, and other adverse impacts. The guiding principle for management derives from the National Historic Preservation Act of 1966 as amended, 16 U.S.C. 470 et seq. and the Archeological Resources Protection Act of 1979 as amended, 16 U.S.C. 47011-mm, which establish legal mandates and protection against identifying sites for the public, etc. The Refuge must ensure archeological and cultural values are described, identified, and taken into consideration prior to implementing projects. It is also essential that new site discoveries are documented. In order to meet these responsibilities, the Refuge intends to maintain an open dialogue with the Regional Historic Preservation Officer (RHPO) and to provide the RHPO with information about new archeological site discoveries. The Refuge will also cooperate with Federal, state, and local agencies, American Indian tribes, the Muscatatuck Wildlife Society, and the public in managing cultural resources on the Refuge.

Strategies:

1. Conduct site-specific surveys prior to ground disturbing projects and protect known archeological, cultural and historic sites.

2. Inform the Regional Historic Preservation Officer early in project planning to ensure compliance with Section 106 of National Historic Preservation Act.

3. In the event of inadvertent discoveries of ancient human remains or artifacts, follow instructions and procedures indicated by the RHPO.

4. Ensure archeological and cultural values are described, identified, and taken into consideration prior to implementing undertakings.

5. Inspect the condition of known cultural resources on the Refuge and report to the RHPO changes in the conditions.

6. Integrate historic preservation with planning and management of other resources and activities.

Chapter 5: Plan Implementation

Introduction

This chapter summarizes the actions, funding, coordination, and monitoring to implement the CCP. As noted in the inside cover of this document, this plan does not constitute a commitment for staffing increases or operational and maintenance increases. These decisions are at the discretion of Congress in overall appropriations, and in budget allocation decisions made at the national and regional levels of the Service.

New and Existing Projects

This CCP outlines an ambitious course of action for the future management of Muscatatuck NWR. It will require considerable staff commitment as well as funding commitment to actively manage the wildlife habitats and to add/improve public use facilities. The Refuge will continually need appropriate operational and maintenance funding to implement the objectives in this plan. A full listing of unfunded Refuge projects and operational needs can be found in Appendix G.

Staffing

Implementing the vision set forth in this CCP will require changes in the organizational structure of the Refuge. Existing staff will direct their time and energy in new directions and new staff members will need to be added to assist in these efforts.

In March of 2008 a national team of Refuge System professionals developed a staffing model to estimate the personnel required to effectively operate and manage the existing 589 field stations of the NWRS. Fifteen factors were used in the evaluation, covering the following topics:

■ total acres, acres actively managed, and number of easement contracts

■ endangered and invasive species populations

Little Blue Heron. Photo credit: Mark Trabue

■ biological management and monitoring, threats and conflicts

■ wilderness management

■ visitor services: visitation, education programs, volunteers, Friends

■ maintenance needs and existing assets

The model attempts to project staffing levels in a systematic, qualitative manner. No model is perfect or the final word in estimating staffing needs, but this type of model is useful for supporting personnel actions and fosters consistent staffing decision-making. The 2008 model projected only the total maximum number of full-time equivalent (FTE) positions needed at each station, not the individual disciplines or specialties. Law enforcement positions were not included in the assessment. In order to implement the staffing model, the final report recommended that each Region adjust the final model numbers as necessary and identify the most appropriate position types for each station.

Table 5: Additional Staffing as Indicated by the 2008 Refuge System Staffing Model

PROPOSED NEW POSITIONS	FTE	RANK
Wildlife Biologist (Invasive Species Management)	1	1
Equipment Operator	1	2
Park Ranger (Interpretation/Volunteer Coordination)	1	3
Biological Science Technician (Invasive Species Management)	1	4
Biological Science Technician (Forestry & Invasive Species)	1	5

The 2008 staffing model results for Muscatatuck NWR included a total of 14 FTE positions, with a subsequent adjustment at the regional level to 11. Using a 2008 baseline staffing of 6 FTE positions the Refuge was asked to identify five additional positions and rank them from greatest to least priority (see Table 5). The additional personnel would expand and improve the quality of the field program, especially invasive species control, the forestry program, water resource management, and environmental education on the Refuge.

The staffing model results illustrate full staffing at Muscatatuck NWR under optimum conditions. Due to the reality of financial constraints and operating budgets within the Service, it may not be possible to reach full staffing levels immediately. However, the amount and quality of management on a refuge heavily depends on the personnel resources available to implement the plan.

Partnership Opportunities

Partnerships are an essential element for the successful accomplishment of goals, objectives, and strategies at Muscatatuck NWR. The objectives outlined in this CCP need the support and the partnerships of federal, state and local agencies, non-governmental organizations and individual citizens. Refuge staff will continue to seek creative partnership opportunities to achieve the vision of the Refuge.

We expect to work with the following notable partners while continuing to develop new partnerships:

- Muscatatuck Wildlife Society
- local Soil and Water Conservation Districts
- local city governments
- Environmental Protection Agency
- Natural Resource Conservation Service
- Purdue Extension
- local Ducks Unlimited chapters
- National Wild Turkey Federation
- Indiana Department of Natural Resources
- Indiana Department of Environmental Management
- local Resource Conservation and Development Councils
- area conservation and birding clubs
- sporting good stores
- Scouting and civic groups
- local Visitor Bureaus
- U.S. Forest Service
- Hayden School Refuge Rangers
- local universities
- The Nature Conservancy
- Sycamore Land Trust

Step-Down Management Plans

The CCP is a plan that provides general concepts and specific wildlife, habitat, and people related objectives. Step-down management plans provide greater detail to managers and employees who will carry out the strategies described in the CCP. The Refuge staff will revise or develop the following step-down plans:

- Habitat Management Plan, including a forest component (5 years)
- Water Management Plan for Restle Unit (2 years)
- Integrated Pest Management Plan (5 years)
- Visitor Services Plan (2 years)
- Fishery Management Plan (5 years)
- Habitat and Wildlife Monitoring Plans (3 years)

Monitoring and Evaluation

The direction set forth in this CCP and specifically identified strategies and projects will be monitored throughout the life of this plan. On a periodic basis, the Regional Office will assemble a station review team whose purpose will be to visit the Refuge and evaluate current activities in light of this plan. The team will review all aspects of Refuge management, including direction, accomplishments and funding. The goals and objectives presented in this CCP will provide the baseline for evaluation of this field station.

Plan Review and Revision

While comprehensive conservation plans are designed to provide guidance for Refuge management over a 15-year period, they are also dynamic and flexible documents that are reviewed regularly and modified when plan review or other Refuge monitoring and evaluation determines that it is necessary.

Service policy calls for an annual review of these plans and revision when significant new information or events necessitate change in order to achieve refuge purposes, vision, and goals. The policy calls for revision, "...when significant new information becomes available, ecological conditions change, major refuge expansion occurs, or when we identify the need to do so during plan review" [602 FW 3].

Plan revisions follow the same procedures and processes used to develop the original CCP. As with a standard CCP planning effort, revisions must follow NEPA requirements and include opportunities for public review and comment. Minor plan revisions that meet the criteria for a categorical exclusion in an EAS may be made in accordance with 550 FW 3.3C.

Appendix A: Finding of No Significant Impact

Finding of No Significant Impact

Environmental Assessment and Comprehensive Conservation Plan for the Muscatatuck National Wildlife Refuge, Indiana

An Environmental Assessment (EA) has been prepared to identify management strategies to meet the conservation goals of Muscatatuck National Wildlife Refuge (NWR). The EA examined the environmental consequences that each management alternative could have on the quality of the physical, biological, and human environment, as required by the National Environmental Policy Act of 1969 (NEPA). The EA evaluated four alternatives for the future management of Muscatatuck NWR.

The alternative selected for implementation on the refuge is *Alternative C*. This preferred alternative directs management towards more historic landscape conditions by expanding forest habitats and decreasing management of constructed wetland units. Former farmland is either transitioned to forest or to open areas in order to increase refuge habitat diversity. This alternative relies on a combination of active management and natural processes to provide quality wildlife habitat for over 80 species of Regional Conservation Priority, including 3 species listed as Federally threatened or endangered. Biological surveys and monitoring activities, invasive species management, and wildlife-dependant recreation opportunities - particularly hunting and fishing, would all increase under the preferred alternative.

For reasons presented above and below, and based on an evaluation of the information contained in the Environmental Assessment, we have determined that the action of adopting Alternative C as the management alternative for Muscatatuck NWR is not a major Federal action which would significantly affect the quality of the human environment, within the meaning of Section 102 (2)(c) of the National Environmental Policy Act of 1969.

Additional Reasons:

- Future management actions will have a neutral or positive impact on the local economy.
- This action will not have an adverse impact on threatened or endangered species.

Supporting References:

- Environmental Assessment
- Comprehensive Conservation Plan

ACTING Regional Director   9/10/09
                                  Date

Appendix B: Glossary

Appendix B: Glossary

Aquatic Species

Includes all freshwater, anadromous and estuarine fishes, freshwater mollusks, freshwater crustaceans and freshwater amphibians.

Archaeological and Cultural Values

Any material remains of past human life or activity greater than 100 years old which are of archaeological interest as defined by Section 4(a) of the Archaeological Resources Protection Act and 43 CFR Part 7.3.

Biodiversity

The variety of life and its processes, including the variety of living organisms, the genetic differences among them, and the communities and ecosystems in which they occur.

Candidate Species

Those species for which the Service has sufficient information on biological vulnerability and threats to propose them for listing.

Compatible Use

A wildlife-dependent recreational use or any other use of a refuge that, in the sound professional judgment of the Director or designee, will not materially interfere with or detract from the fulfillment of the mission of the System or the purposes of the refuge (PL 105-57).

Comprehensive Conservation Plan

A document, completed with public involvement, that describes the desired future condition and provides long-term (15 year planning horizon) guidance to accomplish the purposes of the Refuge System and the individual refuge units.

Conservation

The management of natural resources to prevent loss or waste. Management actions may include preservation, restoration and enhancement.

Conservation Species

The use of all protective methods and procedures necessary to bring any species to the point at which the measures provided are no longer necessary. Such methods and procedures include, but are not limited to, all activities associated with scientific resources management such as research, census, law enforcement, habitat acquisition and maintenance, propagation, live trapping, and transplantation. Conservation is the act of managing a resource to ensure its survival and availability.

Cultural Resources

Cultural resources are defined as "those parts of the physical environment – natural and built – that have cultural value to some kind of sociocultural group... [and] those non-material human social institutions...." (King, p.9). Cultural resources include historic sites, archeological sites and associated artifacts, sacred sites, traditional cultural properties, cultural items (human remains, funerary objects, sacred objects, and objects of cultural patrimony) (McManamon, Francis P. DCA-NPS; letter 12-23-97 to Walla Walla District, COE), and buildings and structures.

Ecosystem

Dynamic and interrelating complex of plant and animal (including humans) communities and their associated non-living environment.

Ecosystem Approach

1) Protecting or restoring the natural function, structure, and species composition of an ecosystem, recognizing that all components are interrelated. 2) Management of natural resources using system-wide concepts to ensure that all plants and animals in ecosystems are maintained at viable levels in native habitats and that basic ecosystem processes are perpetuated indefinitely (Clark and Zaunbrecher 1987).

Endangered Species

A listed species in danger of extinction throughout all or a significant portion of its range.

Forest Fragmentation

Fragmentation may occur when a forested landscape is subdivided into patches. Fragmentation may also occur when numerous openings for such things as fields, roads, and power lines interrupt a continuous forest canopy. The resulting landscape pattern alters habitat connectivity and edge characteristics, influencing a variety of species.

Habitat Enhancement

Improving habitat through alteration, treatment, or other land management of existing habitat to increase habitat value for one or more species without bringing the habitat to a fully restored or naturally occurring condition.

Habitat Protection

Maintain current quality or prevent degradation to habitat. The act of ensuring that habitat quantity and quality do not change, most often as a result of human activities but sometimes in response to unwelcome natural processes or phenomena.

Habitat Restoration

Returns the quantity and quality of habitat to some previous naturally occurring condition, most often some baseline considered suitable and sufficient to support self-sustaining populations of fish and wildlife.

Interjurisdictional Fish

Populations of fish that are managed by two or more states or national or tribal governments because of the scope of their geographic distributions or migrations.

Invasive Species

An alien species whose introduction does or is likely to cause economic or environmental harm or harm to human health.

Migratory Nongame Birds of Management Concern

Those species of nongame birds that (a) are believed to have undergone significant population declines; (b) have small or restricted populations; or (c) are dependent upon restricted or vulnerable habitats.

Migratory Species

Species that move substantial distances to satisfy one or more biological needs, most often to reproduce or escape intolerable cyclic environmental conditions.

National Wildlife Refuge System

All lands and waters and interests therein administered by the Service as wildlife refuges, wildlife ranges, wildlife management areas, waterfowl production areas, and other areas for the protection and conservation of fish and wildlife, including those that are threatened with extinction.

Recovery Plans (species)

Documents developed by the Service that outline tasks necessary to stabilize and recover listed species. Recovery plans include goals for measuring species progress towards recovery, estimated costs and time frames for the recovery process, and an identification of public and private partners that can contribute to implementation of the recovery plan.

Riparian Habitats

Those lands adjacent to streams or rivers that form a transition zone between aquatic and upland systems and are typically dominated by woody vegetation that is of a noticeably different growth form than adjacent vegetation. Riparian areas may or may not meet the definition of wetlands used by Cowardin *et al.* (1979).

Rotation

The period during which a single generation is allowed to grow.

Species of Concern

A species not on the federal list of threatened or endangered species, but a species for which the Service or one of its partners has concerns.

Stakeholders

A person, group, organization, or system that affects or can be affected by an organization's activities. Typical stakeholders in U.S. Fish and Wildlife Service activities include state, tribal, and local government agencies, academic institutions, the scientific community, non-governmental entities including environmental, agricultural, and conservation organizations, trade groups, commercial interests, and private landowners.

Threatened Species

A listed species which is likely to become an endangered species within the foreseeable future throughout all or a significant portion of its range.

Undertaking

A project, activity, or program funded in whole or in part under the direct or indirect jurisdiction of a Federal agency, including those carried out by or on behalf of a Federal agency; those carried out with Federal financial assistance; those requiring a Federal permit, license or approval..." (36 CFR 800.16(y); 12-12-2000), i.e., all Federal actions.

Uplands

All lands not meeting the definition of wetlands, deepwater, or riverine.

Watershed

The area drained by a river or stream and its tributaries.

Wetlands

Lands transitional between terrestrial and aquatic systems where the water table is usually at or near the surface or the land is covered by shallow water (Cowardin *et al.*, 1979. In layman's terms, this habitat category includes marshes, swamps and bogs.

Wildlife-dependent Recreational Use

A use of a refuge involving hunting, fishing, wildlife observation and photography, or environmental education and interpretation.

Appendix C: Species Lists

Bird Species That Occur on Muscatatuck NWR

Family	Common Name	Scientific Name	Probable Abundance by Season				Status	
		A: Abundant, should find on every trip C: Common, should find on 75% of trips U: Uncommon, present but in lesser numbers R: Rare, infrequent or few identifications H: Accidental, not expected at this location O: Occasional					E: Endangered T: Threatened SC: Special Concern	
			Sp	S	F	W	State	Federal
Loons	Common Loon	*Gavia immer*	o	r	o	o		
Grebes	Pied-billed Grebe	*Podilymbus podiceps*	c	u	c	o		
Grebes	Horned Grebe	*Podiceps auritus*	o		o			
Grebes	Red-Necked Grebe	*Podiceps grisegena*	r					
Cormorants	Double-crested Cormorant	*Phalacrocorax auritus*	c	o	c	r		
Herons and Bitterns	American Bittern	*Botaurus lentiginosus*	o	o			E	
Herons and Bitterns	Least Bittern	*Ixobrychus exilis*	o	o	o		E	
Herons and Bitterns	Cattle Egret	*Bubulcus ibis*	r		r			
Herons and Bitterns	Great Egret	*Ardea alba*	u	u	u		SC	
Herons and Bitterns	Snowy Egret	*Egretta thula*	r	r	r			
Herons and Bitterns	Great Blue Heron	*Ardea herodias*	c	c	c	u		
Herons and Bitterns	Little Blue Heron	*Egretta caerulea*	o	o	o			
Herons and Bitterns	Tricolored Heron	*Egretta tricolor*	r	r	r			
Herons and Bitterns	Green Heron	*Butorides virescens*	c	c	u			
Herons and Bitterns	Black-crowned Night Heron	*Nycticorax nycticorax*	u	u	u		E	
Herons and Bitterns	Yellow-crowned Night Heron	*Nyctanassa violacea*	r	r	r		E	
Vultures	Black Vulture	*Coragyps atratus*	o	o	o	o		

Bird Species That Occur on Muscatatuck NWR (Continued)

Family	Common Name	Scientific Name	Sp	S	F	W	State	Federal
			A: Abundant, should find on every trip C: Common, should find on 75% of trips U: Uncommon, present but in lesser numbers R: Rare, infrequent or few identifications H: Accidental, not expected at this location O: Occasional				E: Endangered T: Threatened SC: Special Concern	
Vultures	Turkey Vulture	*Cathartes aura*	c	c	c	o		
Swans, Geese and Ducks	Greater White-fronted Goose	*Anser albifrons*				r		
Swans, Geese and Ducks	Snow Goose	*Chen caerulescens*				r		
Swans, Geese and Ducks	Canada Goose	*Branta canadensis*	a	a	a	a		
Swans, Geese and Ducks	Mute Swan	*Cygnus olor*	o		o	o		
Swans, Geese and Ducks	Tundra Swan	*Cygnus columbianus*	o		o	o		
Swans, Geese and Ducks	Trumpeter Swan	*Cygnus buccinator*				r	E	
Swans, Geese and Ducks	Wood Duck	*Aix sponsa*	a	a	a	c		
Swans, Geese and Ducks	Gadwall	*Anas strepera*	c	o	c	r		
Swans, Geese and Ducks	American Wigeon	*Anas americana*	c		c	o		
Swans, Geese and Ducks	American Black Duck	*Anas rubripes*	c	r	c	u		
Swans, Geese and Ducks	Mallard	*Anas platyrhynchos*	a	c	a	a		
Swans, Geese and Ducks	Blue-winged Teal	*Anas discors*	c	u	c	o		
Swans, Geese and Ducks	Northern Shoveler	*Anas clypeata*	c		c	o		
Swans, Geese and Ducks	Northern Pintail	*Anas acuta*	u		u	r		
Swans, Geese and Ducks	Green-winged Teal	*Anas carolinensis*	c		u	r		
Swans, Geese and Ducks	Canvasback	*Aythya ferina*	o		o	r		
Swans, Geese and Ducks	Redhead	*Aythya americana*	u		u	o		
Swans, Geese and Ducks	Ring-necked Duck	*Aytha collaris*	a		a	u		

Bird Species That Occur on Muscatatuck NWR (Continued)

Probable Abundance by Season:
A: Abundant, should find on every trip
C: Common, should find on 75% of trips
U: Uncommon, present but in lesser numbers
R: Rare, infrequent or few identifications
H: Accidental, not expected at this location
O: Occasional

Status:
E: Endangered
T: Threatened
SC: Special Concern

Family	Common Name	Scientific Name	Sp	S	F	W	State	Federal
Swans, Geese and Ducks	Greater Scaup	Aythya marila	o		o	r		
Swans, Geese and Ducks	Lesser Scaup	Aythya affinis	c		c	u		
Swans, Geese and Ducks	Oldsquaw	Clangula hyemalis	r			r		
Swans, Geese and Ducks	Bufflehead	Bucephala albeola	u		c	u		
Swans, Geese and Ducks	Common Goldeneye	Bucephala clangula	u		u	o		
Swans, Geese and Ducks	Hooded Merganser	Lophodytes cucullatus	u	o	c	o		
Swans, Geese and Ducks	Common Merganser	Mergus merganser	u		o	u		
Swans, Geese and Ducks	Red-breasted Merganser	Mergus serrator	o		o			
Swans, Geese and Ducks	Ruddy Duck	Oxyura jamaicensis	u		u	o		
Hawks and Eagles	Osprey	Pandion haliaetus	u		u		E	
Hawks and Eagles	Bald Eagle	Haliaeetus leucocephalus	o	c	o	o	E	
Hawks and Eagles	Northern Harrier	Circus cyaneus	u	r	u	c	E	
Hawks and Eagles	Sharp-shinned Hawk	Accipiter striatus	u	o	u	u	SC	
Hawks and Eagles	Cooper's Hawk	Accipiter cooperii	u	u	u	u		
Hawks and Eagles	Red-shouldered Hawk	Buteo lineatus	c	c	c	c	SC	
Hawks and Eagles	Broad-winged Hawk	Buteo platypterus	o		o		SC	
Hawks and Eagles	Red-tailed Hawk	Buteo jamaicensis	c	c	c	c		
Hawks and Eagles	Rough-legged Hawk	Buteo lagopus	o		o	o		
Hawks and Eagles	Golden Eagle	Aquila chrysaetos	r		r	r		

Bird Species That Occur on Muscatatuck NWR (Continued)

Family	Common Name	Scientific Name	Probable Abundance by Season				Status	
			Sp	S	F	W	State	Federal
Falcons	American Kestrel	*Falco sparverius*	c	c	c	c		
Falcons	Merlin	*Falco columbarius*	u		u	r		
Falcons	Peregrine Falcon	*Falco peregrinus*	u		u		E	
Upland Game Birds	Ring-necked Pheasant	*Phasianus colchicus*	h	h	h	h		
Upland Game Birds	Ruffed Grouse	*Bonasa umbellus*	r	r	r	r		
Upland Game Birds	Wild Turkey	*Meleagris gallopavo*	c	c	c	c		
Upland Game Birds	Northern Bobwhite Quail	*Colinus virginianus*	c	c	c	c		
Rails and Coots	Yellow Rail	*Coturnicops noveboracensis*	r		r			
Rails and Coots	King Rail	*Rallus elegans*	o	r	r		E	
Rails and Coots	Virginia Rail	*Rallus limicola*	u	o	u		E	
Rails and Coots	Sora	*Porzana carolina*	u	c	u			
Rails and Coots	Common Moorhen	*Gallinula chloropus*	o	o	o		E	
Rails and Coots	American Coot	*Fulica americana*	a	o	a	o		
Cranes	Sandhill Crane	*Grus canadensis*	u	r	u	u	SC	
Shorebirds	Black-bellied Plover	*Pluvialis squatatola*	o	o	o			
Shorebirds	Semipalmated Plover	*Charadrius semipalmatus*	o	o	u			
Shorebirds	Killdeer	*Charadrius vociferus*	c	c	c	o		
Shorebirds	Greater Yellowlegs	*Tringa melanoleuca*	c	c	c		SC	
Shorebirds	Lesser Yellowlegs	*Tringa flavipes*	c	c	c			

Probable Abundance by Season:
A: Abundant, should find on every trip
C: Common, should find on 75% of trips
U: Uncommon, present but in lesser numbers
R: Rare, infrequent or few identifications
H: Accidental, not expected at this location
O: Occasional

Status:
E: Endangered
T: Threatened
SC: Special Concern

Bird Species That Occur on Muscatatuck NWR (Continued)

Family	Common Name	Scientific Name	Probable Abundance by Season (A: Abundant, should find on every trip / C: Common, should find on 75% of trips / U: Uncommon, present but in lesser numbers / R: Rare, infrequent or few identifications / H: Accidental, not expected at this location / O: Occasional)				Status (E: Endangered / T: Threatened / SC: Special Concern)	
			Sp	S	F	W	State	Federal
Shorebirds	Solitary Sandpiper	*Tringa solitaria*	c	c	c		SC	
Shorebirds	Willit	*Catoptrophorus semipalmatus*			u			
Shorebirds	Spotted Sandpiper	*Actitis macularia*	u	o	u			
Shorebirds	Upland Sandpiper	*Bartramia longicauda*	r	r	r		E	
Shorebirds	Ruddy Turnstone	*Arenaria interpres*	r	r	r		SC	
Shorebirds	Semipalmated Sandpiper	*Calidris pusilla*	u	u	u			
Shorebirds	Western Sandpiper	*Calidris mauri*	o	o	o			
Shorebirds	Least Sandpiper	*Calidris minutilla*	u	o	c			
Shorebirds	White-rumped Sandpiper	*Calidris fuscicollis*	o	r	r			
Shorebirds	Baird's Sandpiper	*Calidris bairdii*	o	r	o			
Shorebirds	Pectoral Sandpiper	*Calidris melanotos*	c	c	c			
Shorebirds	Dunlin	*Calidris alpina*	c	c	c			
Shorebirds	Stilt Sandpiper	*Calidris himantopus*	u	u	u			
Shorebirds	Short-billed Dowitcher	*Limnodromus griseus*	u	o	o		SC	
Shorebirds	Long-billed Dowitcher	*Limnodromus scolopaceus*	r	r	r			
Shorebirds	Common Snipe	*Gallinago stenura*	c	c	c	u		
Shorebirds	American Woodcock	*Scolopax minor*	c	u	u	o	SC	
Shorebirds	Wilson's Phalarope	*Phalaropus tricolor*	u	u	u		SC	

Bird Species That Occur on Muscatatuck NWR (Continued)

Family	Common Name	Scientific Name	Probable Abundance by Season A: Abundant, should find on every trip C: Common, should find on 75% of trips U: Uncommon, present but in lesser numbers R: Rare, infrequent or few identifications H: Accidental, not expected at this location O: Occasional				Status E: Endangered T: Threatened SC: Special Concern	
			Sp	S	F	W	State	Federal
Gulls and Terns	Franklin's Gull	*Larus pipixcan*			r	r		
Gulls and Terns	Bonaparte's Gull	*Larus philadelphia*	r		r			
Gulls and Terns	Ring-billed Gull	*Larus delawarensis*	o	r	o	r		
Gulls and Terns	Herring Gull	*Larus argentatus*	r		r			
Gulls and Terns	Caspian Tern	*Sterna caspia*	o		o			
Gulls and Terns	Common Tern	*Sterna hirundo*	o		o			
Gulls and Terns	Forster's Tern	*Sterna forsteri*	o		o			
Gulls and Terns	Least Tern	*Sterna antillarum*	r		r		E	
Gulls and Terns	Black Tern	*Chlidonias niger*	r		r		E	
Doves	Rock Dove	*Columba livia*	u	u	u	u		
Doves	Mourning Dove	*Zenaida macroura*	a	a	a	a		
Cuckoos	Black-billed Cuckoo	*Coccyzus erythropthalmus*	o	o	u			
Cuckoos	Yellow-billed Cuckoo	*Coccyzus americanus*	u	c	c			
Owls	Barn Owl	*Tyto alba*	r	r	r	r	E	
Owls	Eastern Screech Owl	*Otus asio*	c	c	c	c		
Owls	Great Horned Owl	*Bubo virginianus*	c	c	c	c		
Owls	Barred Owl	*Strix varia*	c	c	c	c		
Owls	Long-eared Owl	*Asio otus*	r			r		
Owls	Short-eared Owl	*Asio flammeus*	o		o	o	E	

Bird Species That Occur on Muscatatuck NWR (Continued)

Family	Common Name	Scientific Name	Sp	S	F	W	State	Federal
			Sp: Abundant, should find on every trip / C: Common, should find on 75% of trips / U: Uncommon, present but in lesser numbers / R: Rare, infrequent or few identifications / H: Accidental, not expected at this location / O: Occasional					E: Endangered / T: Threatened / SC: Special Concern
Owls	Northern Saw-whet Owl	*Aegolius acadicus*	r		r	r		
Nighthawks and Nightjars	Common Nighthawk	*Chordeiles minor*	u	a	u		SC	
Nighthawks and Nightjars	Chuck-will's-widow	*Caprimulgus carolinensis*	r	r			SC	
Nighthawks and Nightjars	Whip-poor-will	*Caprimulgus vociferus*	r	u	r			
Swifts	Chimney Swift	*Chaetura pelagica*	c	c	c			
Hummingbirds	Ruby-throated Hummingbird	*Archilochus colubris*	c	c	c			
Kingfishers	Belted Kingfisher	*Ceryle alcyon*	c	c	c	u		
Woodpeckers	Red-headed Woodpecker	*Melanerpes erythrocephalus*	c	c	c	c		
Woodpeckers	Red-bellied Woodpecker	*Melanerpes carolinus*	c	c	c	c		
Woodpeckers	Yellow-bellied Sapsucker	*Sphyrapicus varius*	u	c	u	u		
Woodpeckers	Downy Woodpecker	*Picoides pubescens*	c	c	c	c		
Woodpeckers	Hairy Woodpecker	*Picoides villosus*	c	c	c	c		
Woodpeckers	Northern Flicker	*Colaptes auratus*	c	c	c	c		
Woodpeckers	Pileated Woodpecker	*Dryocopus pileatus*	c	c	c	c		
Flycatchers	Olive-sided Flycatcher	*Contopus cooperi*	o		o			
Flycatchers	Eastern Wood-Pewee	*Contopus virens*	c	c	c			
Flycatchers	Yellow-bellied Flycatcher	*Empidonax flaviventris*	u		u			
Flycatchers	Acadian Flycatcher	*Empidonax virescens*	c	c	c			
Flycatchers	Willow Flycatcher	*Empidonax traillii*	c	c	c			

Bird Species That Occur on Muscatatuck NWR (Continued)

Family	Common Name	Scientific Name	Probable Abundance by Season				Status	
			Sp	S	F	W	State	Federal
Flycatchers	Least Flycatcher	*Empidonax minimus*	u	r	u			
Flycatchers	Eastern Phoebe	*Sayornis phoebe*	c	c	c			
Flycatchers	Great Crested Flycatcher	*Myiarchus crinitus*	c	c	c			
Flycatchers	Eastern Kingbird	*Tyrannus tyrannus*	c	c	c			
Shrikes	Loggerhead Shrike	*Lanius ludovicianus*	r	r	r	r	E	
Shrikes	Northern Shrike	*Lanius excubitor*				r		
Vireos	White-eyed Vireo	*Vireo griseus*	c	c	c			
Vireos	Bell's Vireo	*Vireo bellii*	r	r	r			
Vireos	Yellow-throated Vireo	*Vireo flavifrons*	c	c	c			
Vireos	Blue-headed Vireo	*Vireo solitarius*	u		o			
Vireos	Warbling Vireo	*Vireo gilvus*	c	c	c			
Vireos	Philadelphia Vireo	*Vireo philadelphicus*	u		u			
Vireos	Red-eyed Vireo	*Vireo olivaceus*	c	c	c			
Jays, Magpies and Crows	Blue Jay	*Cyanocitta cristata*	a	a	a	a		
Jays, Magpies and Crows	American Crow	*Corvus caurinus*	a	a	a	a		
Larks	Horned Lark	*Eremophila alpestris*	u	u	u	u		
Swallows	Purple Martin	*Progne subis*	c	c	c			
Swallows	Tree Swallow	*Tachycineta bicolor*	a	a	a			
Swallows	Northern Rough-winged Swallow	*Stelgidopteryx serripennis*	u	u	u			

Status: E: Endangered T: Threatened SC: Special Concern

Probable Abundance by Season: A: Abundant, should find on every trip C: Common, should find on 75% of trips U: Uncommon, present but in lesser numbers R: Rare, infrequent or few identifications H: Accidental, not expected at this location O: Occasional

Bird Species That Occur on Muscatatuck NWR (Continued)

Family	Common Name	Scientific Name	Probable Abundance by Season — A: Abundant, should find on every trip; C: Common, should find on 75% of trips; U: Uncommon, present but in lesser numbers; R: Rare, infrequent or few identifications; H: Accidental, not expected at this location; O: Occasional				Status — E: Endangered; T: Threatened; SC: Special Concern	
			Sp	S	F	W	State	Federal
Swallows	Bank Swallow	*Riparia riparia*	o	o	o			
Swallows	Cliff Swallow	*Petrochelidon pyrrhonota*	r	r	r			
Swallows	Barn Swallow	*Hirundo rustica*	c	c	c			
Chickadees and Titmice	Carolina Chickadee	*Poecile carolinensis*	a	a	a	a		
Chickadees and Titmice	Tufted Titmouse	*Baeolophus bicolor*	a	a	a	a		
Nuthatches	Red-breasted Nuthatch	*Sitta canadensis*	u	u	u	u		
Nuthatches	White-breasted Nuthatch	*Sitta carolinensis*	c	c	c	c		
Creepers	Brown Creeper	*Certhia americana*	u		u	u		
Wrens	Carolina Wren	*Thryothorus ludovicianus*	c	c	c	c		
Wrens	Bewick's Wren	*Thryomanes bewickii*	r	r	r			
Wrens	House Wren	*Troglodytes aedon*	c	c	u			
Wrens	Winter Wren	*Troglodytes troglodytes*	u	c	u	u		
Wrens	Sedge Wren	*Cistothorus platensis*	c	c	c		E	
Wrens	Marsh Wren	*Cistothorus palustris*	u	r	u		E	
Kinglets, Bluebirds, and Thrushes	Golden-crowned Kinglet	*Regulus satrapa*	c	c	c	u		
Kinglets, Bluebirds, and Thrushes	Ruby-crowned Kinglet	*Regulus calendula*	c		c	u		
Kinglets, Bluebirds, and Thrushes	Blue-gray Gnatcatcher	*Polioptila caerulea*	c	c	c			

Bird Species That Occur on Muscatatuck NWR (Continued)

Family	Common Name	Scientific Name	Probable Abundance by Season				Status	
			A: Abundant, should find on every trip C: Common, should find on 75% of trips U: Uncommon, present but in lesser numbers R: Rare, infrequent or few identifications H: Accidental, not expected at this location O: Occasional				E: Endangered T: Threatened SC: Special Concern	
			Sp	S	F	W	State	Federal
Kinglets, Bluebirds, and Thrushes	Eastern Bluebird	Sialia sialis	c	c	c	c		
Kinglets, Bluebirds, and Thrushes	Veery	Catharus fuscescens	u		u			
Kinglets, Bluebirds, and Thrushes	Gray-cheeked Thrush	Catharus minimus	u		u			
Kinglets, Bluebirds, and Thrushes	Swainson's Thrush	Catharus ustulatus	c		c			
Kinglets, Bluebirds, and Thrushes	Hermit Thrush	Catharus guttatus	c		c	o		
Kinglets, Bluebirds, and Thrushes	Wood Thrush	Hylocichla mustelina	c	c	c			
Kinglets, Bluebirds, and Thrushes	American Robin	Turdus migratorius	a	a	a	a		
Mimics	Gray Catbird	Dumetella carolinensis	c	c	c			
Mimics	Northern Mockingbird	Mimus polyglottos	c	c	c	u		
Mimics	Brown Thrasher	Toxostoma rufum	c	c	c	r		
Starlings	European Starling	Sturnus vulgaris	a	a	a	a		
Pipits	American Pipit	Anthus rubescens	o		u	o		
Waxwings	Cedar Waxwing	Bombycilla cedrorum	c	c	c	c		
Warblers	Blue-winged Warbler	Vermivora pinus	c	c	c			

Bird Species That Occur on Muscatatuck NWR (Continued)

Family	Common Name	Scientific Name	Probable Abundance by Season				Status	
			Sp	S	F	W	State	Federal
Warblers	Golden-winged Warbler	*Vermivora chrysoptera*	r		r		E	
Warblers	Tennessee Warbler	*Vermivora peregrina*	c		c			
Warblers	Orange-crowned Warbler	*Vermivora celata*	r		r			
Warblers	Nashville Warbler	*Vermivora ruficapilla*	c		c			
Warblers	Northern Parula	*Parula americana*	u	u	u			
Warblers	Yellow Warbler	*Dendroica petechia*	c	c	c			
Warblers	Chestnut-sided Warbler	*Dendroica pensylvanica*	c		c			
Warblers	Magnolia Warbler	*Dendroica magnolia*	c		c			
Warblers	Cape May Warbler	*Dendroica tigrina*	u		u			
Warblers	Black-throated Blue Warbler	*Dendroica caerulescens*	u		u			
Warblers	Yellow-rumped Warbler	*Dendroica coronata*	c		c	u		
Warblers	Black-throated Green Warbler	*Dendroica virens*	c		c			
Warblers	Blackburnian Warbler	*Dendroica fusca*	u		u			
Warblers	Yellow-throated Warbler	*Dendroica dominica*	c	c	u			
Warblers	Pine Warbler	*Dendroica pinus*	u	u	u			
Warblers	Prairie Warbler	*Dendroica discolor*	c	c	u			
Warblers	Palm Warbler	*Dendroica palmarum*	c		c			
Warblers	Bay-breasted Warbler	*Dendroica castanea*	u		c			
Warblers	Blackpoll Warbler	*Dendroica striata*	c		c			

Status:
E: Endangered
T: Threatened
SC: Special Concern

Probable Abundance by Season:
A: Abundant, should find on every trip
C: Common, should find on 75% of trips
U: Uncommon, present but in lesser numbers
R: Rare, infrequent or few identifications
H: Accidental, not expected at this location
O: Occasional

Bird Species That Occur on Muscatatuck NWR (Continued)

Family	Common Name	Scientific Name	Probable Abundance by Season — A: Abundant, should find on every trip; C: Common, should find on 75% of trips; U: Uncommon, present but in lesser numbers; R: Rare, infrequent or few identifications; H: Accidental, not expected at this location; O: Occasional				Status — E: Endangered; T: Threatened; SC: Special Concern	
			Sp	S	F	W	State	Federal
Warblers	Cerulean Warbler	*Dendroica cerulea*	u	u	u		E	
Warblers	Black-and-white Warbler	*Mniotilta varia*	c	c	c		E	
Warblers	American Redstart	*Setophaga ruticilla*	c	c	c			
Warblers	Prothonotary Warbler	*Protonotaria citrea*	c	c	c			
Warblers	Worm-eating Warbler	*Helmitheros vermivorus*	o	o	o		SC	
Warblers	Ovenbird	*Seiurus aurocapillus*	c	c	c			
Warblers	Northern Waterthrush	*Seiurus noveboracensis*	r		r			
Warblers	Louisiana Waterthrush	*Seiurus motacilla*	u	u	u			
Warblers	Kentucky Warbler	*Oporornis formosus*	c	c	c			
Warblers	Connecticut Warbler	*Oporornis agilis*	o	o	o			
Warblers	Mourning Warbler	*Oporornis philadelphia*	o		o			
Warblers	Common Yellowthroat	*Geothlypic trichas*	c	c	c	r		
Warblers	Hooded Warbler	*Wilsonia citrina*	o	o	o		SC	
Warblers	Wilson's Warbler	*Wilsonia pusilla*	o		o			
Warblers	Canada Warbler	*Wilsonia canadensis*	o		o			
Warblers	Yellow-breasted Chat	*Icteria virens*	c	c	c			
Tanager	Summer Tanager	*Piranga rubra*	u	u	u			
Tanager	Scarlet Tanager	*Piranga olivacea*	c	c	c			

Bird Species That Occur on Muscatatuck NWR (Continued)

Family	Common Name	Scientific Name	Probable Abundance by Season: A: Abundant, should find on every trip; C: Common, should find on 75% of trips; U: Uncommon, present but in lesser numbers; R: Rare, infrequent or few identifications; H: Accidental, not expected at this location; O: Occasional				Status: E: Endangered; T: Threatened; SC: Special Concern	
			Sp	S	F	W	State	Federal
Sparrows, Buntings, and Grosbeaks	Eastern Towhee	Pipilo erythrophthalmus	c	c	c	c		
Sparrows, Buntings, and Grosbeaks	American Tree Sparrow	Spizella arborea	c	c	c	c		
Sparrows, Buntings, and Grosbeaks	Chipping Sparrow	Spizella passerina	c	c	c			
Sparrows, Buntings, and Grosbeaks	Field Sparrow	Spizella pusilla	c	c	c	u		
Sparrows, Buntings, and Grosbeaks	Vesper Sparrow	Pooecetes gramineus	u	o	u	o		
Sparrows, Buntings, and Grosbeaks	Savannah Sparrow	Passerculus sandwichensis	c	o	c	r		
Sparrows, Buntings, and Grosbeaks	Grasshopper Sparrow	Ammodramus savannarum	o	o	o			
Sparrows, Buntings, and Grosbeaks	Henslow's Sparrow	Ammodramus henslowii	o	o	r		E	
Sparrows, Buntings, and Grosbeaks	Le Conte's Sparrow	Ammodramus leconteii	r		r			
Sparrows, Buntings, and Grosbeaks	Nelson's Sharp-tailed Sparrow	Ammodramus nelsoni	r	r	r			
Sparrows, Buntings, and Grosbeaks	Fox Sparrow	Passerella iliaca	c		c	c		

Bird Species That Occur on Muscatatuck NWR (Continued)

Family	Common Name	Scientific Name	Probable Abundance by Season				Status	
			A: Abundant, should find on every trip C: Common, should find on 75% of trips U: Uncommon, present but in lesser numbers R: Rare, infrequent or few identifications H: Accidental, not expected at this location O: Occasional				E: Endangered T: Threatened SC: Special Concern	
			Sp	S	F	W	State	Federal
Sparrows, Buntings, and Grosbeaks	Song Sparrow	*Melospiza melodia*	c	c	c	c		
Sparrows, Buntings, and Grosbeaks	Lincoln's Sparrow	*Melospiza lincolnii*	c		c	r		
Sparrows, Buntings, and Grosbeaks	Swamp Sparrow	*Melospiza georgiana*	c		c	c		
Sparrows, Buntings, and Grosbeaks	White-throated Sparrow	*Zonotrichia albicollis*	c		c	c		
Sparrows, Buntings, and Grosbeaks	White-crowned Sparrow	*Zonotrichia leucophrys*	c		c	c		
Sparrows, Buntings, and Grosbeaks	Dark-eyed Junco	*Junco hyemalis*	c		c	c		
Sparrows, Buntings, and Grosbeaks	Lapland Longspur	*Calcarius lapponicus*				r		
Sparrows, Buntings, and Grosbeaks	Snow Bunting	*Plectrophenax nivalis*				r		
Sparrows, Buntings, and Grosbeaks	Northern Cardinal	*Cardinalis cardinalis*	a	a	a	a		
Sparrows, Buntings, and Grosbeaks	Rose-breasted Grosbeak	*Pheucticus ludovicianus*	c	o	c			
Sparrows, Buntings, and Grosbeaks	Blue Grosbeak	*Guiraca caerulea*	u	u	u			

Bird Species That Occur on Muscatatuck NWR (Continued)

Family	Common Name	Scientific Name	Probable Abundance by Season				Status	
			Sp	S	F	W	State	Federal
Sparrows, Buntings, and Grosbeaks	Indigo Bunting	Passerina cyanea	a	a	a			
Sparrows, Buntings, and Grosbeaks	Dickcissel	Spiza americana	r	r	r			
Blackbirds and Orioles	Bobolink	Dolichonyx oryzivorus	o		r			
Blackbirds and Orioles	Red-winged Blackbird	Agelaius phoeniceus	a	a	a	u		
Blackbirds and Orioles	Eastern Meadowlark	Sturnella magna	a	a	a	u		
Blackbirds and Orioles	Rusty Blackbird	Euphagus carolinus	u		u	u		
Blackbirds and Orioles	Brewer's Blackbird	Euphagus cyanocephalus	r		r			
Blackbirds and Orioles	Common Grackle	Quiscalus quiscula	a	a	a	u		
Blackbirds and Orioles	Brown-headed Cowbird	Molothrus ater	a	a	c	u		
Blackbirds and Orioles	Orchard Oriole	Icterus spurius	c	c	c			
Blackbirds and Orioles	Baltimore Oriole	Icterus galbula	c	c	c			
Finches	Purple Finch	Carpodacus purpureus	c	c	c	c		
Finches	House Finch	Carpodacus mexicanus	c	c	c	c		
Finches	Red Crossbill	Loxia curvirostra				r		
Finches	White-winged Crossbill	Loxia leucoptera				r		
Finches	Common Redpoll	Carduelis flammea				r		
Finches	Pine Siskin	Carduelis pinus	u		u	u		

A: Abundant, should find on every trip
C: Common, should find on 75% of trips
U: Uncommon, present but in lesser numbers
R: Rare, infrequent or few identifications
H: Accidental, not expected at this location
O: Occasional

E: Endangered
T: Threatened
SC: Special Concern

Bird Species That Occur on Muscatatuck NWR (Continued)

Family	Common Name	Scientific Name	Probable Abundance by Season				Status	
			Sp	S	F	W	State	Federal
Finches	American Goldfinch	*Carduelis tristis*	c	c	c	c		
Finches	Evening Grosbeak	*Coccothraustes vespertinus*	r	c	c	r		
Old World Sparrows	House Sparrow	*Passer domesticus*	c	c	c	c		
Extremely Rare or Accidental	Whooping Crane	*Grus americana*						
Extremely Rare or Accidental	Eared Grebe	*Podiceps nigricollis*						
Extremely Rare or Accidental	Western Grebe	*Aechmophorus occidentalis*						
Extremely Rare or Accidental	Glossy Ibis	*Plegadis falcinellus*						
Extremely Rare or Accidental	Cinnamon Teal	*Anas cyanoptera*						
Extremely Rare or Accidental	Ruddy Shelduck	*Tadorna ferruginea*						
Extremely Rare or Accidental	Fulvous Whistling Duck	*Dendrocygna bicolor*						
Extremely Rare or Accidental	White-winged Scoter	*Melanitta fusca*						
Extremely Rare or Accidental	Black Scoter	*Melanitta nigra*						

Probable Abundance by Season legend:
A: Abundant, should find on every trip
C: Common, should find on 75% of trips
U: Uncommon, present but in lesser numbers
R: Rare, infrequent or few identifications
H: Accidental, not expected at this location
O: Occasional

Status legend:
E: Endangered
T: Threatened
SC: Special Concern

Bird Species That Occur on Muscatatuck NWR (Continued)

Family	Common Name	Scientific Name	Probable Abundance by Season				Status	
			A: Abundant, should find on every trip C: Common, should find on 75% of trips U: Uncommon, present but in lesser numbers R: Rare, infrequent or few identifications H: Accidental, not expected at this location O: Occasional				E: Endangered T: Threatened SC: Special Concern	
			Sp	S	F	W	State	Federal
Extremely Rare or Accidental	Surf Scoter	Melanitta perspicillata						
Extremely Rare or Accidental	American Swallow-tailed Kite	Elanoides forficatus						
Extremely Rare or Accidental	Mississippi Kite	Ictinia mississippiensis						
Extremely Rare or Accidental	White Pelican	Pelecanus occidentalis						
Extremely Rare or Accidental	Ruff	Philomachaus pugnax						
Extremely Rare or Accidental	Brambling	Fringilla montifringilla						
Extremely Rare or Accidental	Fish Crow	Corvus ossifragus						
Extremely Rare or Accidental	Varied Thrush	Ixoreus naevius						
Extremely Rare or Accidental	Black-capped Chickadee	Poecile atricapillus						
Extremely Rare or Accidental	Harris Sparrow	Zonotrichia querula						

Butterflies That Occur on Muscatatuck NWR

Family	Common Name	Scientific Name	Status	
			State	Federal
Papilionidae	Spicebush Swallowtail	*Papilio troilus*	Secure	Secure
Papilionidae	Pipevine Swallowtail	*Battus philenor*	Secure	Secure
Papilionidae	Zebra Swallowtail	*Eurytides marcellus*	Secure	Secure
Papilionidae	Black Swallowtail	*Papilio polyxenes asterius*	Secure	Secure
Papilionidae	EasternTiger Swallowtail	*Papilio glaucus*	Secure	Secure
Pieridae	Cabbage White	*Pieris protodice*	SNA	NNA
Pieridae	Checkered White	*Pieris rapae*	Apparently Secure	Apparently Secure
Pieridae	Falcate Orange Tip	*Anthocharis midea*	Apparently Secure?	Apparently Secure/Secure
Pieridae	Alfalfa	*Colias eurytheme*	Secure	Secure
Pieridae	Clouded Sulphur	*Colias philodice*	Secure	Secure
Pieridae	Cloudless Sulphur	*Phoebis sennae*	Secure	Secure
Pieridae	Orange Sulphur	*Colias eurytheme*	Secure	Secure
Lycaenidae	Spring Azure	*Celastrina ladon*	Secure	Secure
Lycaenidae	Eastern Tailed Blue	*Everes comyntas*	Secure	Secure
Lycaenidae	Bronze Copper	*Lycaena hyllus*	Apparently Secure	Secure
Lycaenidae	Little Copper	*Lycaena phlaeas*	Not Ranked	Secure
Lycaenidae	Gray Hairstreak	*Strymon melinus*	Secure	Vulnerable
Lycaenidae	Banded Hairstreak	*Strymon falacer*	Not Ranked	Secure
Lycaenidae	Striped Hairstreak	*Strymon liparops*	Not Ranked	Apparently Secure
Libytheidae	American Snout	*Libytheana bachmannii*	Not Ranked	Secure
Nymphalidae	Great Spangled Fritillary	*Speyeria cybele*	Secure	Secure
Nymphalidae	Meadow Fritillary	*Boloria toddi ammiralis*	Secure	Secure
Nymphalidae	Variegated Fritillary	*Euptoieta claudia*	Apparently Secure	Apparently Secure
Nymphalidae	Pearl Crescent	*Phyciodes tharos*	Secure	Secure
Nymphalidae	Silvery Checkerspot	*Chlosyne nycteis*	Apparently Secure	Apparently Secure
Nymphalidae	Question Mark	*Polygonia progne*	Secure	Secure
Nymphalidae	Hop Merchant (Comma)	*Polygonia interrogationis*	Secure	Secure
Nymphalidae	Eastern Comma	*Polygonia comma*	Secure	Secure
Nymphalidae	Mourning Cloak	*Nymphalis antiopa*	Secure	Secure

Butterflies That Occur on Muscatatuck NWR (Continued)

Family	Common Name	Scientific Name	Status	
			State	Federal
Nymphalidae	Red Admiral	*Vanessa atalanta*	Secure	Secure
Nymphalidae	American Painted Lady	*Vanessa virginiensis*	Secure	Secure
Nymphalidae	Painted Lady	*Vanessa cardui*	Secure	Secure
Nymphalidae	Common Buckeye	*Junonia coenia*	Secure	Secure
Nymphalidae	Red-Spotted Purple	*Basilarchia arthemis astanax*	Not Ranked	Secure
Nymphalidae	Viceroy	*Limenitis archippus*	Secure	Secure
Nymphalidae	Hackberry Emperor	*Asterocampa celtis*	Secure	Secure
Nymphalidae	Tawny Emperor	*Asterocampa clyton*	Secure	Secure
Nymphalidae	Monarch	*Danaus plexippus*	Secure	Secure
Nymphalidae	Common Wood Nymph	*Cercyonis pegala*	Secure	Secure
Nymphalidae	Little Wood Satyr	*Megisto cymela*	Secure	Secure
Hesperiidae	Silver-Spotted Skipper	*Epargyreus clarus*	Secure	Secure
Hesperiidae	Hobomok Skipper	*Poanes hobomok*	Secure	Secure
Hesperiidae	Ocola Skipper	*Panoquina ocola*	Not Ranked	Secure
Hesperiidae	Checkered Skipper	*Pyrgus communis*	Not Ranked	Secure
Hesperiidae	Least Skipper	*Ancyloxypha numitor*	Secure	Secure
Hesperiidae	Tawny-edged Skipper	*Polites themistocles*	Secure	Secure
Hesperiidae	Delaware Skipper	*Anatrytone logan*	Secure	Secure
Hesperiidae	Crossline Skipper	*Polites origenes*	Secure	Secure
Hesperiidae	Zabulon Skipper	*Poanes zabulon*	Secure	Secure
Hesperiidae	Fiery Skipper	*Hylephila phyleus*	Not Ranked	Secure
Hesperiidae	Peck's Skipper	*Polites peckius*	Secure	Secure
Hesperiidae	Dun Skipper	*Euphyes vestris*	Not Ranked	Secure
Nymphalidae	Northern Pealy Eye	*Enodia anthedon*	Imperiled	Secure
Hesperiidae	Dreamy Dusky Wing	*Erynnius icelus*	Secure	Secure
Hesperiidae	Sleepy Dusky Wing	*Erynnius brizo*	Apparently Secure	Secure
Hesperiidae	Horace's Dusky Wing	*Erynnius horatius*	Secure	Secure
Hesperiidae	Wild Indigo Dusky Wing	*Erynnius baptisiae*	Apparently Secure	Secure
Hesperiidae	Northern Broken-dash	*Wallengrenia egeremet*	Secure	Secure
Hesperiidae	Little Glassy Wing	*Pompeius verna*	Secure	Secure
Hesperiidae	Sachem	*Atalopedes campestris*	Not Ranked	Secure

Dragonflies That Occur on Muscatatuck NWR

Common Name	Scientific Name	Status	
		State	Federal
Shadow Darner	*Aeshna umbrosa*	Apparently Secure	Secure
Common Green Darner	*Anax junius*	Secure	Secure
Springtime Darner	*Basiaeschna janata*	Vulnerable	Secure
Fawn Darner	*Boyeria vinosa*	Secure	Secure
Cyrano Darner	*Nasiaeschna pentacantha*	Vulnerable	Secure
Unicorn Clubtail	*Arigomphus villosipes*	Vulnerable	Secure
Ashy Clubtail	*Gomphus lividus*	Apparently Secure	Secure
Lancet Clubtail	*Gomphus exilis*	Apparently Secure	Secure
Common Sanddragon	*Progomphus obscurus*	Vulnerable	Secure
Stream Cruiser	*Didymops transversa*	Vulnerable	Secure
Swift River Cruiser	*Macromia illinoiensis*	Apparently Secure	Secure
Royal River Cruiser	*Macromia taeniolata*	Apparently Secure	Secure
Beaverpond Baskettail	*Epitheca canis*	Critically Imperiled	Secure
Common Baskettail	*Epitheca cynosura*	Apparently Secure	Secure
Prince Baskettail	*Epitheca princeps*	Apparently Secure	Secure
Mocha Emerald	*Somatochlora linearis*	Imperiled	Secure
Calico Pennant	*Celithemis elisa*	Apparently Secure	Secure
Halloween Pennant	*Celithemis eponina*	Apparently Secure	Secure
Double-ringed Pennant	*Celithemis verna*	Critically Imperiled	Secure
Banded Pennant	*Celithemis fasciata*	Apparently Secure	Secure
Eastern Pondhawk	*Erythemis simplicicollis*	Secure	Secure
Spangled Skimmer	*Libellula cyanea*	Apparently Secure	Secure
Blue Corporal	*Libellula deplanata*	Vulnerable	Secure
Slaty Skimmer	*Libellula incesta*	Apparently Secure	Secure
Widow Skimmer	*Libellula luctuosa*	Secure	Secure
Common Whitetail	*Plathemis lydia*	Secure	Secure
Twelve-spotted Skimmer	*Libellula pulchella*	Apparently Secure	Secure
Great Blue Skimmer	*Libellula vibrans*	Vulnerable	Secure
Blue Dasher	*Pachydiplax longipennis*	Secure	Secure

Dragonflies That Occur on Muscatatuck NWR (Continued)

Common Name	Scientific Name	Status	
		State	Federal
Eastern Amberwing	*Perithemis tenera*	Secure	Secure
Autumn Meadowhawk	*Sympetrum vicinum*	Apparently Secure	Secure
Carolina Saddlebags	*Tramea carolina*	Vulnerable	Secure
Black Saddlebags	*Tramea lacerata*	Secure	Secure

Herpetofauna Species That Occur on Muscatatuck NWR

Family	Common Name	Scientific Name	Status			Habitat in Muscatatuck NWR
			State	Federal	Local	
Salamander	Spotted Salamander	*Ambystoma maculatum*	Apparently Secure	Secure	Rare	Hardwood Uplands
Salamander	Marbled Salamander	*Ambystoma opacum*	Apparently Secure	Secure	Rare	Hardwood Uplands
Salamander	Jefferson Salamander	*Ambystoma jeffersonianum*	Apparently Secure	Apparently Secure	Abundant	Hardwood Uplands
Salamander	Smallmouth Salamander	*Ambystoma texanum*	Apparently Secure	Secure	Common	Wet Lowlands
Salamander	Northern Dusky Salamander	*Desmognathus fuscus fuscus*	Apparently Secure	Secure	Uncommon	Sandy Streambeds
Salamander	Northern Slimy Salamander	*Plethodon glutinosus*	Apparently Secure	Secure	Common	Hardwood Uplands
salamander	Four-toed salamander	*Hemidactylium scutatum*	Imperiled	Secure	Rare	Mature Forest with wetlands
Salamander	Redback Salamander	*Plethodon cinereus*	Apparently Secure	Secure	Common	Hardwood Uplands
Salamander	Northern Zigzag Salamander	*Plethodon dorsalis dorsalis*	Apparently Secure	Secure	Rare	Mature Forest with wetlands
Salamander	Red-spotted Newt	*Notophthalmus viridescens viridescens*	Apparently Secure	Secure	Common	All Habitats
Toads	American Toad	*Bufo americanus americanus*	Not Rankd	Secure	Common	Wet Lowlands and Hardwood Uplands
Toads	Fowler's Toad	*Bufo woodhousii fowleri*	Apparently Secure	Secure	Common	Wet Lowlands and Hardwood Uplands
Frogs	Blanchard's Cricket Frog	*Acris crepitans blanchardi*	Not Ranked	Not Ranked	Common	Marsh Edges of Water
Frogs	Western Chorus Frog	*Pseudacris triseriata*	Vulnerable	Secure	Abundant	All Habitats
Frogs	Northern Spring Peeper	*Pseudacris crucifer crucifer*	Not Ranked	Secure	Abundant	Any Water Source
Frogs	Gray Treefrog	*Hyla versicolor*	Apparently Secure	Secure	Abundant	Hardwood Uplands
Frogs	Crawfish Frog	*Rana areolata*	Imperiled	Apparently Secure	Not Ranked	Restle Unit (Last Confirmed 1998)
Frogs	Green Frog	*Rana clamitans melanota*	Apparently Secure	Secure	Abundant	All Permanent Water Sources
Frogs	Bullfrog	*Rana catesbeiana*	Apparently Secure	Secure	Common	All Permanent Water Sources

Herpetofauna Species That Occur on Muscatatuck NWR (Continued)

Family	Common Name	Scientific Name	Status			Habitat in Muscatatuck NWR
			State	Federal	Local	
Frogs	Southern Leopard Frog	*Rana utricularia*	Apparently Secure	Secure	Common	All Habitats
Frogs	Wood Frog	*Rana sylvatica*	Apparently Secure	Secure	Common	Hardwood Uplands
Turtles	Common Snapping Turtle	*Chelydra serpentina serpentina*	Not Ranked	Secure	Common	Any Water Source
Turtles	Common Musk Turtle	*Sternotherus odoratus*	Apparently Secure	Secure	Common	Warm Shallows of Water Source
Turtles	Eastern Box Turtle	*Terrapene carolina carolina*	Vulnerable	Secure	Uncommon	Hardwood Uplands
Turtles	Common Map Turtle	*Graptemys geographica*	Apparently Secure	Secure	Uncommon	Moist Soil Unit #10
Turtles	Ouchita Map Turtle	*Graptemys ouachitensis*	Not Ranked	Secure	Uncommon	Muscatatuck River
Turtles	Midland Painted Turtle	*Chrysemys picta marginata*	Apparently Secure	Secure	Abundant	Any Water Source
Turtles	Red-Eared Slider	*Trachemys scripta elegans*	Not Ranked	Secure	Common	Sue Pond Series of Ponds
Turtles	Spiny Softshell	*Apalone spinifera*	Apparently Secure	Secure	Common	Any Water Source
Lizard	Broad-headed Skink	*Eumeces laticeps*	Apparently Secure	Secure	Not Ranked	Forest and Forest Wetlands
Lizard	Five-Lined Skink	*Eumeces fasciatus*	Not Ranked	Not Ranked	Abundant	Hardwood Uplands and Forest Edge
Snakes	Eastern Gartersnake	*Thamnophis sirtalis sirtalis*	Not Ranked	Not Ranked	Abundant	All Habitats
Snakes	Eastern Ribbonsnake	*Thamnophis sauritus sauritus*	Apparently Secure	Secure	Abundant	All Moist Habitats
Snakes	Northern Watersnake	*Nerodia sipedon sipedon*	Apparently Secure	Secure	Abundant	All Water Habitats
Snakes	Northern Copperbelly Watersnake	*Nerodia erythrogaster neglecta*	Imperiled	Vulnerable	Very Common	Flooded Woodlands
Snakes	Kirtland's Snake	*Clonophis kirtlandii*	Imperiled	Imperiled	Common	Moist Forests and Edges
Snakes	Midland Brownsnake	*Storeria dekayi wrightorum*	Apparently Secure	Secure	Common	Moist Forests and Edges
Snakes	Blue/black Racer	*Coluber constrictor*	Not Ranked	Secure	Common	All Habitats
Snakes	Rough Greensnake	*Opheodrys aestivus*	Vulnerable	Secure	Common	All Edge Habitats

Herpetofauna Species That Occur on Muscatatuck NWR (Continued)

Family	Common Name	Scientific Name	Status			Habitat in Muscatatuck NWR
			State	Federal	Local	
Snakes	Black Rat Snake	*Elaphe obsoleta obsoleta*	Apparently Secure	Secure	Common	Hardwood Uplands
Snakes	Black Kingsnake	*Lampropeltis getula nigra*	Not Ranked	Secure	Very Common	All Habitats
Snakes	Midwest Worm Snake	*Carphophis amoenus helenae*	Apparently Secure	Secure	Probably Common	Hardwood Uplands
Snakes	Ring-necked snake	*Diadophis punctatus*	Not Ranked	Secure	Not Ranked	Most Forests and Edges
Snakes	Eastern Hog-nosed Snake	*Heterodon platirhinos*	Vulnerable	Secure	Not Ranked	Dry, Sandy Uplands

Mammal Species That Occur on Muscatatuck NWR

Family	Common Name	Scientific Name	Source	Status E – Endangered T – Threatened SC – Special Concern	
				State	Federal
Pouched Mammals = *Marsupialia*	Opossum	*Didelphis marsupialis*	Recorded		
Insect Eaters = *Insectivora*	Masked Shrew	*Sorex cinereus*	Suspected		
Insect Eaters = *Insectivora*	Southeastern Shrew	*Sorex longirostris*	Suspected		
Insect Eaters = *Insectivora*	Least Shrew	*Cryptotis parva*	Recorded		
Insect Eaters = *Insectivora*	Shorttail Shrew	*Blarina brevicauda*	Recorded		
Insect Eaters = *Insectivora*	Eastern Mole	*Scalopus aquaticus*	Recorded		
Bats = *Chiroptera*	Little Brown Myotis	*Myotis lucifugus*	Recorded	SC	
Bats = *Chiroptera*	Northern Myotis	*Myotis septentrionalis*	Recorded	SC	
Bats = *Chiroptera*	Indiana Myotis	*Myotis sodalis*	Recorded	E	E
Bats = *Chiroptera*	Silver-Haired Bat	*Lasionycteris noctivagans*	Suspected	SC	
Bats = *Chiroptera*	Eastern Pipistrelle	*Pipistrellus subflavus*	Recorded	SC	
Bats = *Chiroptera*	Big Brown Bat	*Eptesicus fuscus*	Recorded		
Bats = *Chiroptera*	Red Bat	*Lasiurus borealis*	Recorded	SC	
Bats = *Chiroptera*	Hoary Bat	*Lasiurus cinereus*	Recorded	SC	
Bats = *Chiroptera*	Evening Bat	*Nycticeius humeralis*	Recorded	E	
Flesh-eaters = *Carnivora*	Racoon	*Procyon lotor*	Recorded		
Flesh-eaters = *Carnivora*	Least Weasel	*Mustela rixosa*	Recorded	SC	
Flesh-eaters = *Carnivora*	Longtail Weasel	*Mustela frenata*	Recorded		
Flesh-eaters = *Carnivora*	Mink	*Mustela vison*	Recorded		
Flesh-eaters = *Carnivora*	River Otter	*Lutra canadensis*	Recorded	SC	
Flesh-eaters = *Carnivora*	Badger	*Taxidea taxus*	Suspected	SC	
Flesh-eaters = *Carnivora*	Striped Skunk	*Mephitis mephitis*	Recorded		
Flesh-eaters = *Carnivora*	Coyote	*Canis latrans*	Recorded		
Flesh-eaters = *Carnivora*	Red Fox	*Vulpes fulva*	Recorded		
Flesh-eaters = *Carnivora*	Gray Fox	*Urocyon cinereoargenteus*	Recorded		
Flesh-eaters = *Carnivora*	Bobcat	*Lynx rufus*	Recorded	SC	

Mammal Species That Occur on Muscatatuck NWR (Continued)

Family	Common Name	Scientific Name	Source	Status E – Endangered T – Threatened SC – Special Concern	
				State	Federal
Gnawing Mammals = *Rodentia*	Woodchuck	*Marmota monax*	Recorded		
Gnawing Mammals = *Rodentia*	Southern Flying Squirrel	*Glaucomys volans*	Recorded		
Gnawing Mammals = *Rodentia*	Eastern Chipmunk	*Tamias striatus*	Recorded		
Gnawing Mammals = *Rodentia*	Eastern Gray Squirrel	*Sciurus carolinensis*	Recorded		
Gnawing Mammals = *Rodentia*	Eastern Fox Squirrel	*Sciurus niger*	Recorded		
Gnawing Mammals = *Rodentia*	Beaver	*Castor canadensis*	Recorded		
Gnawing Mammals = *Rodentia*	Deer Mouse	*Peromyscus maniculatus*	Recorded		
Gnawing Mammals = *Rodentia*	White-Footed Mouse	*Peromyscus leucopus*	Recorded		
Gnawing Mammals = *Rodentia*	Southern Bog Lemming	*Synaptomys cooperi*	Suspected		
Gnawing Mammals = *Rodentia*	Meadow Vole	*Microtus pennsylvanicus*	Recorded		
Gnawing Mammals = *Rodentia*	Prairie Vole	*Microtus ochrogaster*	Recorded		
Gnawing Mammals = *Rodentia*	Woodland Vole	*Microtus pinetorum*	Suspected		
Gnawing Mammals = *Rodentia*	Muskrat	*Ondatra zibethica*	Recorded		
Gnawing Mammals = *Rodentia*	Norway Rat	*Rattus norvegicus*	Recorded		
Gnawing Mammals = *Rodentia*	House Mouse	*Mus musculus*	Recorded		
Gnawing Mammals = *Rodentia*	Eastern Cottontail	*Sylvilagus floridanus*	Recorded		
Deer = *Cervidae*	Whitetail Deer	*Odocoileus virginianus*	Recorded		

Mussel Species Found on Muscatatuck NWR

Subfamily	Common Name	Scientific Name	Status (State)	Status (Federal)
Corbiculidae	Asiatic Clam	*Corbicula fluminea*	SNA	NNA
Anodontinae	Cylindrical Papershell	*Anodontoides ferussacianus*	Vulnerable	Secure
Anodontinae	White Heelsplitter	*Lasmigona complanata*	Apparently Secure	Secure
Anodontinae	Giant Floater	*Pyganodon grandis*	Apparently Secure	Secure
Anodontinae	Flutedshell	*Lasmigona costata*	Apparently Secure	Secure
Anodontinae	Paper Pondshell	*Utterbackia imbecillis*	Apparently Secure	Secure
Unioninae	Threeridge	*Amblema plicata*	Apparently Secure	Secure
Unioninae	Spike	*Elliptio dialata*	Vulnerable	Secure
Unioninae	Wabash Pigtoe	*Fusconaia flava*	Apparently Secure	Secure
Unioninae	Elephantear	*Elliptio crassidens*	Apparently Secure	Secure
Unioninae	Washboard	*Megalonaias nervosa*	Apparently Secure	Secure
Unioninae	Pimpleback	*Quadrula pustulosa*	Apparently Secure	Secure
Unioninae	Mapleleaf	*Quadrula quadrula*	Apparently Secure	Secure
Unioninae	Pistolgrip	*Tritogonia verrucosa*	Apparently Secure	Apparently Secure/ Secure
Unioninae	Pondhorn	*Uniomerus tetralasmus*	Possibly Extirpated	Secure
Lampsilinae	Plain Pocketbook	*Lampsilis cardium*	Apparently Secure	Secure
Lampsilinae	Fatmucket	*Lampsilis siliquoidea*	Apparently Secure	Secure
Lampsilinae	Deertoe	*Truncilla truncata*	Vulnerable	Secure
Lampsilinae	Yellow Sandshell	*Lampsilis teres*	Imperiled	Secure
Lampsilinae	Fragile Papershell	*Leptodea fragilis*	Apparently Secure	Secure

Mussel Species Found on Muscatatuck NWR (Continued)

Subfamily	Common Name	Scientific Name	Status (State)	Status (Federal)
Lampsilinae	Pondmussel	*Ligumia subrostrata*	Critically Imperiled	Secure
Lampsilinae	Pink Heelsplitter	*Potamilus alatus*	Apparently Secure	Secure
Lampsilinae	Lilliput	*Toxolasma parvus*	Imperiled	Secure
Lampsilinae	Little Spectaclecase	*Villosa lienosa*	Imperiled	Secure

The Fishes of Muscatatuck NWR

Common Name	Scientific Name	Federal	State	Family	Exotic
bowfin	*Amia calva*	Secure	Apparently Secure	Amiidae	
pirate perch	*Aphredoderus sayanus*	Secure	Apparently Secure	Aphredoderidae	
brook silverside	*Labidesthes sicculus*	Secure	Apparently Secure	Atherinopsidae	
river carpsucker	*Carpiodes carpio*	Secure	Apparently Secure	Catostomidae	
quillback	*Carpiodes cyprinus*	Secure	Apparently Secure	Catostomidae	
highfin carpsucker***	*Carpiodes velifer*	Apparently Secure	Apparently Secure	Catostomidae	
white sucker	*Catostomus commersonii*	Secure	Apparently Secure	Catostomidae	
creek chubsucker	*Erimyzon oblongus*	Secure	Apparently Secure	Catostomidae	
northern hogsucker	*Hypentelium nigricans*	Secure	Apparently Secure	Catostomidae	
smallmouth buffalo	*Ictiobus bubalus*	Secure	Apparently Secure	Catostomidae	
bigmouth buffalo	*Ictiobus cyprinellus*	Secure	Apparently Secure	Catostomidae	
spotted sucker	*Minytrema melanops*	Secure	Apparently Secure	Catostomidae	
silver redhorse	*Moxostoma anisurum*	Secure	Apparently Secure	Catostomidae	
river redhorse***	*Moxostoma carinatum*	Apparently Secure	Vulnerable	Catostomidae	
black redhorse	*Moxostoma duquesnei*	Secure	Apparently Secure	Catostomidae	
golden redhorse	*Moxostoma erythrurum*	Secure	Apparently Secure	Catostomidae	
shorthead redhorse	*Moxostoma macrolepidotum*	Secure	Apparently Secure	Catostomidae	
rock bass	*Ambloplites rupestris*	Secure	Apparently Secure	Centrarchidae	
flier	*Centrarchus macropterus*	Secure	Apparently Secure	Centrarchidae	
green sunfish	*Lepomis cyanellus*	Secure	Apparently Secure	Centrarchidae	
pumpkinseed sunfish	*Lepomis gibbosus*	Secure	Apparently Secure	Centrarchidae	
warmouth	*Lepomis gulosus*	Secure	Apparently Secure	Centrarchidae	
bluegill	*Lepomis macrochirus*	Secure	Apparently Secure	Centrarchidae	
longear sunfish	*Lepomis megalotis*	Secure	Apparently Secure	Centrarchidae	
redear sunfish	*Lepomis microlophus*	Secure	Apparently Secure	Centrarchidae	
redspotted sunfish	*Lepomis miniatus*	Secure	Vulnerable	Centrarchidae	
smallmouth bass	*Micropterus dolomieu*	Secure	Apparently Secure	Centrarchidae	

The Fishes of Muscatatuck NWR (Continued)

Common Name	Scientific Name	Federal	State	Family	Exotic
spotted bass	*Micropterus punctulatus*	Secure	Apparently Secure	Centrarchidae	
largemouth bass	*Micropterus salmoides*	Secure	Apparently Secure	Centrarchidae	
white crappie	*Pomoxis annularis*	Secure	Apparently Secure	Centrarchidae	
black crappie	*Pomoxis nigromaculatus*	Secure	Apparently Secure	Centrarchidae	
gizzard shad	*Dorosoma cepedianum*	Secure	Apparently Secure	Clupeidae	
central stoneroller minnow	*Campostoma anomalum*	Secure	Apparently Secure	Cyprinidae	
goldfish***	*Carassius auratus*	NNA	SNA	Cyprinidae	Exotic
spotfin shiner	*Cyprinella spiloptera*	Secure	Apparently Secure	Cyprinidae	
steelcolor shiner	*Cyprinella whipplei*	Secure	Apparently Secure	Cyprinidae	
carp	*Cyprinus carpio*	NNA	SNA	Cyprinidae	Exotic
silverjaw minnow	*Ericymba buccata*	Secure	Apparently Secure	Cyprinidae	
streamline chub[b]	*Erimystax dissimilis*	Apparently Secure	Apparently Secure	Cyprinidae	
Mississippi silvery minnow	*Hybognathus nuchalis*	Secure	Apparently Secure	Cyprinidae	
bigeye chub	*Hybopsis amblops*	Secure	Imperiled	Cyprinidae	
common shiner[b]	*Luxilis cornutus*	Secure	Apparently Secure	Cyprinidae	
striped shiner	*Luxilus chrysocephalus*	Secure	Apparently Secure	Cyprinidae	
redfin shiner	*Lythrurus umbratilis*	Secure	Apparently Secure	Cyprinidae	
silver chub[b]	*Macrhybopsis storeriana*	Secure	Apparently Secure	Cyprinidae	
golden shiner	*Notemigonus crysoleucas*	Secure	Apparently Secure	Cyprinidae	
emerald shiner	*Notropis atherinoides*	Secure	Apparently Secure	Cyprinidae	
bigeye shiner	*Notropis boops*	Secure	Apparently Secure	Cyprinidae	
silver shiner	*Notropis photogenis*	Secure	Apparently Secure	Cyprinidae	
rosyface shiner***	*Notropis rubellus*	Secure	Apparently Secure	Cyprinidae	
sand shiner***	*Notropis stramineus*	Apparently Secure	Apparently Secure	Cyprinidae	
mimic shiner[b]	*Notropis volucellus*	Secure	Apparently Secure	Cyprinidae	
suckermouth minnow	*Phenacobius mirabilis*	Secure	Apparently Secure	Cyprinidae	
bluntnose minnow	*Pimephales notatus*	Secure	Apparently Secure	Cyprinidae	

The Fishes of Muscatatuck NWR (Continued)

Common Name	Scientific Name	Federal	State	Family	Exotic
fathead minnow***	*Pimephales promelas*	Secure	Apparently Secure	Cyprinidae	
bullhead minnow	*Pimephales vigilax*	Secure	Apparently Secure	Cyprinidae	
blacknose dace	*Rhinichthys atratulus*	Secure	Apparently Secure	Cyprinidae	
creek chub	*Semotilus atromaculatus*	Secure	Apparently Secure	Cyprinidae	
grass pickerel	*Esox americanus vermiculatus*	Secure	Apparently Secure	Esocidae	
northern pike	*Esox lucius*	Secure	Apparently Secure	Esocidae	
muskellunge	*Esox masquinongy*	Secure	Apparently Secure	Esocidae	
northern studfish[a]	*Fundulus catenatus*	Secure	Imperiled	Fundulidae	
blackstripe topminnow	*Fundulus notatus*	Secure	Apparently Secure	Fundulidae	
black bullhead	*Ameiurus melas*	Secure	Apparently Secure	Ictaluridae	
yellow bullhead	*Ameiurus natalis*	Secure	Apparently Secure	Ictaluridae	
brown bullhead	*Ameiurus nebulosus*	Secure	Apparently Secure	Ictaluridae	
channel catfish	*Ictalurus punctatus*	Secure	Apparently Secure	Ictaluridae	
mountain madtom	*Noturus eleutherus*	Apparently Secure	Apparently Secure	Ictaluridae	
stonecat[b]	*Noturus flavus*	Secure	Apparently Secure	Ictaluridae	
tadpole madtom	*Noturus gyrinus*	Secure	Apparently Secure	Ictaluridae	
brindled madtom	*Noturus miurus*	Secure	Vulnerable	Ictaluridae	
flathead catfish	*Pylodictis olivaris*	Secure	Apparently Secure	Ictaluridae	
longnose gar	*Lepisosteus osseus*	Secure	Apparently Secure	Lepisosteidae	
shortnose gar***	*Lepisosteus platostomus*	Secure	Apparently Secure	Lepisosteidae	
eastern sand darter	*Ammocrypta pellucida*	Vulnerable	Vulnerable	Percidae	
mud darter	*Etheostoma asprigene*	Apparently Secure	Apparently Secure	Percidae	
greenside darter	*Etheostoma blennioides*	Secure	Apparently Secure	Percidae	
rainbow darter	*Etheostoma caeruleum*	Secure	Apparently Secure	Percidae	
fantail darter	*Etheostoma flabellare*	Secure	Apparently Secure	Percidae	
harlequin darter	*Etheostoma histrio*	Secure	Vulnerable	Percidae	
johnny darter	*Etheostoma nigrum*	Secure	Apparently Secure	Percidae	
orangethroat darter	*Etheostoma spectabile*	Secure	Apparently Secure	Percidae	
yellow perch	*Perca flavescens*	Secure	Apparently Secure	Percidae	

The Fishes of Muscatatuck NWR (Continued)

Common Name	Scientific Name	Federal	State	Family	Exotic
logperch	*Percina caprodes semifasciata*	Secure	Apparently Secure	Percidae	
blackside darter	*Percina maculata*	Secure	Apparently Secure	Percidae	
slenderhead darter	*Percina phoxocephala*	Secure	Apparently Secure	Percidae	
dusky darter	*Percina sciera*	Secure	Apparently Secure	Percidae	
chestnut lamprey	*Ichthyomyzon castaneus*	Apparently Secure	Apparently Secure	Petromyzontidae	
American brook lamprey	*Lampetra appendix*	Apparently Secure	Vulnerable	Petromyzontidae	
mosquitofish	*Gambusia affinis*	NNA	SNA	Poeciliidae	Exotic
freshwater drum	*Aplodinotus grunniens*	Secure	Apparently Secure	Sciaenidae	
central mudminnow	*Umbra limi*	Secure	Apparently Secure	Umbridae	
[a] Historic record believed to now be extirpated					
[b] Historic record that may no longer persist in the system					
***Species suspected but not verified					

Appendix D: Regional Conservation Priority Species at Muscatatuck NWR

Regional Conservation Priority Species at Muscatatuck NWR

Species or Group	Scientific Name	Habitat	Concerns
Birds[a]			
American Bittern	(*Botaurus lentiginosus*)	Palustrine, Grasslands	Uncommon/declining
Least Bittern	(*Ixobrychus exilis*)	Palustrine	Uncommon/declining
Black-crowned Night-Heron	(*Nycticorax nycticorax*)	Lacustrine, Palustrine, Riverine	Rare/declining
Double Crested Cormorant	(*Phalacrocorax auritus*)	Lacustrine, Riverine (large rivers, shorelines), Forests (islands)	"Nuisance" (management plan available)
Snow Goose	(*Chen caerulescens*)	Lacustrine, Palustrine	Recreational/economic value, "Nuisance" (management plan in preparation)
Canada Goose – Resident	(*Branta canadensis*)	Lacustrine, Palustrine	Recreation/nuisance
Canada Goose – Migrant Populations	(*Branta canadensis*)	Lacustrine, Palustrine	Recreation
Trumpeter Swan	(*Cygnus buccinator*)	Lacustrine, Palustrine, Riverine	Recreational/ economic value
Wood Duck	(*Aix sponsa*)	Palustrine, Riverine, Forests	Recreation
American Black Duck	(*Anas rubripes*)	Lacustrine, Palustrine (shrub/scrub)	Recreation/economic value
Mallard	(*Anas platyrhynchos*)	Palustrine, Forests	Recreation
Blue-winged Teal	(*Anas discors*)	Palustrine, Grasslands	Recreational/economic value
Northern Pintail	(*Anas acuta*)	Palustrine, Grasslands	Recreational/economic value. Declining
Canvasback	(*Aythya valisineria*)	Lacustrine, Palustrine, Riverine	Recreational/economic value
Lesser Scaup	(*Aythya affinis*)	Lacustrine, Palustrine, Riverine (large rivers, shorelines)	Recreational/economic value, Declining
Bald Eagle	(*Haliaeetus leucocephalus*)	Lacustrine, Riverine, Forests	Economic value
Northern Harrier	(*Circus cyaneus*)	Palustrine, Grasslands	Uncommon/declining
Yellow Rail	(*Coturnicops noveboracensis*)	Palustrine (wet meadow)	Uncommon/declining
King Rail	(*Rallus elegans*)	Palustrine	Rare/declining
Common Moorhen	(*Gallinula chloropus*)	Palustrine	Uncommon/declining
Whooping Crane – Eastern Population	(*Grus americana*)	Palustrine	Experimental population
Upland Sandpiper	(*Bartramia longicauda*)	Grasslands	Rare/declining

Regional Conservation Priority Species at Muscatatuck NWR (Continued)

Species or Group	Scientific Name	Habitat	Concerns
Stilt Sandpiper	(*Calidris himantopus*)	Lacustrine, Palustrine, Riverine	Uncommon/declining
Short-billed Dowitcher	(*Limnodromus griseus*)	Lacustrine, Palustrine, Riverine	Uncommon/declining
American Woodcock	(*Scolopax minor*)	Palustrine, Forests (early successional)	Recreation, economic value. Declining
Wilson's Phalarope	(*Phalaropus tricolor*)	Lacustrine, Palustrine	Uncommon/declining
Common Tern - Great Lakes Population	(*Sterna hirundo*)	Lacustrine	Uncommon/declining (status assessment under way)
Forster's Tern	(*Sterna forsteri*)	Lacustrine, Palustrine	Uncommon/declining
Least Tern - Interior Population	(*Sterna antillarum*)	Palustrine	Endangered
Black Tern	(*Chlidonias niger*)	Lacustrine, Palustrine	Uncommon/declining (status assessment completed and conservation needs identified)
Black-billed Cuckoo	(*Coccyzus erythropthalmus*)	Forests, Shrublands	Uncommon/declining
Barn Owl	(*Tyto alba*)	Grasslands	Rare/declining
Long-eared Owl	(*Asio otus*)	Forests	Rare/declining (status unknown)
Short-eared Owl	(*Asio flammeus*)	Grasslands	Rare/declining
Chuck-will's-widow	(*Caprimulgus carolinensis*)	Forests	Rare/declining
Whip-poor-will	(*Caprimulgus vociferus*)	Forests	Uncommon/declining
Red-headed Woodpecker	(*Melanerpes erythrocephalus*)	Forests	Rare/declining
Northern Flicker	(*Colaptes auratus*)	Forests	Fairly common/declining
Olive-sided Flycatcher	(*Contopus cooperi*)	Forests (coniferous)	Uncommon/declining
Acadian Flycatcher	(*Empidonax virescens*)	Forests	Uncommon/declining
Loggerhead Shrike	(*Lanius ludovicianus*)	Grasslands, Shrublands	Rare/declining
Bell's Vireo	(*Vireo bellii*)	Palustrine, Shrublands	Uncommon/declining
Bewick's Wren	(*Thryomanes bewickii*)	Shrublands, Forests (early successional)	Rare/declining
Sedge Wren	(*Cistothorus platensis*)	Palustrine (wet meadows)	Uncommon/declining
Wood Thrush	(*Hylocichla mustelina*)	Forests	Uncommon/declining
Blue-winged Warbler	(*Vermivora pinus*)	Shrublands, Forests (early successional)	Uncommon/decling
Golden-winged Warbler	(*Vermivora chrysoptera*)	Shrublands, Forests (early successional)	Uncommon/declining

Regional Conservation Priority Species at Muscatatuck NWR (Continued)

Species or Group	Scientific Name	Habitat	Concerns
Prairie Warbler	(*Dendroica discolor*)	Shrublands, Forests (early successional)	Uncommon/declining
Cerulean Warbler	(*Dendroica cerulea*)	Forests	Uncommon/declining
Prothonotary Warbler	(*Protonotaria citrea*)	Forests (bottomland)	Fairly Common/declining
Worm-eating Warbler	(*Helmitheros vermivorus*)	Forests	Uncommon/declining
Louisiana Waterthrush	(*Seiurus motacilla*)	Riverine, Forests	Uncommon/declining
Kentucky Warbler	(*Oporornis formosus*)	Forests	Uncommon/declining
Canada Warbler	(*Wilsonia canadensis*)	Forests (mixed)	Uncommon/declining
Field Sparrow	(*Spizella pusilla*)	Grasslands, Shrublands	Fairly common/declining
Grasshopper Sparrow	(*Ammodramus savannarum*)	Grasslands	Uncommon/declining
Henslow's Sparrow	(*Ammodramus henslowii*)	Grasslands	Rare/declining?
Le Conte's Sparrow	(*Ammodramus leconteii*)	Palustrine (wet meadows), Grasslands	Uncommon/declining
Nelson's Sharp-tailed Sparrow	(*Ammodramus nelsoni*)	Palustrine (marshes)	Uncommon/declining
Dickcissel	(*Spiza americana*)	Palustrine	Fairly common/declining
Bobolink	(*Dolichonyx oryzivorus*)	Grasslands	Fairly common/declining
Eastern Meadowlark	(*Sturnella magna*)	Grasslands	Uncommon/declining
Rusty Blackbird	(*Euphagus carolinus*)	Forests	Uncommon/declining
Orchard Oriole	(*Icterus spurius*)	Forests (early successional), Palustrine	Fairly common/declining?
Mammals			
Indiana Bat	(*Myotis sodalist*)	Caves, Mines, Forests	Endangered
Reptiles			
Copperbelly water snake - Southern population	(*Nerodia erythrogaster neglecta*)	Palustrine (swamps), Forests (upland, bottomland)	Rare/declining
Fish			
Eastern sand darter	(*Ammocrypta pellucida*)	Riverine (streams, main channels)	Rare/declining
Mussels			
Threeridge	(*Amblema plicata*)	Riverine (mud/sand/gravel in small to large rivers and impoundments)	Recreational/economic value
Washboard	(*Megalonaias nervosa*)	Riverine (mud/sand/gravel in medium to large rivers)	Recreational/economic value

Regional Conservation Priority Species at Muscatatuck NWR (Continued)

Species or Group	Scientific Name	Habitat	Concerns
Pimpleback	(*Quadrula pustulosa pustulosa*)	Riverine (mud/sand/gravel in medium to large river)	Recreational/economic value (commercial)
Pistolgrip	(*Tritogonia verrucosa*)	Riverine (mud/sand/gravel in medium to large rivers)	Rare/declining (range overlaps commercial harvested areas)
Asiatic clam	(*Corbicula fluminea*)	Riverine	"Nuisance"
Plants			
N/A			

a. *In December 2008 the RCPS bird list was updated from the original January 2002 version.*

Appendix E: Compliance Requirements

Appendix E / Compliance Requirements

Rivers and Harbor Act (1899) (33 U.S.C. 403)

Section 10 of this Act requires the authorization by the U.S. Army Corps of Engineers prior to any work in, on, over, or under a navigable water of the United States.

Antiquities Act of 1906. 16 U.S.C. 431 et seq.

Authorizes the scientific investigation of antiquities on Federal land and provides penalties for unauthorized removal of objects taken or collected without a permit.

Migratory Bird Treaty Act, 16 U.S.C. 703 et seq.

Designates the protection of migratory birds as a Federal responsibility. This Act enables the setting of seasons, and other regulations including the closing of areas, Federal or non Federal, to the hunting of migratory birds.

Migratory Bird Conservation Act, 16 U.S.C. 715 et seq.

Establishes procedures for acquisition by purchase, rental, or gift of areas approved by the Migratory Bird Conservation Commission.

Fish and Wildlife Coordination Act 16 U.S.C. 661 et seq. (1934)

Requires that the Fish and Wildlife Service and state fish and wildlife agencies be consulted whenever water is to be impounded, diverted or modified under a Federal permit or license. The Service and state agency recommend measures to prevent the loss of biological resources, or to mitigate or compensate for the damage. The project proponent must take biological resource values into account and adopt justifiable protection measures to obtain maximum overall project benefits. A 1958 amendment added provisions to recognize the vital contribution of wildlife resources to the Nation and to require equal consideration and coordination of wildlife conservation with other water resources development programs. It also authorized the Secretary of Interior to provide public fishing areas and accept donations of lands and funds.

Migratory Bird Hunting Stamp Act. Also known as the Duck Stamp Act, 16 U.S.C. 718 et seq. (1934)

Requires every waterfowl hunter 16 years of age or older to carry a stamp and earmarks proceeds of the Duck Stamps to buy or lease waterfowl habitat. A 1958 amendment authorizes the acquisition of small wetland and pothole areas to be designated as 'Waterfowl Production Areas,' which may be acquired without the limitations and requirements of the Migratory Bird Conservation Act.

Historic Sites, Buildings and Antiquities Act. Also known as the Historic Sites Act of 1935, 16 U.S.C. 461 et seq.

Declares it a national policy to preserve historic sites and objects of national significance, including those located on refuges. Provides procedures for designation, acquisition, administration, and protection of such sites.

Refuge Revenue Sharing Act, 16 U.S.C. 715s (1935)

Requires revenue sharing provisions to all fee-title ownerships that are administered solely or primarily by the Secretary through the Service.

Transfer of Certain Real Property for Wildlife Conservation Purposes Act, 16 U.S.C. 667b-667d (1948)

Provides that upon a determination by the Administrator of the General Services Administration, real property no longer needed by a Federal agency can be transferred without reimbursement to the Secretary of Interior if the land has particular value for migratory birds, or to a state agency for other wildlife conservation purposes.

Federal Records Act of 1950, 44 U.S.C. 31

Directs the preservation of evidence of the government's organization, functions, policies, decisions, operations, and activities, as well as basic historical and other information.

Fish and Wildlife Act of 1956, 16 U.S.C. 742a et seq.

Established a comprehensive national fish and wildlife policy and broadened the authority for acquisition and development of refuges.

Refuge Recreation Act, 16 U.S.C. 460k et seq. (1962)

Allows the use of refuges for recreation when such uses are compatible with the refuge's primary purposes and when sufficient funds are available to manage the uses.

Wilderness Act of 1964, 16 U.S.C. 1131 et seq.

Directed the Secretary of Interior, within 10 years, to review every roadless area of 5,000 or more acres and every roadless island (regardless of size) within National Wildlife Refuge and National Park Systems and to recommend to the President the suitability of each such area or island for inclusion in the National Wilderness Preservation System, with final decisions made by Congress. The Secretary of Agriculture was directed to study and recommend suitable areas in the National Forest System.

Land and Water Conservation Fund Act of 1965, 16 U.S.C. 460 et seq.

Uses the receipts from the sale of surplus Federal land, outer continental shelf oil and gas sales, and other sources for land acquisition under several authorities.

National Wildlife Refuge System Administration Act of 1966, 16 U.S.C. 668dd, 668ee

Defines the National Wildlife Refuge System and authorizes the Secretary to permit any use of a refuge provided such use is compatible with the major purposes for which the refuge was established. The Refuge Improvement Act clearly defines a unifying mission for the Refuge System; establishes the legitimacy and appropriateness of the six priority public uses (hunting, fishing, wildlife observation and photography, or environmental education and interpretation); establishes a formal process for determining compatibility; established the responsibilities of the Secretary of Interior for managing and protecting the System; and requires a Comprehensive Conservation Plan for each refuge by the year 2012. This Act amended portions of the Refuge Recreation Act and National Wildlife Refuge System Administration Act of 1966.

National Historic Preservation Act, 16 U.S.C. 470 et seq. (1966)

Establishes as policy that the Federal Government is to provide leadership in the preservation of the nation's prehistoric and historic resources. Section 106 requires Federal agencies to consider impacts their undertakings could have on historic properties; Section 110 requires Federal agencies to manage historic properties, e.g., to document historic properties prior to destruction or damage; Section 101 requires Federal agencies to consider Indian tribal values in historic preservation programs, and requires each Federal agency to establish a program leading to inventory of all historic properties on its land.

Architectural Barriers Act of 1968, 42 U.S.C. 4151 et seq.

Requires federally owned, leased, or funded buildings and facilities to be accessible to persons with disabilities.

National Environmental Policy Act of 1969, 42 U.S.C. 4321 et seq.

Requires the disclosure of the environmental impacts of any major Federal action significantly affecting the quality of the human environment.

Uniform Relocation Assistance and Real Property Acquisition Policies Act of 1970, 42 U.S.C. 4601 et seq.

Provides for uniform and equitable treatment of persons who sell their homes, businesses, or farms to the Service. The Act requires that any purchase offer be no less than the fair market value of the property.

Endangered Species Act of 1973, 16 U.S.C. 1531 et seq.

Requires all Federal agencies to carry out programs for the conservation of endangered and threatened species.

Rehabilitation Act of 1973, 29 U.S.C. 701 et seq.

Requires programmatic accessibility in addition to physical accessibility for all facilities and programs funded by the Federal government to ensure that anybody can participate in any program.

Archaeological and Historic Preservation Act 16 U.S.C.469-469c

Directs the preservation of historic and archaeological data in Federal construction projects.

Clean Water Act of 1977, 33 U.S.C. 1251

Requires consultation with the Corps of Engineers (404 permits) for major wetland modifications.

Surface Mining Control and Reclamation Act of 1977, 30 U.S.C. 1201 et seq.

Regulates surface mining activities and reclamation of coal-mined lands. Further regulates the coal industry by designating certain areas as unsuitable for coal mining operations.

Executive Order 11988 (1977)

Each Federal agency shall provide leadership and take action to reduce the risk of flood loss and minimize the impact of floods on human safety, and preserve the natural and beneficial values served by the floodplains.

Executive Order 11990

Executive Order 11990 directs Federal agencies to (1) minimize destruction, loss, or degradation of wetlands and (2) preserve and enhance the natural and beneficial values of wetlands when a practical alternative exists.

Executive Order 12372 (Intergovernmental Review of Federal Programs)

Directs the Service to send copies of the Environmental Assessment to state planning agencies for review.

American Indian Religious Freedom Act, 42 U.S.C. 1996, 1996a (1976)

Directs agencies to consult with native traditional religious leaders to determine appropriate policy changes necessary to protect and preserve American Indian religious cultural rights and practices.

Fish and Wildlife Improvement Act of 1978, 16 U.S.C. 742a

Improves the administration of fish and wildlife programs and amends several earlier laws including the Refuge Recreation Act, the National Wildlife Refuge System Administration Act, and the Fish and Wildlife Act of 1956. It authorizes the Secretary to accept gifts and bequests of real and personal property on behalf of the United States. It also authorizes the use of volunteers on Service projects and appropriations to carry out a volunteer program.

Archaeological Resources Protection Act of 1979, 16 U.S.C. 470aa et seq.

Protects materials of archaeological interest from unauthorized removal or destruction and requires Federal managers to develop plans and schedules to locate archaeological resources.

Farmland Protection Policy Act, Public Law 97-98, 7 U.S.C. 4201 (1981)

Minimizes the extent to which Federal programs contribute to the unnecessary and irreversible conversion of farmland to nonagricultural uses.

Emergency Wetlands Resources Act of 1986, 16 U.S.C. 3901 et seq.

Promotes the conservation of migratory waterfowl and offsets or prevents the serious loss of wetlands by the acquisition of wetlands and other essential habitats.

Federal Noxious Weed Act of 1974, 7 U.S.C. 2801 et seq.

Requires the use of integrated management systems to control or contain undesirable plant species, and an interdisciplinary approach with the cooperation of other federal and state agencies.

Native American Graves Protection and Repatriation Act, 25 U.S.C. 3001 et seq. (1990)

Requires Federal agencies and museums to inventory, determine ownership of, and repatriate cultural items under their control or possession.

Americans with Disabilities Act of 1990, 42 U.S.C. 12101 et seq.

Prohibits discrimination in public accommodations and services.

Executive Order 12898 (1994)

Establishes environmental justice as a Federal government priority and directs all Federal agencies to make environmental justice part of their mission. Environmental justice calls for fair distribution of environmental hazards.

Executive Order 12996 Management and General Public Use of the National Wildlife Refuge System (1996)

Defines the mission, purpose, and priority public uses of the National Wildlife Refuge System. It also presents four principles to guide management of the System.

Executive Order 13007 Indian Sacred Sites (1996)

Directs Federal land management agencies to accommodate access to and ceremonial use of Indian sacred sites by Indian religious practitioners, avoid adversely affecting the physical integrity of such sacred sites, and where appropriate, maintain the confidentiality of sacred sites.

National Wildlife Refuge System Improvement Act of 1997, 16 U.S.C. 668dd

Considered the "Organic Act of the National Wildlife Refuge System. Defines the mission of the System, designates priority wildlife-dependent public uses, and calls for comprehensive refuge planning. Section 6 requires the Service to make a determination of compatibility of existing, new and changing uses of Refuge land; and Section 7 requires the Service to identify and describe the archaeological and cultural values of the refuge.

The Act also directs the administration of the Refuge System to ensure the biological integrity, diversity, and environmental health of the System. According to the U.S. FWS Service Manual (601 FW3) this refers to the maintenance of existing elements, and where appropriate the restoration of lost or severely degraded elements. Integrity pertains to biotic composition, structure, and function at genetic, organismal, and community levels. Diversity includes protection of the broad variety of living organisms, genetic distinctions, and community compositions. Environmental health recognizes the importance of both biotic and abiotic features and processes in the System. The standard of measure for each of these terms is defined using historic conditions,

or conditions and processes present prior to substantial anthropogenic changes, as indicated by the best available science and sound professional judgment.

National Wildlife Refuge System Volunteer and Community Partnership Enhancement Act of 1998, 16 U.S.C. 742a

Amends the Fish and Wildlife Act of 1956 to promote volunteer programs and community partnerships for the benefit of national wildlife refuges, and for other purposes.

National Trails System Act, 16 U.S.C. 1241 et seq. (1968)

Assigns responsibility to the Secretary of Interior and thus the Service to protect the historic and recreational values of congressionally designated National Historic Trail sites.

Treasury and General Government Appropriations Act, Pub. L. 106-554, §1(a)(3), Dec. 21, 2000, 114 Stat. 2763, 2763A–125

In December 2002, Congress required federal agencies to publish their own guidelines for ensuring and maximizing the quality, objectivity, utility, and integrity of information that they disseminate to the public (44 U.S.C. 3502). The amended language is included in Section 515(a). The Office of Budget and Management (OMB) directed agencies to develop their own guidelines to address the requirements of the law. The Department of the Interior instructed bureaus to prepare separate guidelines on how they would apply the Act. The U.S. Fish and Wildlife Service has developed "Information Quality Guidelines" to address the law.

Cultural Resources and Historic Preservation

The National Wildlife Refuge System Improvement Act of 1997, Section 6, requires the Service to make a determination of compatibility of existing, new and changing uses of Refuge land; and Section 7 requires the Service to identify and describe the archaeological and cultural values of the refuge.

The National Historic Preservation Act (NHPA), Section 106, requires Federal agencies to consider impacts their undertakings could have on historic properties; Section 110 requires Federal agencies to manage historic properties, e.g., to document historic properties prior to destruction or damage; Section 101 requires Federal agencies consider Indian tribal values in historic preservation programs, and requires each Federal agency to establish a program leading to inventory of all historic properties on its land.

The Archaeological Resources Protection Act of 1979 (ARPA) prohibits unauthorized disturbance of archeological resources on Federal and Indian land; and other matters. Section 10 requires establishing "a program to increase public awareness" of archeological resources. Section 14 requires plans to survey lands and a schedule for surveying lands with "the most scientifically valuable archaeological resources." This Act requires protection of all archeological sites more than 100 years old (not just sites meeting the criteria for the National Register) on Federal land, and requires archeological investigations on Federal land be performed in the public interest by qualified persons.

The Native American Graves Protection and Repatriation Act of 1990 (NAGPRA) imposes serious delays on a project when human remains or other cultural items are encountered in the absence of a plan.

The American Indian Religious Freedom Act (AIRFA) iterates the right of Native Americans to free exercise of traditional religions and use of sacred places.

EO 13007, Indian Sacred Sites (1996), directs Federal agencies to accommodate access to and ceremonial use, to avoid adverse effects and avoid blocking access, and to enter into early consultation.

Restle Unit Deed Restrictions

The property shall be known and posted as the Restle Wildlife Management Area.

Grantee shall perpetually manage the real estate as a wetland habitat for native wildlife and plant enhancement and protection.

In order to further wetland habitat development, the construction of dams, levees, spillways and associated water level and flow control devices shall be permitted, as well as plantings appropriate to their maintenance. Water level manipulation for wetland management purposes shall be permitted, even though some native plants and animals may be damaged by such management.

Control of woody vegetation is permitted.

No timbering, burning, hunting, trapping, or fishing shall be permitted, except that plant harvesting or controlled burning for the protection of the wetland or research into the protection of wetlands are permitted. Wildlife harvesting within the levee constructed by the Fish and Wildlife Service in 1990 is also permitted for the protection of the wetland within the levee. The permitted activities specified in this paragraph are to be conducted only by personnel of the grantee or their designees for that specific purpose.

No herbicides or insecticides shall be used on the real estate, except that if the native plant or animal habitat is threatened by the excessive growth of native species or the invasion or excessive growth of species alien to the area, herbicides or insecticides may be used for the limited purposes of controlling such populations.

No construction of buildings shall be permitted except for observation blinds and wildlife study structures, nesting boxes, and other animal habitat improvement structures.

No general access of the public to the area shall be permitted. Barbara Restle, her children and their spouses, and her grandchildren will continue to have access to the property for wildlife observation purposes. Access to persons other than grantee's agents, officers, and employees shall be permitted by the grantee only on written application for educational, research, or habitat development purposes deemed consistent with the goals of this grant.

No commercial sale of any resources from the property shall be permitted.

The Sassafras Chapter of the National Audubon Society shall be allowed to review management of the property on an annual basis. To this end, a representative of the Sassafras Audubon Society, as designated by the Sassafras Audubon Society Board of Directors must be allowed to enter the property at least once every three months. Prior to entering the project the Sassafras Audubon Society representative will notify the Fish and Wildlife Service at least one week in advance of the date of the inspection of the property.

Appendix F: Appropriate Use Determinations

Appropriate Refuge Uses

The Service's Appropriate Use Policy describes the initial decision process a refuge manager follows when first considering whether or not to allow a proposed use on a refuge. The refuge manager must first find a use to be appropriate before undertaking a compatibility review of the use and outlining the stipulations of the use.

This policy clarifies and expands on the compatibility policy (603 FW 2.10D(1)), which describes when refuge managers should deny a proposed use without determining compatibility. If we find a proposed use is not appropriate, we will not allow the use and will not prepare a compatibility determination. By screening out proposed uses not appropriate to the refuge, the refuge manager avoids unnecessary compatibility reviews. By following the process for finding the appropriateness of a use, we strengthen and fulfill the Refuge System mission. Although a refuge use may be both appropriate and compatible, the refuge manager retains the authority to not allow the use or modify the use.

Background for this policy as it applies to Muscatatuck NWR is found in the following statutory authorities:

- *National Wildlife Refuge System Administration Act of 1966*, as amended by the *National Wildlife Refuge System Improvement Act of 1997* (16 U.S.C. 668dd-668ee). This law provides the authority for establishing policies and regulations governing refuge uses, including the authority to prohibit certain harmful activities. The Administration Act does not authorize any particular use, but rather authorizes the Secretary of the Interior to allow uses only when they are compatible. The Improvement Act provides the Refuge System mission and includes specific directives and a clear hierarchy of public uses on the Refuge System.

- *Refuge Recreation Act of 1962*, (16 U.S.C. 460k). This law authorizes the Secretary of the Interior to allow public recreation in areas of the Refuge System when the use is an "appropriate incidental or secondary use."

This policy does NOT apply to:

- Situations where reserved rights or legal mandates provide we must allow certain uses.

- Refuge Management Activities. Refuge management activities conducted by the Refuge System or a Refuge System-authorized agent are designed to conserve fish, wildlife, and plants and their habitats. These activities are used to fulfill a refuge purpose(s) or the Refuge System mission, and are based on the best available science and sound professional judgment.

Uses that have been administratively determined to be appropriate are:

- *Six wildlife-dependent recreational uses.* As defined by the National Wildlife Refuge System Improvement Act of 1997 (Improvement Act), the six wildlife-dependent recreational uses (hunting, fishing, wildlife observation and photography, and environmental education and interpretation) are determined to be appropriate. However, the refuge manager must still determine if these uses are compatible.

- *Take of fish and wildlife under state regulations.* States have regulations concerning take of wildlife that includes hunting, fishing, and trapping. We consider take of wildlife under such regulations appropriate. However, the refuge manager must determine if the activity is compatible before allowing it on a refuge.

Refuge uses must meet at least one of the following four conditions to be deemed appropriate:

- It is a wildlife-dependent recreational use of a refuge as identified in the Improvement Act.

- It contributes to fulfilling the refuge purpose(s), the Refuge System mission, or goals or objectives described in a refuge management plan approved after the Improvement Act was signed into law.

- The use involves the take of fish and wildlife under state regulations.

- The refuge manager has evaluated the use following the guidelines in this policy and found that it is appropriate. The criteria used by the manager to evaluate appropriateness can be found on each of the appropriate use forms included in this appendix. Also included under this condition are 'specialized uses,' or uses that require specific authorization from the Refuge System, often in the form of a special use permit, letter of authorization, or other permit document. These uses do not include uses already granted by a prior existing right. We make appropriateness findings for specialized uses on a case-by-case basis.

Finding of Appropriateness of a Refuge Use

Refuge Name: **Muscatatuck National Wildlife Refuge**

Use: **Farming and Haying**

This exhibit is not required for wildlife-dependent recreational uses, forms of take regulated by the State, or uses already described in a refuge CCP or step-down management plan approved after October 9, 1997.

Decision Criteria:	YES	NO
(a) Do we have jurisdiction over the use?	X	
(b) Does the use comply with applicable laws and regulations (Federal, State, tribal, and local)?	X	
(c) Is the use consistent with applicable Executive orders and Department and Service policies?	X	
(d) Is the use consistent with public safety?	X	
(e) Is the use consistent with goals and objectives in an approved management plan or other document?	X	
(f) Has an earlier documented analysis not denied the use or is this the first time the use has been proposed?	X	
(g) Is the use manageable within available budget and staff?	X	
(h) Will this be manageable in the future within existing resources?	X	
(i) Does the use contribute to the public's understanding and appreciation of the refuge's natural or cultural resources, or is the use beneficial to the refuge's natural or cultural resources?	X	
(j) Can the use be accommodated without impairing existing wildlife-dependent recreational uses or reducing the potential to provide quality (see section 1.6D. for description), compatible, wildlife-dependent recreation into the future?	X	

Where we do not have jurisdiction over the use ("no" to (a)), there is no need to evaluate it further as we cannot control the use. Uses that are illegal, inconsistent with existing policy, or unsafe ("no" to (b), (c), or (d)) may not be found appropriate. If the answer is "no" to any of the other questions above, we will generally not allow the use.

If indicated, the refuge manager has consulted with State fish and wildlife agencies.   **Yes X**   **No** _____

When the refuge manager finds the use appropriate based on sound professional judgment, the refuge manager must justify the use in writing on an attached sheet and obtain the refuge supervisor's concurrence.

Based on an overall assessment of these factors, my summary conclusion is that the proposed use is:

Not Appropriate _____   Appropriate __X__

Refuge Manager: _Mo Webbe_____   Date: _9/8/09___

If found to be Not Appropriate, the refuge supervisor does not need to sign concurrence if the use is a new use.
If an existing use is found Not Appropriate outside the CCP process, the refuge supervisor must sign concurrence.
If found to be Appropriate, the refuge supervisor must sign concurrence.

cting

Refuge Supervisor: _Sandra M. Sichanis_____   Date: _9/11/09___

A compatibility determination is required before the use may be allowed.

Finding of Appropriateness of a Refuge Use

Refuge Name: **Muscatatuck National Wildlife Refuge**

Use: **Wild Food / Shed Antler Collecting**

This exhibit is not required for wildlife-dependent recreational uses, forms of take regulated by the State, or uses already described in a refuge CCP or step-down management plan approved after October 9, 1997.

Decision Criteria:	YES	NO
(a) Do we have jurisdiction over the use?	X	
(b) Does the use comply with applicable laws and regulations (Federal, State, tribal, and local)?	X	
(c) Is the use consistent with applicable Executive orders and Department and Service policies?	X	
(d) Is the use consistent with public safety?	X	
(e) Is the use consistent with goals and objectives in an approved management plan or other document?	X	
(f) Has an earlier documented analysis not denied the use or is this the first time the use has been proposed?	X	
(g) Is the use manageable within available budget and staff?	X	
(h) Will this be manageable in the future within existing resources?	X	
(i) Does the use contribute to the public's understanding and appreciation of the refuge's natural or cultural resources, or is the use beneficial to the refuge's natural or cultural resources?	X	
(j) Can the use be accommodated without impairing existing wildlife-dependent recreational uses or reducing the potential to provide quality (see section 1.6D. for description), compatible, wildlife-dependent recreation into the future?	X	

Where we do not have jurisdiction over the use ("no" to (a)), there is no need to evaluate it further as we cannot control the use. Uses that are illegal, inconsistent with existing policy, or unsafe ("no" to (b), (c), or (d)) may not be found appropriate. If the answer is "no" to any of the other questions above, we will generally not allow the use.

If indicated, the refuge manager has consulted with State fish and wildlife agencies.   **Yes   X**   **No_____**

When the refuge manager finds the use appropriate based on sound professional judgment, the refuge manager must justify the use in writing on an attached sheet and obtain the refuge supervisor's concurrence.

Based on an overall assessment of these factors, my summary conclusion is that the proposed use is:

Not Appropriate _____   Appropriate   X

Refuge Manager:_____   Date: 9/8/09

If found to be Not Appropriate, the refuge supervisor does not need to sign concurrence if the use is a new use.
If an existing use is found Not Appropriate outside the CCP process, the refuge supervisor must sign concurrence.
If found to be Appropriate, the refuge supervisor must sign concurrence.

Acting Refuge Supervisor:_____   Date: 9/11/09

A compatibility determination is required before the use may be allowed.

Finding of Appropriateness of a Refuge Use

Refuge Name: **Muscatatuck National Wildlife Refuge**

Use: **Research Projects by Third Parties**

This exhibit is not required for wildlife-dependent recreational uses, forms of take regulated by the State, or uses already described in a refuge CCP or step-down management plan approved after October 9, 1997.

Decision Criteria:	YES	NO
(a) Do we have jurisdiction over the use?	X	
(b) Does the use comply with applicable laws and regulations (Federal, State, tribal, and local)?	X	
(c) Is the use consistent with applicable Executive orders and Department and Service policies?	X	
(d) Is the use consistent with public safety?	X	
(e) Is the use consistent with goals and objectives in an approved management plan or other document?	X	
(f) Has an earlier documented analysis not denied the use or is this the first time the use has been proposed?	X	
(g) Is the use manageable within available budget and staff?	X	
(h) Will this be manageable in the future within existing resources?	X	
(i) Does the use contribute to the public's understanding and appreciation of the refuge's natural or cultural resources, or is the use beneficial to the refuge's natural or cultural resources?	X	
(j) Can the use be accommodated without impairing existing wildlife-dependent recreational uses or reducing the potential to provide quality (see section 1.6D. for description), compatible, wildlife-dependent recreation into the future?	X	

Where we do not have jurisdiction over the use ("no" to (a)), there is no need to evaluate it further as we cannot control the use. Uses that are illegal, inconsistent with existing policy, or unsafe ("no" to (b), (c), or (d)) may not be found appropriate. If the answer is "no" to any of the other questions above, we will generally not allow the use.

If indicated, the refuge manager has consulted with State fish and wildlife agencies.   Yes _X_   No _____

When the refuge manager finds the use appropriate based on sound professional judgment, the refuge manager must justify the use in writing on an attached sheet and obtain the refuge supervisor's concurrence.

Based on an overall assessment of these factors, my summary conclusion is that the proposed use is:

Not Appropriate _____   Appropriate _X_

Refuge Manager: _____   Date: 9/8/09

If found to be Not Appropriate, the refuge supervisor does not need to sign concurrence if the use is a new use.
If an existing use is found Not Appropriate outside the CCP process, the refuge supervisor must sign concurrence.
If found to be Appropriate, the refuge supervisor must sign concurrence.

Acting Refuge Supervisor: _____   Date: 9/11/09

A compatibility determination is required before the use may be allowed.

Appendix G: Deferred Maintenance and Improvement Projects and New Projects

Project Number	Deferred Maintenance & Improvement Projects	Description	Estimated Cost
Deferred Maintenance & Improvement			
2005230736	R3 DM 99 Muscatatuck Levee MSU 1 General Rehab	Seasonally Flooded Const. Impoundments	$10,755
2005230751	R3 DM 99 Muscatatuck Levee MSU 2 General Rehab	Seasonally Flooded Const. Impoundments	$8,892
2005230769	R3 DM 99 Muscatatuck Levee MSU 4 General Rehab	Seasonally Flooded Const. Impoundments	$10,438
2005230778	R3 DM 99 Muscatatuck Levee MSU 4 North General Rehab	Seasonally Flooded Const. Impoundments	$27,369
2005230786	R3 DM 99 Muscatatuck Levee MSU 5 General Rehab	Seasonally Flooded Const. Impoundments	$21,592
2005230953	R3 DM 99 Muscatatuck Levee Sheryl General Rehab	Fishing	$26,486
2005230984	R3 DM 99 Muscatatuck Levee Endicott South General Rehab	Seasonally Flooded Const. Impoundments	$47,616
2005230987	R3 DM 99 Muscatatuck Levee Sand Hill Ponds General Rehab	Fishing	$13,122
2005232382	R3 DM 99 Muscatatuck Levee Persimmon Ponds General Rehab	Fishing	$15,451
2005232398	DM Child Repair Erosion on M-7 Masher Dike	Seasonally Flooded Const. Impoundments	$52,000
2005232414	R3 DM 99 Muscatatuck Levee Lake Linda General Rehab	Fishing	$58,511
2005232420	R3 DM 99 Muscatatuck Road Service to Shop Area General Rehab	Observation & Photog.	$33,621
2005232429	R3 DM 99 Muscatatuck Levee Pfaffenburger M-6 General Rehab	Seasonally Flooded Const. Impoundments	$38,151
2005232511	R3 DM 99 Muscatatuck Levee Sue Pond General Rehab	Migratory Waterbirds	$51,586
2005241814	R3 DM 99 Muscatatuck WCS Richart General Rehab	Fishing	$7,646
2005241831	R3 DM 99 Muscatatuck WCS M4 to Storm Creek General Rehab	Seasonally Flooded Const. Impoundments	$8,583
2005241839	R3 DM 99 Muscatatuck WCS M5 to Storm Creek General Rehab	Seasonally Flooded Const. Impoundments	$8,583
2005241844	R3 DM 99 Muscatatuck WCS M6 Outlet General Rehab	Seasonally Flooded Const. Impoundments	$12,379
2006402270	R3 DM 99 Muscatatuck WCS Moss Lake General Rehab	Seasonally Flooded Const. Impoundments	$16,359
2006402682	DM Child Bridge Mutton Creek General Rehab	Public Access Roads	$20,000
2006402685	DM Child Bridge StormCreek General Rehab	Public Access Roads	$20,000

Project Number	Deferred Maintenance & Improvement Projects	Description	Estimated Cost
2006402686	R3 DM 99 Muscatatuck Bridge Public M3 (Storm 500 N)	Public Access Roads	$8,105
2006402687	DM Child Bridge M4 West Entrance Decking Replacement	Public Access Roads	$20,000
2006403233	R3 DM 99 Muscatatuck Dam Low Hazard Richart	Fishing	$13,939
2006403235	R3 DM 99 Muscatatuck Dam Low Hazard Stanfield	Fishing	$8,307
2006403238	R3 DM 99 Muscatatuck Dam Low Hazard Moss Lake	Seasonally Flooded Const. Impoundments	$19,385
2006410096	R3 DM 99 Muscatatuck Observation Deck Endicott General Rehab	Observation & Photog.	$8,997
2006410097	R3 DM 99 Muscatatuck Pavillon Haackman Overlook General Rehab	Observation & Photog.	$6,385
2006410098	R3 VFE 99 Muscatatuck Fishing Pier Lake Linda General Rehab	Fishing	$5,851
2007744088	R3 RRP Muscatatuck Preliminary Engineering (Rte 010)	Public Access Roads	$260,000
2007744089	R3 RRP Muscatatuck County Line Road (Rte 010)	Public Access Roads	$304,103
2007744090	R3 RRP Muscatatuck 400N Road (Rte 011)	Public Access Roads	$230,894
2007744091	R3 RRP Muscatatuck 500N Road (Rte 102)	Public Access Roads	$76,589
2007744094	R3 RRP Muscatatuck Visitor Center FHWA Rte 901	Public Access Roads	$5,346
2007744095	R3 RRP Muscatatuck Check Station Loop A FHWA Rte 904	Public Access Roads	$10,499
2007744101	R3 RRP Muscatatuck Visitor Center FHWA Rte 902	Public Access Roads	$13,347
2007744104	R3 RRP Muscatatuck Stanfield Lake Boat Ramp FHWA Rte 906	Fishing	$5,621
2007744105	R3 RRP Muscatatuck Myers Cabin South Roadside FHWA Rte 910	Public Access Roads	$1,544
2007744107	R3 RRP Muscatatuck Road Public FHWA Rte 010 Hwy 50 to VC	Public Access Roads	$57,723
2007744108	R3 RRP Muscatatuck Turkey Trail FHWA Rte 912	Public Access Roads	$7,170
2007744109	R3 RRP Muscatatuck Stanfield Lake Loop FHWA Rte 917	Public Access Roads	$4,949
2007744115	R3 RRP Muscatatuck Stanfield Lake Loop FHWA Rte 917	Public Access Roads	$1,737
2007744121	R3 RRP Muscatatuck Bird Trail FHWA Rte 921	Public Access Roads	$3,443
2008866101	R3 FY09 Trails Muscatatuck Richart Trail	Observation & Photog.	$10,000
2008866107	R3 FY09 Trails Muscatatuck Bird Trail	Observation & Photog.	$15,000
2008866110	R3 FY09 Trails Muscatatuck Turkey Trail	Observation & Photog.	$32,000
2008867009	R3 DM 99 Muscatatuck Public Fishing Peir / Dock, Stanfield Lake	Fishing	$7,527
2008867341	R3 DM 99 Muscatatuck Dike - Wood Duck 320' General Rehab	Seasonally Flooded Const. Impoundments	$7,759

Project Number	Deferred Maintenance & Improvement Projects	Description	Estimated Cost
2008867388	R3 DM 99 Muscatatuck Dike, MSU - 3 GENERAL Rehab	Seasonally Flooded Const. Impoundments	$25,928
2008867411	R3 DM 99 Muscatatuck Dike – S Wagner GENERAL Rehab	Seasonally Flooded Const. Impoundments	$6,405
2008867418	R3 DM 99 Muscatatuck Dike – W Wagner General Rehab	Seasonally Flooded Const. Impoundments	$5,103
2008867431	R3 DM 99 Muscatatuck Dike – Monroe County General Rehab	Seasonally Flooded Const. Impoundments	$11,497
2008837452	R3 DM 99 Muscatatuck Dike – McDonald South General Rehab	Seasonally Flooded Const. Impoundments	$5,475
2008867560	R3 RRP Muscatatuck Road Public Route 103 - 1225 E	Public Access Roads	$72,187
2008867851	R3 RRP Muscatatuck Signs - Trail Public Hiking	Observation & Photog., & Interpretation	$13,964
	Total		$1,795,918

Project Number	New and Construction Projects	Description	Estimated Cost
2007718327	Designs to Improve Moist Soil and Green Tree Habitat CIEG CHILD	Bottomland Hardwood Forest	$80,000
2007718329	Improve Moist Soil and Green Tree Habitat CINC CHILD	Bottomland Hardwood Forest	$900,000
2007741744	R3 VFE Child Muscatatuck Construct Visitor Center Pavilian Roof	Interpretation	$82,000
2007741749	R3 VFE Muscatatuck Install Restle Unit Interpretive Signs and Observation Deck Repair	Observation & Photog.	$15,000
2007741750	R3 VFE Muscatatuck Hackman Overlook Structure Improvements	Observation & Photog.	$10,000
2007742988	R312 VFE CINC Muscatatuck Construct Kiosks at Four Locations	Observation & Photog., & Interpretation	$40,000
2008863562	Construct 8-Person Fire Bunkhouse	Support for all Goals	$450,000
	Tree Planting (Approx.) 970 Acres over the life of the CCP	Upland & Bottomland Hardwood Forests	$77,000
	Timber Stand Improvement on (Approx.) 5,000 Acres over the life of the CCP, add one Biological Technician.	Upland & Bottomland Hardwood Forests	$132,000
	General Shoreline Improvements to Fishing Areas and Boat Launching Ramp	Fishing	$100,000
	Accessible Wildlife Viewing Platform/Deck at the "Shop Field"/Crane Viewing Area	Observation & Photog., & Interpretation	$100,000
	Conduct a Hydrological Survey of the Seep Springs RNA	Seep Springs RNA	$70,500
	Conduct Refuge-wide Invasive Plant Surveys Every 5 Years	Invasive Plant Species	$180,000
	Close West Entrance (Cty. Rd. 400 N.), Move Gate, Add Turn-around Circles, (Rte.011)	Public Access Roads	$150,000
	Expand Environmental Education and Volunteer Staffing	Visitor Services Staffing	$95,000
	Hydrologic Study of Southern Moist Soil Units	Hydrologic Study	$80,000
	Manage Invasive Plant Control Program and Expand Staffing	Invasives Management	$252,000
	Expanded Wildlife Monitoring	Wildlife Monitoring	$181,000
Total			$2,994,500

Appendix H: Literature Cited

Literature Cited

National Audubon Society. 2008. Important bird areas in the U.S. Available at: http://www.audubon.org/bird/iba/

Blaustein, A. R., D. B. Wake, and W. P. Sousa. 1994. Amphibian declines: judging stability, persistence, and susceptibility of populations to local and global extinctions. Conservation Biology 8(1):60-71.

Blossey, B. 2004. Before, during and after: the need for long-term monitoring in invasive plant species management. Biological Invasions 1(2):301-311

Carter, T. 2007. Unpublished data. Report to Muscatatuck NWR. 3pp.

Collins, B. S. and L. L. Battaglia. 2002. Microenvironmental heterogeneity and *Quercus michauxii* regeneration in experimental gaps. Forest Ecology and Management 155(1): 279-290.

Conant, J. R. and J. T. Collins. 1991. A Field Guide to Reptiles and Amphibians: Eastern and Central North America. Houghton Mifflin Company, Boston.

Cox, C. 1991. Pesticised and birds: from DDT to today's poisons. Journal of Pesticide Reform11(4): 2-6.

Curry, J. R. 2001. Dragonflies of Indiana. Indiana Academy of Science, Indianapolis, Indiana.

Donalty, S., S. E. Henke, and C. L. Kerr. 2003. Use of winter food plots by nongame wildlife species. Wildlife Society Bulletin 31(3):774-778.

FedStats. United States Government. 2002. http://www.fedstats.gov/.

Fisher, B.E. Unpublished correspondence to MNWR with results of a mussel survey conducted in 2007. Indiana Department of Natural Resources, Edinburgh IN. 9pp

Fisher, J. T. and L. Wilkinson. 2005. The response of mammals to forest fire and timber harvest in the North American boreal forest. Mammal Review 35(1):51-81.

Forest Service. 2007. Forest inventory and analysis strategic plan: a history of success a dynamic future. United States Department of Agriculture.

Gray, M. J., R. M. Kaminski, G. Weerakkody, B. D. Leopold, and K. C. Jensen. 1999. Aquatic invertebrate and plant responses following mechanical manipulations of moist-soil habitat. Wildlife Society Bulletin 27(3): 770-779.

Harmon J.L. 1996. Survey of the freshwater mussels (Bivalvia: Unionidae) of the Muscatatuck National Wildlife Refuge. Unpublished manuscript, Franklin IN. 8pp.

Harper, C. A. 2007. Strategies for managing early succession habitat for wildlife. Weed Technology 21(4):932-937.

Haukos, D. A. and L. M. Smith. 1993. Moist-soil Management of Playa Lakes for migrating and wintering ducks. Wildlife Society Bulletin 21(3):288-298.

Herkert, J. R. 1994. The effects of habitat fragmentation on Midwestern grassland bird communities. Ecological Applications 4(3):461-471.

Homoya, M. 2007. Personal communication. Botanist/ecologist for Indiana Natural Heritage Program. Indiana Department of Natural Recourses.

Houlahan, J. E., C. S Findlay, B. R. Schmidt, A. H. Mayer, and S. L. Kuzmin. 2000. Quantitative evidence for global amphibian population declines. Nature 404(6779):752-755.

Indiana Department of Natural Resources. 2000. Indiana Statewide Outdoor Recreation Plan 2000-2004: a new millennium, a new tradition. Indianapolis, Indiana.

Indiana Department of Natural Resources. 2005. Indiana comprehensive wildlife strategy 10/01/05. Project Coordinator C. Gremillion-Smith. Indiana Department of Natural Resources, Indianapolis. 103pp, plus appendices.

Indiana Department of Natural Resources, Division of Outdoor Recreation. 2006. Hoosiers on the Move: The Indiana State Trails, Greenways, and Bikeways Plan. Indianapolis, Indiana.

Indiana Department of Natural Resources. 2008. 2008 Indiana fish consumption advisory. Accessed July 24, 2008. http://in.gov/isdh/files/2008_FCA_Booklet.pdf

Jackson, M. T. *editor.* 1997. The Natural Heritage of Indiana. Indiana University Press, Bloomington and Indianapolis, Indiana.

Jacquart, E., M. Homoya, and L. Casebere. 2002. Natural communities of Indiana: 7/1/02 working draft. Indiana Department of Natural Resources, Division of Nature Preserves, Indianapolis, IN.

Johnson, S.A., H.D. Walker, C.S. Hudson, T.R. Hewitt, and J.S. Thompson. 2007. Prospects for restoring river otters in Indiana. Proceedings of the Indiana Academy of Science 116(1):71-83

Kingsbury, B. A. 1997. Habitat requirements of the copperbelly water snake, *Nerodia erthrogaster neglecta.* Indiana-Purdue University, Fort Wayne, Indiana.

Kozlowski, T. T. 2002. Physiological-ecological impacts of flooding on riparian forest ecosystems. Wetlands 22(3):550-561.

Lindsey, A. A. 1997. Walking in Wilderness. Pp 113-123, in M. T. Jackson (ed.) The Natural Heritage of Indiana. Indiana University Press, Bloomington. 482pp.

Marshall, D.L., G.L. Helt, B.G. Nagel. 2007. Interim Soil Survey of Jennings County, Indiana. U.S Department of Agriculture, Natural Resources Conservation Service

Marshall, J. C., B. A. Kingsbury, and D. J. Minchella. *In press.* Microsatellite variation, population structure, and bottlenecks in the threatened copperbelly water snake. Conservation Genetics.

McWilliams-Munson, R. 1996. Contaminant Assessment Process Manual, Muscatatuck National Wildlife Refuge: Preliminary Report of Findings.

Nagel, B.G., R.C. Wingard, Jr., G.R. Struben. 1990. Soil Survey of Jackson County, Indiana. U.S Department of Agriculture, Soil Conservation Service. U.S. Government Printing Office, Washington D.C.

National Climatic Data Center, National Oceanic and Atmospheric Administration. Asheville, NC.

National Wildlife Refuge System Improvement Act of 1997 Public Law 105-57

Nickell, A.K., W.D. Hosteter, S. H. Brownfield, A. Rivera, 1976. Soil Survey of Jennings County, Indiana. U.S Department of Agriculture, Soil Conservation Service. U.S. Government Printing Office, Washington D.C.

Patrick, R. and D. M. Palavage. 1994. The value of species as indicators of water quality. Proceedings of the Academy of Natural Sciences of Philadelphia 145:55-92.

Pimentel, D., R. Zuniga, and D. Morrison. 2005. Update on the environmental and economic cost associated with alien-invasive species in the United States. Ecological Economics 52(3):273-288.

Pruitt, S. and J. Szymanski. 1997. Endangered and threatened wildlife and plants; determination of threatened status for the northern population of the copperbelly water snake. Federal Register 62:4183-4193

Robinson, S. K., F. R. Thompson III, T. M. Donovan, D. R. Whitehead, and J. Faaborg. 1995. Regional forest fragmentation and the nesting success of migratory birds. Science 267(5206):1987-1990

Roe, J. H., B. A. Kingsbury, and N. R. Herbert. 2003. Wetland and upland use patterns in semi-aquatic snakes: implications for wetland conservation. Wetlands 23(4): 1003-1014

Rooney, T. P. and D. M. Waller. 2003. Direct and indirect effects of white-tailed deer in forest ecosystems. Forest Ecology and Management 181(1):165-176.

Sallabanks, R., J. R. Walters, and J. A. Collazo. 2000. Breeding bird abundance in bottomland hardwood forests: habitat, edge, and patch size effects. The Condor 102(4): 748-758

Sieracki, J.L., T.E. Burk, and J.H. Schomaker. 2002. Muscatatuck NWR vegetation cover spatial database (2000). Staff Paper Series Number 159, Department of Forest Resources. College of Natural Resources. U. of Minn., Minneapolis, MN. 62pp.

Simon, T.P. 2008. Preliminary diagnosis of contaminant patterns in streams and rivers of the National Wildlife Refuges in Indiana. Project ID:1261-3N34. U.S. Fish and Wildlife Service, Environmental Contaminants Program, Bloomington, Indiana. 970 pp.

Slusher, B.R. and D. Welch. 2001. Site conservation plan for Beanblossom Bottoms. Sycamore Land Trust, Bloomington. 25pp.

Smith, L. M. and J. A. Kadlec. 1983. Seed banks and their role during drawdown of a North American marsh. The Journal of Applies Ecology 20(2):673-684.

STATS Indiana. 2007. Indiana Business Research Center at Indiana University's Kelley School of Business, Bloomington, Indiana.

Tang, Z, B. A. Engel, B. C. Pijanowski, and K. J. Lim. 2005. Forecasting land use change and its environmental impact at a watershed scale. Journal of Environmental Management 76(1): 35-45

Thomas, J. A. 1981. Soil Survey of Monroe County, Indiana. U.S Department of Agriculture, Soil Conservation Service. U.S. Government Printing Office, Washington D.C.

Twedt, D. J., R. R. Wilson, and A. S. Keister. 2007. Spatial models of northern bobwhite populations for conservation planning. Journal of Wildlife Management 71(6):1808-1818.

U.S. Census Bureau. 2008. State and County QuickFacts. Data derived from Population Estimates, Census of Population and Housing, Small Area Income and Poverty Estimates, State and County Housing Unit Estimates, County Business Patterns, Nonemployer Statistics, Economic Census, Survey of Business Owners, Building Permits, Consolidated Federal Funds Report. Accessed July 22, 2008. http://quickfacts.census.gov/qfd/states/18/18079.html.

U.S. Fish & Wildlife Service. 2004. Annual Report of Lands Under Control of the U.S. Fish and Wildlife Service.

U.S. Fish & Wildlife Service. 1999. Fish & Wildlife Resource Conservation Priorities: Region 3.

U.S. Geological Survey. 2001. National Land Cover Database Zone 60 Land Cover Layer

Waide, R. B., M. R. Willig, C. F. Steiner, G. Mittelbach, L. Gough, S. I. Dodson, G. P. Juday, and R. Parmenter. 1999. The relationship between productivity and species richness. Annual Review of Ecology and Systematics 30:257-300

Wake, D. B. 1991. Declining amphibian populations. Science 253(5022):860.

Wayne, W. J. 1956. Thickness of Drift and Bedrock Physiography of Indiana North of the Wisconsin Glacial Boundary. Report of Progress No. 7. Geological Survey, Indiana Department of Conservation, Bloomington, Indiana.

Whitaker, J.O., Jr. 1995. Survey of bats at Muscatatuck National Wildlife Refuge, in Jackson and Jennings County, Indiana. Report to J.F. New & Associates. 21pp

Woodall, C., D. Johnson, J. Gallion, C. Perry, B. Butler, R. Piva, E. Jepsen, D. Nowak, and P. Marshall. 2005. Indiana's forests 1999-2003 (Part A). Resour. Bull. NC-253A. St. Paul, MN: U.S. Department of Arrgriculture, Forest Service, North Central Research Station. 94 p.

Appendix I: List of Preparers

List of Preparers

Refuge Staff

- Marc Webber, Refuge Manager

- Susan Knowles, Wildlife Refuge Specialist

- Donna Stanley, Outdoor Recreation Planner

- Dan Wood, Wildlife Biologist

- Frank Polyak, Park Ranger

Regional Planning Staff

- Jared Bowman, Refuge Planner

- Gabriel DeAlessio, Wildlife Biologist/ Cartographer

- Jane Hodgins, Technical Writer/Editor

- John Schomaker, Refuge Planner (retired)

Appendix J: Response to Comments on the Draft CCP

Response to Comments

Initial drafts of Muscatatuck National Wildlife Refuge's CCP and EA were released to stakeholders and the public on April 6, 2009. After 53 days of public comment, including an open house held at the Refuge visitor center on April 23, 2009, 40 written comment submissions were made containing more than 150 individual comments. Most comments were received from members of the general public, but comments were also submitted by representatives of the Indiana Department of Natural Resources, the Sierra Club's Winding Waters Group, The Nature Conservancy, Earlham College, and Groundsmith Consulting.

The comments were well distributed across all subject areas, including wildlife, habitat, water resources, hunting, fishing, education, other public uses, facilities and infrastructure, and planning. In general, the public expressed an appreciation for the excellent outdoor recreation and wildlife viewing opportunities at the Refuge, and wants to see these opportunities balanced with the preservation of quality habitat and healthy wildlife populations.

Comments both supported and opposed a number of management actions proposed in the environmental assessment's range of alternatives, including closure of the west entrance, paving the auto tour route, charging an entrance fee, restoring man-made wetland areas to native forest, allowing boats and electric trolling motors on fishing lakes, and decreasing farming acreage. Additionally, there seemed to be universal approval for extending Refuge hours, protecting the unique Acid Seep Springs Research Natural Area, increasing outreach and education to children, and more aggressively controlling invasive species.

Each comment was carefully considered and, where appropriate, changes were made to the CCP in response to the thoughts and concerns expressed. The full range of comment submissions is represented in the sections below, but similar or duplicate comments were grouped or eliminated to reduce redundancy. Comments are grouped by subject, and a response has been provided to each by Refuge staff.

The Refuge thanks all of the individuals who submitted comments and feedback during this CCP process.

Wildlife

Comment 1: Non-game Wildlife

There should be a greater emphasis on managing for non-game wildlife, such as upland ponds for amphibians.

Response: Non-game wildlife comprises a substantial part of the biodiversity of Muscatatuck NWR. Refuge staff and visiting scientists working under special use permits conduct extensive monitoring of herpetofauna (reptiles and amphibians) and insect fauna annually. Most management actions convey direct benefits to non-game fauna including moist soil and forest management practices.

For example, the Refuge is well known for its' thriving population of the state-listed endangered copperbelly watersnake, which preys primarily on amphibians. The Refuge has more than 80 ponds and marshes with many of the former associated with house and farm sites that were built by private land owners before the Refuge was acquired, and they support a wide diversity and abundance of amphibians. Additionally, more than 60 percent of the Refuge is classified as wetland, much of which is bottomland hardwood forest that is excellent amphibian habitat.

The CCP will promote expansion of the bottomland hardwood forest and improved management of moist soil units, which should increase the abundance of amphibians, non-game birds, bats, and some other mammal species.

Comment 2: Invasive Plants

Invasive plants are a real problem on the Refuge and controlling them should be a priority in the CCP.

Response: Muscatatuck NWR staff, along with staff at our Regional Office, recognize the grave threat posed by invasive plants at the Refuge and throughout the region and country. One of our high priority staffing needs identified in this CCP and in agency staffing reviews is the addition of an invasive species biologist along with biological science technicians to conduct invasive plant removal work, and filling a vacant equipment operator position.

We have also identified the need to thoroughly map the presence and distribution of all invasive species on the Refuge so that we can prioritize our control activities on those invasive plants that pose the greatest threat to the Refuge.

Every summer, using our best available information, Refuge staff have been locating and controlling Japanese stiltgrass, a recent invader that threatens forest communities. We also monitor for and control high-risk invasive plants such as purple loosestrife, kudzu, oriental bittersweet, and others as outbreaks are discovered. We depend on auxiliary staff such as STEP student employees and interns to do the majority of our on-the-ground invasives fieldwork, and a percentage of the money spent on the station's biology program goes into controlling invasive species. See "Objective 1.5: Invasive Plant Species" on page 56 of the CCP for additional information on proposed management of invasive plant species.

Comment 3: Controlling Invasive Plants – Fire

Fire is not an effective way to control invasive plants, mechanical or chemical treatments are more effective.

Response: The Refuge has not used fire to control invasive plants, and has not used fire as a part of prescribed management since 2000. We use both established chemical and mechanical treatments on invasive plants with good success at Muscatatuck NWR.

If reinstated, prescribed fire would be used for general improvement of the condition of forests, grasslands, and moist soil units. Although there are no current plans to use fire for invasive plant control, the Refuge maintains this treatment as an adaptive management option if identified by the scientific literature as the most effective strategy to eradicate a species of invasive plant.

Comment 4: Feral Hogs

Feral hogs are now found in areas adjacent to the Refuge and should be added to the invasive or nuisance animal lists.

Response: To date, no evidence of feral hogs has been found on the Refuge. However, the range of feral hogs in Indiana is expanding, and Muscatatuck NWR staff are on the look-out for signs and reports from visitors of sightings.

Comment 5: Beavers, Mink, Muskrats, Otters

The Refuge should allow trappers to remove the problematic beavers and mink.

Don't remove too many beavers, muskrats, and otters.

Response: Most predators on beaver, mink, river otter, and muskrat are either extirpated from Indiana or occur in such low numbers as to have little effect on the populations of these species. As a result, beaver and muskrat are not only abundant throughout Indiana and on the Refuge, but these two animals damage Refuge infrastructure and disrupt habitat management activities.

Beaver build dams that flood sensitive habitats, killing trees and rare plants, and disrupt water management that is timed to produce the maximum amount of food for migrating waterfowl. Muskrat burrow into dikes and dams causing damage and the risk of failure of the structures. Populations of both species need to be reduced for the benefit of most other species that use the Refuge. To this end, control of beavers under a permit from the Indiana DNR began in the fall of 2008, and control of muskrat will begin in late 2009 or 2010.

River otters were reintroduced into Indiana in 1995, and the Refuge was one of the reintroductions sites. Since then, their population has increased throughout the state, and they were removed from the state's endangered species list in 2005. River otters are not causing any known damage at Muscatatuck NWR, and no specific management activities are currently planned. They may be reducing numbers of sport fish to the detriment of recreational fishing, but this effect may benefit local amphibian populations.

Mink numbers on the Refuge are unknown. They are an active predator and an integral part of the Refuge ecosystem, and no specific monitoring or control activities are planned.

Comment 6: Deer Control

You should have a 10-foot fence to keep deer inside the Refuge.

Response: Deer at Muscatatuck NWR are part of the larger population of the area, and immigration and emigration helps keep the herd healthy from a genetic and disease resistance perspective. An active and expanding hunt program in partnership with Indiana DNR provides population management and valuable recreational and harvest opportunities for participants. A fence would be extremely costly to build and maintain, would negatively impact a number of other species, and likely be ineffective due to failures and vandalism.

Habitat

Comment 7: Forest Management

Don't passively allow areas to revert back to forest, but actively manage the transition by planting with desired trees and using timber stand improvement practices to increase value and decrease invasives.

Response: Refuge staff recognizes the desirability of returning former farm fields to upland and bottomland hardwood forest supporting the maximum diversity of plant and animal life as quickly as possible. To this end, Refuge management has secured funding for planting trees.

From 1966-2000, approximately 82 acres were planted. Since 2000, an additional 30 acres were planted in 2004, 15 acres in 2007, 19 acres in 2008, and 28 acres in 2009. Over the course of the CCP, 970 acres of former farmland will revert to forest through a combination of natural succession and tree planting. Tree planting is relatively expensive, and acquiring the necessary funding for planting 970 acres in 15 years will require extensive staff efforts and collaboration with other conservation partners.

Timber stand improvement practices were recommended to Refuge staff during the Biological Review of Muscatatuck NWR Management in 2007. Forest management is proposed in the CCP as a part of the Habitat Management Plan, and pending the availability of funding, will be completed within 5 years of completing this CCP. This plan will provide a prescription for active forest management that is expected to call for application of timber stand improvement where needed.

Comment 8: Converting Wetlands to Forest

No wetland areas should be allowed to revert back to forest. This is not a national forest, and too few wetlands remain on the landscape.

Increased forest cover does not meet the establishment purpose of the Refuge – promoting waterfowl, deep woods habitat requires 20,000 acres of forest, and continuous forest cover reduces edge habitat needed by birds.

Response: Muscatatuck NWR presents numerous competing priorities for habitat management. The CCP eliminates some moist soil units in order to return areas of the Refuge to habitats resembling pre-settlement conditions and benefit specific species, but other moist soil units will be retained for waterfowl, migratory birds, and other species.

Prior to settlement and land clearing for agriculture by Europeans, southern Indiana and the location of the Refuge was a combination of bottomland and upland hardwood forests dominated by beech-maple communities with significant oak-hickory community elements also present. There were relatively few standing bodies of water such as lakes and ponds, and most open water existed as ephemeral marshes and wetland created by seasonal rains and floods, and the damming of creeks and streams by beaver.

The moist soil units proposed for conversion to forest are very difficult to maintain and keep in prime condition due to their location in the floodplain of the Vernon Fork of the Muscatatuck River. The forest expansions planned may serve the deep forest requirements of species such as the Cerulean Warbler, but will primarily benefit the endangered Indiana bat that breeds on the Refuge and cavity nesting waterfowl such as Wood Ducks and Hooded Mergansers.

Muscatatuck NWR's constructed moist soil units provide the opportunity to create feeding areas for migratory waterfowl and shorebirds, brood rearing areas for resident breeding waterfowl such as Wood Ducks and resident geese, and habitat for herpetofauna (reptiles and amphibians). However, increases in bottomland hardwood forests, which are also classified as wetland habitats, will also serve herpetofauna, provide a return to a more natural cycle of flooding and drainage to the Refuge's waterfowl sanctuary area, and ultimately provide more trees for cavity nesting species such as Wood Ducks, a species of waterfowl the Refuge is directed to support by the Refuge purposes.

Furthermore, conversion of moist soil units 8-10 to bottomland forest, while taking away some impounded wetlands, will convert most of the existing wetland area into a more diverse mosaic of wetland habitats that will have sloughs, channels, and ephemeral ponds. These new wetlands will either be actively restored or allowed to form naturally from habitat succession to the benefit of native herpetofauna and other wildlife and native plants.

Finally, the loss of brood rearing habitat for cavity nesting species is considered to be insignificant, as a large reservoir of brood rearing habitat will persist within the Moss Lake summer pool footprint, estimated to be more than adequate for the anticipated demand.

Comment 9: Cooperative Farming

Farming provides a valuable food source for wildlife, discourages the spread of invasives, and it should be continued at the Refuge.

I would like to see areas in the southeast section of the Refuge planted to crops.

Actively convert some cropland into forest, but plant additional acreage to crops.

There should be more cropland on the Refuge, and in large enough patches to attract good farmers.

I am concerned about the loss of farmland and feel the Refuge should continue this use. It could be used to generate revenue for Refuge maintenance and operations.

Response: Reducing cropland acreage is not unique to Muscatatuck NWR. The Service has been reducing its use of cropland as a management strategy on national wildlife refuges for several years. The U.S. Fish and Wildlife Service Biological Integrity, Diversity and Environmental Health Policy developed in response to the National Wildlife Refuge System Improvement Act of 1997 calls for refuges to restore their lands to natural conditions and historic vegetative communities.

Muscatatuck NWR has been gradually reducing the number of acres in its Cooperative Farming program since shortly after establishment in 1966. The primary reasons for this reduction are to reduce fragmentation of forest habitats and to restore more acreage to natural habitats. The remaining acres in the Cooperative Farming program are slated to be restored to diverse native grassland areas to promote species diversity and continue to provide the wildlife viewing opportunities they currently support. Conversion of these acres out of farming will only take place when proper restoration activities can be planned and implemented so as to protect these acres from being overrun by invasive species.

The Service portion (25 percent) of the annual Cooperative Farming harvest is left on the Refuge for wildlife consumption. However, the use of this resource by migratory waterfowl is low, and most of the harvest is eaten by resident species such as deer, turkey, and resident geese, none of which require food supplementation. In the case of deer and resident geese, supporting higher populations of these animals can be detrimental to habitat restoration efforts elsewhere on the Refuge, and to neighboring private property.

The southeast section of the Refuge is converting through natural succession to a mixture of upland and bottomland hardwood forest to provide for larger continuous blocks of forest habitats. Additional farming acres in this location would only create more fragmentation of habitat, smaller continuous blocks of forest, and decreased vegetative diversity on the Refuge.

The Service portion of yields from Cooperative Farming is left in the fields for wildlife use. If the Refuge share of crops is harvested, it is only available for later retrieval from commercial elevators and storage facilities for use as food for wildlife on a national wildlife refuge. If crops grown on refuges are sold, proceeds go into the

Service's general fund and are not directly available to the Refuge where the harvest originated.

Water Resources

Comment 10: Creek Water Levels

Keep the water levels in Storm and Mutton Creeks low so upstream landowners don't get inundated.

Response: Refuge staff recognize the problems caused by flooding in the low lying areas of Jackson and Jennings Counties.

Mutton and Storm Creeks were ditched and straightened in the 19th century, and pass through the Refuge en route to the Vernon Fork of the Muscatatuck River. Drainage can be slowed by many factors including log jams, beaver dams, siltation, and discharge through the Moss Lake water control structure. The construction of the latter was completed after an extensive Environmental Impact Statement that included calculations associated with the watershed and land use in the area. Also, land use in the area has continued to change dramatically since Refuge establishment with urban development resulting in more frequent flooding, increases in flood duration, and greater pressures on drainage systems.

In response to high water levels in Refuge creeks, we are taking the following steps:

- Refuge staff began controlling the beaver population in the fall of 2008.
- Refuge staff are regularly patrolling both Storm and Mutton Creeks to map the locations of dams and log jams and record water level staging caused by these obstructions.
- Dams and log jams are regularly broken with hand tools, and Refuge staff are investigating the potential for more effective solutions using construction equipment such as backhoes and excavators.
- Two of the six bays in the Moss Lake Water Control Structure (MLWCS) will be converted from top draining stop-log type dams to bottom draining screw-gate type control structures in the summer of 2009. The bottom draining structures will allow for faster drainage of water, removal of more of the silt load, and easier, more responsive water level

manipulation. If the results obtained from these changes in the MLWCS result in positive outcomes and more screw-gates would further improve conditions, additional stop log bays will be replaced with screw-gate structures in 2010-12.

Additionally, past management caused the winter pool level in Moss Lake to be 3 feet higher (543.0 msl) than the summer pool level (540.0 msl) by adding stop logs in the water control structure each October. In the fall of 2007, the Refuge changed its management approach and no longer actively impounds water above 540 msl, resulting in levels in Mutton and Storm Creeks that are generally 3 feet lower than previous conditions – barring additional restrictions in flow due to beaver dams and log jams.

Comment 11: Seep Springs RNA

Restore the natural hydrology of the acid seep springs area and the adjacent floodplain forest by replacing the culvert on the south end of the area and by eliminating a portion of the M6 pond.

Response: Comments from our state partners and the public on the Seep Springs Research Natural Area have prompted us to revise the objective in the CCP.

Extensive efforts are under way and are described in this CCP to restore the natural hydrology of the Seep Springs RNA through a diagnosis of the problems and an evaluation of the impacts of potential corrective measures. "Objective 1.6: Seep Springs Research Natural Area" on page 57 and strategies for management of the RNA have been updated from the draft version of this document to provide more detailed information on the problems associated with the hydrology in this area, and the short- and long-term responses planned by Refuge staff to restore the area to historic conditions.

Hunting

Comment 12: Refuge Hunting Program

Not only should there be no expansion of hunting as called for in the preferred alternative, but this place should be a 'Refuge' for wildlife where no hunting at all is allowed.

Duck hunting should not be allowed.

Close hunting in the area extending from just south of the west entrance road to Stanfield Lake.

Response: Hunting is one of the six priority public uses on national wildlife refuges as identified in the National Wildlife Refuge System Improvement Act of 1997. The other five priority public uses are: fishing, interpretation, environmental education, wildlife observation and photography.

Refuges are required to permit hunting when it is compatible with the purposes for which the Refuge was established, and not otherwise in conflict with requirements of applicable laws and regulations such as the Endangered Species Act, or refuge management plans.

Waterfowl hunting is not allowed at Muscatatuck NWR because of the Refuge's relatively small size, the fact that most bodies of water on the Refuge are managed to produce food for migrating waterfowl, and because of the disruption hunting would cause to migrant waterbirds that use the Refuge.

The area from just south of the west entrance road to Stanfield Lake includes areas open to hunting species in the Refuge's hunt program. Much of the western portion of this area is part of the waterfowl sanctuary area and is closed to all public uses except during National Wildlife Refuge Week, when day-hiking is allowed.

East of the waterfowl sanctuary, hunting occurs in the area south of Stanfield Lake and east of County Line Road for rabbit, quail, squirrel, turkey, and deer. Hunting also takes place in the area between County Line Road and the waterfowl sanctuary for deer and turkey, which is considered by hunters to be one of the better hunting areas on the Refuge. The East and West River Trails occur in this area, and under the CCP will not be maintained but rather will be allowed to revert back to natural habitat conditions. Otherwise, all Refuge trails occur in the northeast portion of the Refuge in a no-hunting area so that other visitors are able to avoid hunting areas during hunting seasons. Please refer to "Public Use, Hunting, at Muscatatuck NWR" on page 38 of the CCP for further clarification of hunting areas on the Refuge.

Comment 13: Population Monitoring

Monitor rabbit, quail, squirrel, turkey, and deer before and after the hunting season.

Response: Rabbit, quail, squirrel, turkey and deer are resident wildlife species that are abundant and widespread in Indiana and are not state or federally listed threatened or endangered species. Refuge staffing levels do not permit direct monitoring of these species because of the higher priority work needed to manage listed species, control invasive species, and manage and restore habitat.

The Refuge generally follows the Indiana DNR's management actions by allowing hunting of these species during state seasons within state limits. Where exceptions occur, they are generally more restrictive and call for shorter hunting periods on limited sections of the Refuge to limit conflicts with other Refuge management activities or public uses, and also provide sanctuary for these animals. Deer and turkey hunts are managed in consultation with the Indiana DNR, and the permit draws are conducted by the DNR for the Refuge. Hunter reports and interviews are used to determine the effect and quality of the hunts.

The number of hunters participating in rabbit, quail, and squirrel hunts is unknown because no permit system or check-in is required for these hunts. All evidence suggests that hunter numbers for these animals are low, and their impacts on respective populations negligible.

Comment 14: Hunter Orange

There is no need for hunter orange during the turkey, archery, or squirrel seasons.

Response: The Refuge hunting programs follows Indiana DNR regulations to the extent that they meet Refuge needs, and exceeds the regulations as necessary to promote safe use of the Refuge by the hunting and non-hunting user groups. Hunter orange will be required for all Refuge hunts except the turkey hunt.

Hunter orange clothing and accessories do not disturb most game species or negatively affect hunts. Muscatatuck NWR is a multiple-use facility with the non-hunting public allowed onto the property and within hunting areas during hunts. Hunter orange greatly improves the visibility of hunters to both non-hunters and hunters alike. This step is being taken to improve overall safety and reduce conflicts during Refuge hunts.

Fishing

Comment 15: Fishing Lakes

Fishing should not be allowed at Mallard and Display Ponds.

Response: We agree. Mallard and Display Ponds will be removed from the Refuge fishing program. Under the CCP they will be allowed to revert to bottomland hardwood forest. Because of this, their small dams will not be repaired if they fail following implementation of the CCP.

Comment 16: Seasonal Fishing

Fishing disrupts birds during the late fall, winter, and early spring. It should only be allowed between May and October.

Response: Muscatatuck NWR hosts mostly shallow water use by dabbling ducks and courting Wood Ducks and Wood Ducks with their broods. Fishing at Muscatatuck NWR occurs only on some of our relatively deep lakes and ponds, and along the north bank of the Vernon Fork of the Muscatatuck River. These deeper water habitats are not preferred or routinely used by these species. The disruption to waterfowl use by fishing is minimal, and fishing of these areas has been determined to be compatible with Refuge purposes, and is therefore allowed.

Additionally, fishing is one of the six priority public uses on national wildlife refuges as identified in the National Wildlife Refuge System Improvement Act of 1997. The other five priority public uses are: hunting, interpretation, environmental education, wildlife observation and photography.

Comment 17: Stocking

All fishing ponds and lakes should be stocked annually.

Response: The stocking of fish solely for the purpose of enhancing recreational fisheries is not allowed under the U.S. Fish and Wildlife Service's Biological Integrity Policy, which was developed as a result of the National Wildlife Refuge System Improvement Act of 1997. Stocking is a management practice used on refuges only to rebuild populations of native and rare fish species that are depleted.

Comment 18: Motor Use

The use of electric motors for fishing should be allowed as soon as possible.

No motors of any kind should be allowed on fishing lakes, they aren't big enough.

The use of trolling motors could ruin the fisheries on Stanfield Lake.

Response: Historically, boating has only been allowed on Stanfield Lake using oars and paddles for propulsion, and no motors. However, this makes boating difficult or impossible for persons physically unable to paddle or row a boat. The management decision to allow the use of electric trolling motors is intended to make boat fishing accessible to a wider range of Refuge visitors. However, gasoline powered motors attached to boats will still be prohibited.

Because Stanfield Lake is a relatively small lake (125 acres), monitoring of fish populations to determine baseline population levels will be conducted before allowing the use of electric trolling motors, and will continue thereafter in an effort to assess the impact of electric trolling motor use on the fish population and on the quality of the fishing opportunity. Should the use of motors lead to a decline in fish abundance or changes in community assemblages, Refuge staff will adapt management to include a limited number of boat launches per day, implement slot limits or aggregate creel limits, or use implement other management actions to protect Refuge fish populations.

Comment 19: Lakes with Boat Use

Lakes in addition to Stanfield should be opened to boat use, including Richart and Linda.

Allow canoes and kayaks on other fishing lakes.

Response: In the interest of maintaining high-quality recreational fishing, small boats including canoes and kayaks are not allowed on the small lakes (Linda and Sheryl) and ponds (Persimmon and Sand Hill) that are in the Refuge Fishing Program. Float tubes and waders are currently allowed and will continue to be allowed on these bodies of water under the CCP. Richart Lake does not have a launching facility. Extensive use by canoe and kayaks would lead to bank and shoreline erosion and damage the few launch areas available near Refuge roads, and is therefore not allowed.

Float tubes and waders are currently allowed on Richart Lake and will continue to be allowed there under the CCP.

Comment 20: Boat Length Restrictions

Review watercraft boat restrictions.

Response: The Refuge does not currently restrict watercraft size or allow motors of any kind. Under the CCP, electric trolling motors will be allowed on Stanfield Lake. A small concrete launching ramp is available to facilitate launching of small, shallow draft boats. Large or deep draft boats are not recommended due to the small size of the ramp and shallowness of waters adjacent to the ramp, and gasoline powered motors cannot be used or attached to boats launched at Stanfield Lake.

Comment 21: Stanfield Lake Boat Dock Channel

The dock channel on Stanfield Lake should be extended, and the area around it deepened and regularly cleaned of vegetation and moss.

Response: Stanfield Lake does not have a boat dock but rather a concrete boat launching ramp. Silt that accumulates on the ramp is periodically removed to facilitate boat launching and recovery. Stanfield Lake is a relatively shallow constructed lake, and there is no boating channel into the lake from the ramp. Small, shallow draft boats are recommended, and the Refuge does not plan to dredge a channel to permit access to larger boats than those that have historically used the lake despite the new allowance of electric trolling motors. However, due to overall siltation in the lake, the area in front of the ramp may also become shallower. Refuge staff will monitor the depth near the ramp to determine conditions and post advisories. Removal of sediment may be considered if the facility becomes unusable in the future. All water bodies at the Refuge become heavily covered with algae seasonally, and it is not possible to control this growth with available resources or within the limits of policy regarding

the application of chemicals. Although inconvenient, algae and aquatic weed growth does not prohibit boat access to the lake.

Outreach and Education

Comment 22: Youth Education

I strongly encourage the Refuge to increase their programming for children.

I support working with additional schools for environmental education.

Response: Refuge staff strongly support this recommendation. At present the Refuge supports environmental education through a number of on- and off-site programs every year, the largest of which is the on-site annual "Conservation Field Days Programs" that provides environmental education opportunities to third grade students in Jackson and Jennings Counties. Current staffing levels do not support additional growth in our environmental education or outreach programs. Refuge staff have made the addition of an Environmental Educator position a priority in regional and national Service staffing plans and exercises.

Comment 23: Website

Provide additional web updates and bird viewing updates.

Response: We are working on improving our website by adding local events and information of interest. Development of our improved site will begin in 2009.

Other Public Use

Comment 24: Entrance Fees

The public should not have to pay entrance fees to use the Refuge. Use collection boxes instead.

An entrance fee is a good idea. You should also offer annual passes and honor NPS passes.

Instate an entrance fee between April and October, with fee exceptions for days with Refuge programs and for members of the Muscatatuck Wildlife Society.

Don't add an entrance fee, this tactic did not work in the past.

Response: Several times during development of the Draft CCP, Refuge and Regional Office staff discussed the possibility of charging an entrance fee to provide funding for Refuge operations. An entrance fee was proposed in two of the four alternatives evaluated in the Environmental Assessment, however neither of those alternatives were selected as the preferred alternative. The CCP does not propose an entrance fee.

An entrance fee was charged in 1988 and 1989 with collections being made with the use of an "iron ranger" or collection box system. Recently, Regional policy regarding the amount of operational funding provided to each refuge changed, resulting in an increase to each station. As a result of this increase, staff determined that the benefits of additional funding raised through a fee program would not outweigh the negative impact on visitors and support from the neighboring community.

Comment 25: Refuge Hours

I strongly support extended Refuge hours for additional wildlife viewing and photography. Sunrise and sunset are the best times of the day for these activities.

Response: Under the CCP, Refuge hours will be extended to one hour before sunrise to one hour after sunset daily. This action will not only provide improved wildlife viewing and photography opportunities, but will increase the time available for hunting and fishing on the Refuge.

Comment 26: Law Enforcement

More patrolling needs to occur after normal business hours.

Response: We agree. Criminal activity on public land, which ranges from poaching to producing illicit drugs, often occurs after hours. It is also important that law enforcement occurs during peak hours, however, which makes scheduling a challenge.

Refuge law enforcement staff are shared between all three of the national wildlife refuges located in the state of Indiana, further reducing the time available for patrols on any one refuge, including Muscatatuck NWR.

Refuge Officers and managers recognize the unique scheduling needs for law enforcement and do everything possible, including partnering and coordinating with Indiana DNR Conservation Officers, to promote the presence of law enforcement during prime public use time as well as during off-peak hours.

Comment 27: Sanctuary Area Access

The sanctuary area of the Refuge should be opened to the public for wildlife viewing during the non-nesting periods of the year, or on some periodic basis.

Response: Waterfowl sanctuary is very important to fulfilling the purpose of the Refuge "...as an inviolate sanctuary...for migrating birds" and it requires significant limitations on public access.

Currently, the waterfowl sanctuary area is open to walk-in traffic one week a year during National Wildlife Refuge Week, and for vehicle tours during certain special events. The CCP retains this limited access.

Approximately 70 percent of all waterfowl use at the Refuge in 2008 occurred in the waterfowl sanctuary, and we believe that it is imperative that we protect this area from disturbance during the migration period that runs from late October through April. Additionally, other waterbird species such as Great Blue Herons, King Rails, and shorebirds utilize this area during the breeding season, as do Wood Ducks and Hooded Mergansers for brood rearing and feeding habitat.

Comment 28: Seasonal Wildlife Viewing Access

Please do not limit visitor access during peak migration periods, these are the best time of the year to view wildlife.

Response: Above all else, the National Wildlife Refuge System Improvement Act states that wildlife comes first on national wildlife refuges (Fish and Wildlife Service Manual 602 FW 1). In keeping with this direction, the Refuge will limit access to some areas to reduce disturbance of migratory birds and other wildlife.

The Refuge's "upper" moist soil units (M1-6), as well as McDonald Marsh North and Sue Pond, are being rehabilitated and managed to provide more food for waterfowl than in the past. Waterfowl use of these units will be reduced if foot traffic is permitted along all sides of the levees that border the units. The Refuge plans to seasonally close these levees to foot traffic to attract waterfowl to the area and reduce disturbance of these birds during migration, when it's important that they consume as much food as possible and conserve their energy.

Reducing foot traffic will not eliminate the opportunity to view waterfowl and other wildlife during these times of the year. People can still use Refuge public roads that border these units, including the auto tour route. More food and less disturbance may result in increased use of Refuge by birds, which may in turn lead to better wildlife viewing opportunities overall.

Comment 29: Water Drip for Bird Viewing

Water drips are a great way to increase bird activity, and additional drips should be placed near the visitor center.

Response: Refuge staff will look into the possibility of implementing this recommendation with the application of hose lines and solar powered pumps.

Facilities and Infrastructure

Comment 30: West Entrance

The west entrance should be closed to reduce traffic cutting through the Refuge and reduce associated dust.

I do not support the closure of the west entrance. It is necessary in emergencies, when primary roads are closed, and allows quick access to/from the Refuge maintenance shop.

Response: Refuge and Regional Office staff have been concerned about traffic cutting through the Refuge between Highways 50 and 31 for many years. The Service wants to encourage quality visits by individuals who have the Refuge as a

destination, encourage driving within speed limits to reduce dust and noise that disturb wildlife and other visitors, and discourage passage through the Refuge when Refuge roads are used only to reach another destination. We believe that closing the west entrance will achieve these results.

In addition, the closure may discourage heavy vehicle traffic, which contributes to higher annual road maintenance costs. Finally, all Refuge informational facilities – kiosks, the visitor center, and offices – are located just inside the gates along the entrance off of Highway 50. Promoting the use of this entrance enhances the Refuge's ability to provide visitors with orientation materials, advisories, and information on activities, events, road conditions, and other Refuge-related information.

Refuge staff recognize that closing the West Entrance Road will inconvenience some visitors. We think that benefits resulting from reduced pass-through use will significantly increase the quality of Refuge visits and reduce disturbance to wildlife.

We understand and appreciate the concern about emergency access. A gate will be installed at the West Entrance Road that could be opened during emergencies or under other special conditions.

Comment 31: Paving Refuge Roads

In addition to the prohibitive cost, paving Refuge roads will encourage people to drive faster and create additional hazards for other visitors, will create unnatural barriers for wildlife, and will increase vehicle/animal collisions.

The Refuge roads should be paved to keep down the dust for both people and wildlife, and reduce maintenance.

The roads on the Refuge need more maintenance.

Closing any Refuge roads is a bad idea because it could limit access to the elderly and disabled.

Response: Refuge staff recognize that paving Refuge roads would be costly and have both positive and negative implications and effects.

Refuge staff do not believe paving the roads will create a barrier to wildlife movement or increase the risk of wildlife being killed by cars. Paved surfaces may effectively reduce the number of animals struck on the road because drivers will be able to come to a controlled stop faster on pavement than on gravel. Refuge staff members are unaware of any reports indicating that narrow paved roads are any more of a barrier to wildlife movement than gravel roads.

While paved roads have the potential to increase the occurrence of speeding, closing the Refuge west entrance and eliminating through traffic should counteract this trend. Furthermore, law enforcement patrols will be adjusted to address any increase in speeding. Speed limiting features such as speed humps may be included in paved road design to further reduce speed on straight stretches, or in areas where people or wildlife congregate.

Gravel roads, while less expensive to install and maintain overall, have higher annual costs in both materials and labor. Refuge road sections are periodically overtopped by flood waters that sweep away gravel and generally damage the road bed, necessitating frequent repairs. Gravel must be replaced annually due to flooding events and a general degeneration of conditions from vehicle use. Dust is a significant problem in the summer and fall. It reduces the quality of visitor experiences and makes hiking and biking along Refuge roads undesirable. Vehicle traffic on gravel roads is also louder than on pavement, increasing wildlife disturbance and decreasing visitor enjoyment of the Refuge.

Muscatatuck NWR has only one maintenance staff member to handle all maintenance tasks. A second equipment operator position is authorized but has not been filled due to budget shortfalls. Filling this position is listed as the top staffing priority for the Refuge when funding becomes available.

No Refuge roads are proposed for closure in the CCP, only the west entrance.

Comment 32: Road Drainage

Maintain water drainage on and adjacent to Refuge roads.

Response: Efforts are made to keep roads and their drainage ditches open, safe, and in as good a condition as resources permit.

Maintaining drainage ditches and roads is challenging at Muscatatuck NWR. Many reaches of Refuge roads are in floodplain areas and are regularly overtopped and eroded during heavy

rain and flooding. Drainage ditches routinely fill with road gravel and eroded sediment, and are damaged by fast moving drainage during rain and flooding events. Trees and limbs that fall during high winds associated with storms clog drainages and redirect water flow onto roads, causing further damage.

Keeping up with these demands will require additional maintenance personnel including a second equipment operator and, when the budget allows, filling that position will be a high priority.

Comment 33: East and West River Trails

I use the East and West River Trails regularly and would be disappointed if they were let go.

Provide more parking for the River Trails.

Response: We understand that some visitors will be disappointed, but the Refuge does not have the resources to maintain the river trails. The East and West River Trails are located in the southern part of the Refuge near the Vernon Fork of the Muscatatuck River and are 3 and 4 miles long, respectively. Objective 3.3 in the CCP calls for discontinuing maintenance of the trails and allowing them to revert back to natural habitat conditions.

This change will eventually add approximately 8.5 acres of bottomland forest habitat to the Refuge. The area of the River Trails will still be open to public use, but will become more primitive as the vegetation grows back. Unlike parks, national wildlife refuges do not usually have extensive trail networks but rather allow public uses across the landscape and provide a small number of trails to accommodate users who do not wish to walk through undeveloped areas.

Because they are in the floodplain of the river, the East and West River Trails are periodically inundated with water and impacted by debris from flooding. Refuge staff do not have the time to properly clear and mow these trails, and current mowing and clearing has been taken on by the Refuge Friends Group, the Muscatatuck Wildlife Society, through a contract with a private vendor. Conditions have deteriorated in recent years and more maintenance is required in the form of mowing, log removal and grading.

Comment 34: Renaming Trails

One of the trails in the area of the old Hunt family farm should be re-named to honor the family.

> **Response:** The process to rename the Richart trail to the Hunt-Richart Trail in honor of the Hunt family and their long history on the site of the Richart Trail is under way.

Comment 35: Overlooks

Modify or rebuild the structure if necessary, but don't remove Hackman Overlook because it memorializes a family from the area.

Remove the Richart Lake gazebo and the North Endicott handicapped viewing platform.

Remove the Hackman overlook because it attracts vandals, or remove everything except the floor and handrails.

I like the addition of a Sandhill Crane overlook area.

> **Response:** Overlooks provide improved viewing access and draw the public to areas with good wildlife viewing opportunities. Objective 3.3 of the CCP describes plans to maintain the Endicott Overlook, build a new overlook near the Maintenance Shop where migrating cranes often congregate and deer and turkey are commonly seen, and modify or remove the Hackman Overlook off the Richart Trail on the shore of Richart Lake.
>
> The Hackman Overlook was built with funds donated by the Hackman family, and every effort will be made to retain it in a modified state. However, it requires repair and modification to discourage vandalism and to reduce safety risks to visitors because of its isolated location. Refuge staff are investigating the feasibility of removing the roof, windows, and sidewalls to leave an open platform with railings. Without cover from rain or sun, people will be less inclined to loiter and vandalize the facility, but it will still provide a good view out over the lake for wildlife observation and photography.

Comment 36: Mowing

There should be more mowing around the main entrance, the entry road, the visitor center, and the parking lots.

> **Response:** Mowing is a big undertaking at Muscatatuck NWR, and is only part of the Refuge's maintenance responsibilities. Yet, it is vital to public safety and access, and is sometimes necessary for wildlife management activities.
>
> When the budget allows, it is our intention to increase our maintenance staff in order to address all maintenance needs, including mowing.

Refuge Planning

Comment 37: Planning Frequency

Plans should be re-visited more frequently than every 15 years.

> **Response:** We agree. Chapter 5 of the CCP states that the plan will be reviewed periodically. Service policy is more specific. It directs us to review the CCP at least once annually to decide if revisions are necessary (FWS 602 FW 3).
>
> The same policy goes on to direct refuges to:
>
> > "Revise the CCP when significant new information becomes available, ecological conditions change, major refuge expansion occurs, or when we identify the need to do so during plan review. This should occur every 15 years or sooner, if necessary."
>
> In addition to the CCP, Refuge staff prepare a number of topic-specific management plans and step-down plans on a regular basis. Step-down management plans take general or broad goals and objectives and flesh out the fine details, such as strategies, tactics, and other direct management actions.
>
> Six step-down plans focused on habitat, water management, pest management, visitor services, fishery management, and habitat and wildlife monitoring are scheduled to be completed within the next 5 years. See Chapter 5 of the CCP for details.